The
Roman Rituals

Translated by K.W. Kesler

Translated by K. W. KESLER (MARCH, 1997 – 2011)
Taken from Aramaic text, and through early Hebrew translations
as well as digressive Greek.

ISBN: 148005187X
ISBN-13: 978-1480051874

DEDICATION

To all of those who made this journey in my life possible. And especially
to a friend, Scotty, who told me repeatedly growing up
that "God loves, you, he loves me, and he loves us all."
And that I would later remind him, that in the end, "God is love, and he
holds us all dear regardless of who or what we do."

CONTENTS

Other books by the Author…..

Demonology 101

Demonology 201: The knowledge of Banishment

**If you have any questions or comments,
please feel free to ask through
www.demon101.com**

ACKNOWLEDGMENTS

It is here that a wide variety of people have helped me. I began this project actually in 1997. I took about two years off between 1999 and 2001, but Ironically began working back on the project at 4 o'clock in the morning on September 11th, 2001. I remember working for a few hours, and even though I was facing exhaustion, seeing the images on the TV that would keep me up until 8 am on 9-12-2001. It was a few days later I came back to work again on it, and kept at it for the past years. My Brother in Law, Todd was a great amount of inspiration on this project as his knowledge helped guide me from time to time as he was great source of knowledge on Occult subjects.

I would like to thank Dr. Ian Phillips, and Dr. Vera Bacto of The Vatican for their patience in helping me acquire the proper documents (and in the right order) to make this project complete. I also must thank Father Kevin John Patrick McDonald, Grand Prior of the Archivio Segreto Vaticano archives at the Vatican. (who also shows some of the best hospitality for a "Yank" stuck in Italy for 3 months, and is one of the best cooks in Europe!)

1

BLESSINGS AND OTHER SACRAMENTALS

INTRODUCTION

A subheading to the above heading could well be: "The Sacramentals--Christ in Daily Life." In the ordination service, the Church, through the bishop, anoints and blesses the hands of the newly made priest, accompanying the action with these words: "May it please you, O Lord, to consecrate and sanctify these hands by this anointing and our blessing; that whatever they bless may be blessed, and whatever they consecrate may be consecrated in the name of our Lord Jesus Christ." By this and other ceremonies in the rite for ordination the young priest has it impressed on him that his sacramental ministry, namely, the power to offer sacrifice, the duty of preaching the word of God in Mass and of distributing the Bread of life to the people, the duty of administering the other sacraments, the duty of dispensing blessings and other sacramentals--that all these constitute the main reason for his being what he is, a mediator between God and men, the dispenser of God's mysteries.

For a priest all else must be kept subordinate to his sacramental ministry. In the first age of the Church the apostles, as soon as they discovered that other works were interfering with their strictly priestly ministrations, ordained other men as deacons or assistants, whose function it was to take over a large share of those activities not absolutely required of pastors of souls. So nowadays too the priest can find auxiliaries to aid him in the office of teaching, in the good work of visiting the sick and seeking out the stray sheep, intending to the needs of the poor and the widows and orphans, in keeping files and financial books, in running parish organizations and recreational programs. But he cannot turn over to them his sacramental powers, neither the greater ones of consecrating at Mass, of baptizing, of absolving, of anointing, nor even the lesser ones of bestowing on persons and objects the official blessing of the Church. Her sacramentals, then, ought not to be "the twentieth-century stepchildren of Mother Church," as someone has referred to them.

If it is true that in the world of today conditions are not conducive to a high evaluation and appreciation of the seven sacraments of Christ, then surely it can be admitted all the more readily that the sacramentals fare even worse. If a certain measure of humility and simplicity is needed by man to recognize God at work with, and in, and for us in the greater mysteries, the Eucharist and the other sacraments, it is required even in greater measure to recognize His action in those consecratory acts which are lesser than those seven, namely, the sacramentals. Pride and sophistication are a hindrance to understanding that God, when He created the universe,consecrated all creation, not alone man, but every lower form; and that Christ, in redeeming the world after the Fall, removed the curse fallen on creation, not only from man but from the lesser species as well. Thus for a long time the sacramental acts such as the many consecrations and blessings of the Church have been, if not actually disdained, looked upon with apathy and indifference by her children. So much so that some are apt to be disedified rather than edified when they are made aware that the Church has a mind to speak a blessing on horse, silkworm, bonfire, beer, bridal chamber, medicine, or lard.

God's ultimate purpose in creating the world is the

manifestation of His goodness and excellence, and a communication of them in part to His creatures. Consequently, creation's first reason for existence is to glorify the Creator. Human beings fulfill this obligation to glorify God by living in conformity with the laws which govern human existence, but they do so more nobly still in those positive acts of religion, sacrifice, sacraments, social and private prayer, consecrations, and blessings. For in this latter way man does not praise God in isolation, but he is united with the praise which his elder brother, Jesus Christ, everlastingly renders to the Blessed Trinity. Irrational creatures fulfill their obligation also in their existence and functions, according to the laws that govern their nature. This is their silent voice of praise. But lower creation too is destined to take part in the direct and positive act of praising the Creator. The psalms and canticles leave no doubt about this. The fall of man caused lower creatures to be separated from God, for they were bound to God through mankind. And they became once more consecrated in the redemption, not purely for their own sake, but for the purposes of higher creation. Therefore, in union with man, and in union with the God-man, the rest of creation participates in the praise which without ceasing raises its voice to the adorable Trinity.In the Epistle to the Romans St. Paul records that the complete emancipation of creation will not be effected until the end of time. But ever since our Lord transfigured lower creatures by employing them in sacramental ways--consider His use of bread, wine, water, oil, sacred signs-- material things have been participating with Him and with man in divine worship. And where Christ left off, the Church continues. The consecration and transfiguration of the creatures of God is done through sacraments and sacramentals. The passion and resurrection of Jesus notwithstanding, the individual man is not justified until the fruit of these momentous acts is communicated to him by way of sacramental sanctification. Lower creatures in similar fashion are freed from their enslavement by being sacramentalized. Before the Church will use them in the service of God or of men, she wills that first they be exorcised of any allegiance to Satan, then sanctified by her consecratory hand.

Certainly there is a difference of kind and of efficacy

between the seven sacraments and the lesser sacraments called sacramentals. There is a difference of degree in the seven sacraments themselves. One is not so necessary or sublime as another. Furthermore, it is not true to say without qualification that one distinction between sacraments and sacramentals is that the former owe their institution to Christ, the latter to the Church. For some of the sacramentals definitely come directly from Christ, exactly how many and actually which ones is not clear. There is one sacramental, however, of whose origin there is not a particle of doubt. This is the mandatum, the washing of feet, carried out by our Lord at the Last Supper, and today still used in the liturgy of Maundy Thursday. What requires stressing here is that men should not belittle the sacramentals because of the fact that they owe their institution in greatest part not to the positive will and act of Christ, but instead to the will and act of the Church. For in the light of the doctrine of the mystical body both have a sacred origin, the sacraments from the personal, historical Christ, the sacraments from the mystic Christ--Christ living and working in His mystical bride, the Church. The sacramentals are aptly designated as extensions and radiation of the sacraments. Both are sources of divine life; both have an identical purpose, divine life. They have, moreover, an identical cause, the passion and resurrection of Jesus Christ; albeit they differ in nature, efficacy, and intensity.

Because man is weakened by sin both in his mental and physical faculties, he needs in striving for salvation, in addition to the sacraments themselves, other supernatural aids constantly at hand, in order to overcome his own inherent weakness as well as the obstacles put in his way by creature things. These auxiliaries, the sacramentals, are the many powerful supports by which man's course to heaven can be lightened, affording protection against the enemies of his soul and promoting bodily well-being in the interests of the soul. As the code of Canon Law defines them: sacramentals are objects and actions which the Church is wont to use, somewhat as she uses the sacraments, in order to obtain through her intercession effects, especially effects of a spiritual nature. As Christ has endowed with infallible grace the outward signs by which sacraments are effected, so in a similar way the

Church has endowed with spiritual powers the outward signs by which sacramentals are constituted. And why are such simple things like the sacramentals so efficacious in the life of grace? Because their efficacy is dependent on the power of the Church's impetration, and not solely on the devotion of the subject who uses them. We say that the sacraments work "ex opere operato," that is, in virtue of the outward signs that are posited. On the other hand, we are accustomed to hear that the sacramentals work "ex opere operantis," which would mean in virtue of the intensity of devotion in those who use them. Yet this is only part of the truth. The thing is cast in an altogether different light when it is stated in full precision, namely, that the sacramentals work "ex opere operantis Ecclesiae," which means that their efficacy is in first place dependent on the power of the Church's intercession, and only secondly on the devout dispositions of the subject concerned. Back in the Middle Ages, William of Paris stated: "The efficacy of the sacramentals is rooted in the nobility of the Church, which is so pleasing to God and so beloved by Him that she never meets with a refusal from Him. The matter could hardly be expressed better. Owing to the resurgence of the doctrine of the mystical body, it has been granted to our times to view the Church once more in her true nature as the body of Christ, flesh of His flesh, bone of His bone, more intimate a part of Him than a bride is of her bridegroom. Therefore, it is not exactly improper to speak of an efficacy "ex opera operato" in the case of sacramentals. For example, an altar that receives the consecration of the Church is consecrated and remains consecrated, no matter how fervent and devout was the bishop who performed the consecration.

Sacramentals have been classified in many ways. But a simple and clear way of classifying them is to divide them into three groups. First, those that lay the basis for divine worship by creating the place and the atmosphere, by raising up certain persons--apart from bishops, priests, and deacons--officially designated to perform divine worship, and by supplying the appurtenances necessary for divine worship, for example: (a) the consecration of a church and an altar, or the consecration of a cemetery; (b) the blessing of an abbot, of monks and virgins, of the ministers in minor orders; (c) the consecration of a chalice or paten, the consecration of a church bell, the blessing of vestments, etc. Second, those used in the course of celebrating Mass and administering the sacraments; for example, the incantation of the altar, the reading of the Gospel, the last blessing, or the giving of salt and the anointing in baptism. Third, those that extend from the worship in church to the Christian home and family circle, to the occupations of farming, industry, and trades; for example, the blessing of a home, field, animals, printing presses, fire-engine, etc.

Although we have stressed the truth that the sacramentals derive their efficacy chiefly from the intercessory power of the Church, we may not minimize the role played by man's own subjective dispositions. The sacraments, too, for that matter, demand something of the individual recipient--at the very least that the subject place no obstacle in the way of grace. But in the case of the sacramentals man's cooperation has a very large part to play if they are to attain their full purpose. Their function is to provide an atmosphere in which the virtue of religion can thrive, and to produce a psychological reaction in man, to raise his thoughts and aspirations out of the realm of the profane and up to the realm of the sacred, to fix his heart on the things of the spirit, to impress on his consciousness God's will for him and God's providence always hovering over him.

Before ascending into heaven our Lord, in His infinite wisdom and love, bequeathed to His followers the seven sacraments, which were to occupy the center of their religious life, to be like so many milestones for them on the journey to heaven. But He also foresaw that the periphery of the Christian life could be sanctified by further supports of a lesser kind, supernatural helps that would be constantly at hand, even every hour, serving to consecrate the works and activities of the day and to lighten its burdens and sorrows. Thus He indicated to the apostles in broad lines how they might make use of other signs and symbols in furthering the work of sanctifying souls. Seeing that the Master Himself had employed the sign of the cross, the act of exorcism, the washing of feet at the Last Supper, and had commanded them to do like things in His name, the apostles were soon imitating Him, performing exorcisms and blessing creatures, as St. Paul has testified in 1 Timothy 4.5. Certainly the Church was inspired by the Holy Spirit, when, following the apostolic period, she began to introduce rites that we now call sacramentals, such as the solemn blessing of baptismal water, of oils, salt, and bread, of first-fruits, and the blessing of milk and honey in connection with first holy communion of the neophytes on Easter morning, to mention only some of the ceremonies that very early embellished the celebration of Mass and the administration of the other sacraments. How wrong were men like Luther and Harnack when they asserted that the sacramentals of the Catholic Church were an invention of the Middle Ages, and scarcely better than a return to the legalistic rites of the Talmud and the Pharisees. In response to the natural craving of man for ritual and ceremonial, for tokens and memorials, the Church gave her children, instead of "panis et circenses," blessed bread and religious processions, instead of antiques, sacred relics and medals. The legitimate demands of a Christian people were as much a factor as the will of the Church herself in promoting the development and the multiplication of pious ceremonies. Soon every province of life was consecrated by the Church's benediction. From the church edifice the sacramentals widen out to embrace the totality of Christian life. Home and hearth, granary and workshop, field and meadow, vineyard and orchard, fountain and river receive a consecration. In private life there was a blessing for the wife who had recently conceived and one for the woman in the pangs of labor; a blessing for the lad who had just reached the age when he could be introduced to the ABC's, and one for the young man about to sprout his first beard; for the sick, blessed medicaments of water, salt, bread, and herbs, instead of a doctor, harder to come by then than even now. Public life also had its blessings, a blessing of a king and queen, emperor and empress, a blessing of a knight and his accouterments of sword and lance, a blessing of public penitents, of pilgrims, of crusaders. In time of plague and famine, a deprecatory blessing against rats, mice, locusts, and noxious vermin. In time of calamity, a blessing to protect the people against fire, wind, earthquake, and flood.

7

In all this, to be sure, abuse and superstition eventually crept in, especially in the later Middle Ages. When diocesan synods failed to stem such misuse of sacred things, Paul V finally stepped in, and by a Bull of June 16, 1614, published the official Roman Ritual for the universal Church, to which model all diocesan rituals were thenceforth to conform. But in the seventeenth and eighteenth centuries the abuse was revived, particularly through the religious orders, who printed private collections of blessings and especially exorcisms with prayers and formulas of such a nature as to outdo even the superstitions of the late Middle Ages. Perhaps it is a conscientious fear of reviving superstition that prompts us to be so hesitant about restoring the sacramentals to their onetime place of honor. Or perhaps, as we say, you can't turn back the clock. Young men no longer grow beards, save for an exceptional group, and professional exterminators have arisen to make short shrift of every kind of pest, from bedbug to termite.

Admittedly we would look foolish trying to revive some of the olden pious customs. Yet there are a good many sacramentals, most of those given in this ritual, that could be resurrected to considerable profit. With some efforts at instruction and with continual encouragement, the people's sensibilities as to their significance and value would be aroused, as it has been shown where it has been tried.

It should be noted to the reader, this is NOT the basic version. This version was translated through many different sources, and more importantly re-set to update the meaning into modern age. If you are unaware of Catholic rituals and ceremonies, one might want to glance over this section and then move along. IT IS NOT ADVISED FOR SOMEONE INEXPERIANCED IN OCCULT LAWS, RITUALS AND CEREMONIES TO ATTEMPT THE RITE OF EXORCISM.

2

GENERAL RULES CONCERNING BLESSINGS
(FOR ADMINISTERING THE SACRAMENTS)

1. RITE FOR PROVIDING HOLY WATER

Some minor changes have been made in this rite, such as the omission of certain words, putting salt into the water only once, and the use of the short conclusion for the orations (see "Ephemerides Liturgicae" 75 [1961] 426). The holy-water font is a counterpart of the baptismal font; and the sacramental use of holy water is related to the great sacrament of water, baptism.
Easter is the day par excellence for baptism, and every Sunday is a little Easter. Consequently, on the Lord's day the Church blesses water to be used in the ceremony of renewal of baptism, for as often as she sprinkles us with the blessed water a sign is given us of that sacrament which once bestowed the gift of life. The rubrics

direct that the water may be blessed either in the church proper or in the sacristy. For the edification of the people it might be well to perform this blessing in the sight of the people, at least occasionally. The practice of putting salt into the water comes no doubt from the incident of the miraculous cure of the poisonous well (see 4 Kings 2.19-21), where the prophet Eliseus used salt to purify the water of the well.

1. On Sundays, or whenever this blessing takes place, salt and fresh water are prepared in the church or in the sacristy. The priest, vested in surplice and purple stole, says:

Priest: "Our help is in the name of the Lord."
All: "Who made heaven and earth."

2. The exorcism of salt follows: God's creature, salt, I cast out the demon from you by the living God, by the true God, by the holy God, by God who ordered you to be thrown into the water-spring by Eliseus to heal it of its barrenness. May you be a purified salt, a means of health for those who believe, a medicine for body and soul for all who make use of you. May all evil fancies of the foul fiend, his malice and cunning, be driven afar from the place where you are sprinkled. And let every unclean spirit be repulsed by Him who is coming to judge both the living and the dead and the world by fire.

All: Amen.

Let us pray: "Almighty everlasting God, we humbly appeal to your mercy and goodness to graciously bless this creature, salt, which you have given for mankind's use. May all who use it find in it a remedy for body and mind. And may everything that it touches or sprinkles be freed from uncleanness and any influence of the evil spirit; through Christ our Lord.

All: Amen.

Exorcism of the water: God's creature, water, I cast out the demon from you in the name of God   the Father almighty, in the name of

Jesus Christ, His Son, our Lord, and in the power of the Holy Spirit. May you be a purified water, empowered to drive afar all power of the enemy, in fact, to root out and banish the enemy himself, along with his fallen angels. We ask this through the power of our Lord Jesus Christ, who is coming to judge both the living and the dead and the world by fire.
All: Amen.

Let us pray: O God, who for man's welfare established the most wonderful mysteries in the substance of water, hearken to our prayer, and pour forth your blessing on this element now being prepared with various purifying rites. May this creature of yours, when used in your mysteries and endowed with your grace, serve to cast out demons and to banish disease. May everything that this water sprinkles in the homes and gatherings of the faithful be delivered from all that is unclean and hurtful; let no breath of contagion hover there, no taint of corruption; let all the wiles of the lurking enemy come to nothing. By the sprinkling of this water may everything opposed to the safety and peace of the occupants of these homes be banished, so that in calling on your holy name they may know the well-being they desire, and be protected from every peril; through Christ our Lord.
All: Amen.

3. Now the priest pours the salt into the water in the form of a cross, saying:May this salt and water be mixed together; in the name of the Father, and of the Son, and of the Holy Spirit.
All: Amen.

P: The Lord be with you.

All: May He also be with you.

Let us pray: God, source of irresistible might and king of an invincible realm, the ever-glorious conqueror; who restrain the force of the adversary, silencing the uproar of his rage, and valiantly
subduing his wickedness; in awe and humility we beg you, Lord, to regard with favor this creature thing of salt and water, to let the

light of your kindness shine upon it, and to hallow it with the dew of your mercy; so that wherever it is sprinkled and your holy name is invoked, every assault of the unclean spirit may be baffled, and all dread of the serpent's venom be cast out. To us who entreat your mercy grant that the Holy Spirit may be with us wherever we may be; through Christ our Lord.
All: Amen.

4. On Sundays after the water is blessed and before Mass begins the celebrant sprinkles the altar, himself, the ministers, and the people as prescribed in the Missal and in the ceremony of the Ritual given below.

5. Christ's faithful are permitted to take holy water home with them to sprinkle the sick, their homes, fields, vineyards, and the like. It is recommended too that they put it in fonts in the various rooms, so that they may use it to bless themselves daily and frequently.

2. THE SUNDAY BLESSING WITH HOLY WATER

There has been a slight change made in this ceremony--the priest no longer says the Miserere while he sprinkles the people (see "Ephemerides Liturgicae" 75 [1961] 426), and the wording of the rubric for Passiontime and Eastertime also has been altered. The significance of this blessing is touched on in the commentary given above, and the frequent omission of this blessing is noted with regret. Some say that it interferes with the introit procession, but some solution could be found.

The priest who is to offer the Mass, vested in cope of the proper color, comes to the altar, and as he kneels on the step with the ministrants (also in Eastertime) he receives the aspersory from the deacon. First he sprinkles the altar three times (simultaneously intoning the antiphon), then himself, and then he stands and sprinkles the ministrants. The choir takes up the singing of the antiphon, during which time the celebrant sprinkles the clergy and the people. The proper antiphons are given below (for the music for these see the music supplement).

Antiphon outside Eastertime

Purify me with hyssop, * Lord, and I shall be clean of sin. Wash
me, and I shall be whiter than snow. Ps. 50.1. Have mercy on me,
God, * in your great kindness. V. Glory be to the Father, and to the
Son, and to the Holy Spirit. * As it was in the beginning, is now,
and ever shall be, world without end. Amen. Purify me with
hyssop, Lord, and I shall be clean of sin. Wash me, and I shall be
whiter than snow.

The antiphon is sung thus at the sprinkling with holy water on all
Sundays outside Eastertime; but the doxology is not said during
Passiontime, and the antiphon is repeated right after the psalm
verse.

During Eastertime, from Easter Sunday until Pentecost inclusive
the following antiphon is sung:

Antiphon during Eastertime

I saw water flowing out from beneath the threshold of the temple,
alleluia; and all to whom this water came were saved, and they
shall say, alleluia, alleluia. Ps. 117. Give thanks to the Lord, for He
is good, for His mercy endures forever. V. Glory be to the Father,
and to the Son, and to the Holy Spirit. As it was in the beginning,
is now, and ever shall be, world without end. Amen. I saw water
flowing out from beneath the threshold of the temple, alleluia; and
all to whom this water came were saved, and they shall say,
alleluia, alleluia.

The first antiphon given above is resumed on Trinity Sunday.

On Easter Sunday, in churches where there is a baptismal font, the
water used for the sprinkling is that which has been blessed during
the Easter Vigil, that which was taken from the font before the

holy oils were poured in.

After the singing of the antiphon the priest, who by this time has returned to the altar, stands at the foot of the altar, and with hands folded chants the following:

P: Lord, show us your mercy (alleluia).

All: And grant us your salvation (alleluia).

P: Lord, heed my prayer.

All: And let my cry be heard by you.

P: The Lord be with you.

All: May He also be with you.

Let us pray.
Hear us, holy Lord and Father, almighty everlasting God, and in your goodness send your holy angel from heaven to watch over and protect all who are assembled in this dwelling, to be with them and give them comfort and encouragement; through Christ our Lord.

All: Amen.

3. BLESSING OF WINE

On the Feast of St. John, Apostle and Evangelist

At the end of the principal Mass on the feast of St. John, Apostle and Evangelist, after the last Gospel, the priest, retaining all vestments except the maniple, blesses wine brought by the people. This is done in memory and in honor of St. John, who drank without any ill effects the poisoned wine offered to him by his enemies.

P: Our help is in the name of the Lord.
All: Who made heaven and earth.
P: The Lord be with you.
All: May He also be with you.

Let us pray.
If it please you, Lord God, bless and consecrate this vessel of wine (or any other beverage) by the power of your right hand; and grant that, through the merits of St. John, apostle and evangelist, all your faithful who drink of it may find it a help and a protection. As the blessed John drank the poisoned potion without any ill effects, so may all who today drink the blessed
wine in his honor be delivered from poisoning and similar harmful things. And as they offer themselves body and soul to you, may they obtain pardon of all their sins; through Christ our Lord.
All: Amen.

Lord, bless this creature drink, so that it may be a health-giving medicine to all who use it; and grant by your grace that all who taste of it may enjoy bodily and spiritual health in calling on your holy name; through Christ our Lord.
All: Amen.

May the blessing of almighty God, Father, Son, and Holy Spirit, come on this wine (or any other beverage) and remain always.
All: Amen.

It is sprinkled with holy water. If the blessing is given privately outside of Mass, the priest is vested in surplice and stole and performs the ceremony as given above.

4. ANOTHER FORM FOR BLESSING WINE

on the Feast of St. John, Apostle and Evangelist.
At the end of Mass, after the last Gospel, the following is said:

Psalm 22

(For this psalm see Rite for Baptism of Children)

After the psalm: Lord, have mercy. Christ, have mercy. Lord, have mercy. Our Father (the rest inaudibly until:)

P: And lead us not into temptation.

All: But deliver us from evil.

P: Save your servants.

All: Who trust in you, my God.

P: Lord, send them aid from your holy place.

All: And watch over them from Sion.

P: Let the enemy have no power over them.

All: And the son of iniquity be powerless to harm them.

P: Then if they drink anything deadly.

All: It will not harm them.

P: Lord, heed my prayer.

All: And let my cry be heard by you.

P: The Lord be with you.

All: May He also be with you.

Let us pray. Holy Lord, almighty Father, everlasting God, who willed that your Son, co-eternal and consubstantial with you, come down from heaven and in the fulness of time be made flesh for a time of the blessed Virgin Mary, in order to seek the lost and wayward sheep and carry it on His shoulders to the sheepfold, and

to heal the man fallen among robbers of his wounds by pouring in oil and wine; may you bless and sanctify this wine which you have vintaged for man's drink. Let all who taste or drink of it on this holy feastday have health of body and soul; by your grace let it be a solace to the man who is on a journey and bring him safely to his destination; through Christ our Lord.
All: Amen.

Let us pray.
Lord Jesus Christ, who spoke of yourself as the true vine and the apostles as the branches, and who willed to plant a chosen vineyard of all who love you, bless this wine and empower it with your blessing; so that all who taste or drink of it may, through the intercession of your beloved disciple John, apostle and evangelist, be spared every deadly and poisonous affliction and enjoy bodily and spiritual well-being. We ask this of you who live and reign forever and ever.
All: Amen.

Let us pray.
God, who in creating the world brought forth for mankind bread as food and wine as drink, bread to nourish the body and wine to cheer the heart; who conferred on blessed John, your beloved disciple, such great favor that not only did he himself escape the poisoned potion, but could restore life by your power to others who were dead from poison; grant to all who drink this
wine spiritual gladness and everlasting life; through Christ our Lord.
All: Amen.

It is sprinkled with holy water.

5. BLESSING OF EPIPHANY WATER

On the Eve of Epiphany

(Approved by the Congregation of Sacred Rites, Dec. 6, 1890)

{This blessing comes from the Orient, where the Church has long emphasized in her celebration of Epiphany the mystery of our Lord's baptism, and by analogy our baptism. This aspect is not neglected in western Christendom, although in practice we have concentrated on the visit of the Magi. Many years before the Latin Rite officially adopted the blessing of Epiphany water, Diocesan rituals, notably in lower Italy, had contained such a blessing.}

1. At the appointed time the celebrant, vested in white cope (if a bishop, the mitre is worn but removed during the prayers), and the deacon and subdeacon, vested in white dalmatic and tunic respectively, come before the altar. They are preceded by acolytes, who carry the processional cross and lighted candles (which are put in their proper place), and by the other clergy. A vessel of water and a container of salt are in readiness in the sanctuary.

First the Litany of the Saints is sung, during which time all kneel. After the invocation "That you grant eternal rest," etc. the celebrant rises and sings the following two invocations, the second in a higher key:

That you bless   this water. R. We beg you to hear us. That you bless   and sanctify   this water R. We beg you to hear us.

Then the chanters continue the litany up to and including the last Lord, have mercy.

After this the celebrant chants Our Father the rest inaudibly until:

P: And lead us not into temptation.

All: But deliver us from evil.

2. Then the following psalms are sung:

Psalm 28

(For this psalm see Rite for Baptism of Adults)

Psalm 45

P: God is our refuge and our strength, * an ever-present help in distress.

All: Therefore we fear not, though the earth be shaken and mountains plunge into the depths of the sea;

P: Though its waters rage and foam * and the mountains quake at its surging.

All: The Lord of hosts is with us; * our stronghold is the God of Jacob.

P: There is a stream whose runlets gladden the city of God, * the holy dwelling of the Most High.

All: God is in its midst; it shall not be disturbed; * God will help it at the break of dawn.

P: Though nations are in turmoil, kingdoms totter, * His voice resounds, the earth melts away;

All: The Lord of hosts is with us; * our stronghold is the God of Jacob.

P: Come, see the deeds of the Lord, * the astounding things He has wrought on earth.

All: He has stopped wars to the end of the earth; * the bow he breaks; He splinters the spears; He burns the shields with fire.

P: Desist, and confess that I am God, * exalted among the nations, exalted upon the earth.

All: The Lord of hosts is with us; * our stronghold is the God of Jacob.

P: Glory be to the Father.

All: As it was in the beginning.

Psalm 146

P: Praise the Lord, for He is good; * sing praise to our God, for He is gracious; it is fitting to praise Him.

All: The Lord rebuilds Jerusalem; * the dispersed of Israel He gathers.

P: He heals the brokenhearted * and binds up their wounds.

All: He tells the number of the stars; * He calls each by name.

P: Great is our Lord and mighty in power; * to His wisdom there is no limit.

All: The Lord sustains the lowly; * the wicked He casts to the ground.

P: Sing to the Lord with thanksgiving; * sing praise with the harp to our God.

All: Who covers the heavens with clouds, * who provides rain for the earth;

P: Who makes grass sprout on the mountains * and herbs for the service of men;

All: Who gives food to the cattle, * and to the young ravens when they cry to Him.

P: He delights not in the strength of the steed, * nor is He pleased with the fleetness of men.

All: The Lord is pleased with those who fear Him, * with those who hope for His kindness.

P: Glory be to the Father.

All: As it was in the beginning.

The celebrant then chants:

Exorcism against Satan and the apostate angels

In the name of our Lord Jesus   Christ and by His power, we cast you out, every unclean spirit, every devilish power, every assault of the infernal adversary, every legion, every diabolical group and sect; begone and stay far from the Church of God, from all who are made in the image of God and redeemed by the precious blood of the divine   Lamb. Never again dare, you cunning serpent, to deceive the human race, to persecute the Church of God, nor to strike the chosen of God and to sift them as wheat. For it is the Most High God who commands you,   He to whom you heretofore in your great pride considered yourself equal; He who desires that all men might be saved and come to the knowledge of truth. God the Father   commands you. God the Son commands you. God the Holy   Spirit commands you. The majesty of Christ, the eternal Word of God made flesh commands you; He who for the salvation of our race, the race that was lost through your envy, humbled Himself and became obedient even unto death; He who built His Church upon a solid rock, and proclaimed that the gates of hell should never prevail against her, and that He would remain with her all days, even to the end of the world. The sacred mystery of the cross   commands you, as well as the power of all the mysteries of Christian faith. The exalted Virgin Mary, Mother of God   commands you, who in her lowliness crushed your proud head from the first moment of her Immaculate

Conception. The faith of the holy apostles Peter and Paul and the other apostles commands you. The blood of the martyrs and the devout intercession of all holy men and women commands you.

Therefore, accursed dragon and every diabolical legion, we adjure you by the living   God, by the true God, by the holy God, by the God who so loved the world that He gave His only-begotten Son, that whoever believes in Him shall not perish but shall have life everlasting; cease your deception of the human race and your giving them to drink of the poison of everlasting damnation; desist from harming the Church and fettering her freedom. Begone Satan, you father and teacher of lies and enemy of mankind. Give place to Christ in whom you found none of your works; give place to the one, holy, Catholic, and apostolic Church, which Christ Himself purchased with His blood. May you be brought low under God's mighty hand. May you tremble and flee as we call upon the holy and awesome name of Jesus, before whom hell quakes, and to whom the virtues, powers, and dominations are subject; whom the cherubim and seraphim praise with unwearied voices, saying: Holy, holy, holy, Lord God of hosts!

Next the choir sings the following antiphon and canticle:

Antiphon

Today the Church is espoused to her heavenly bridegroom, for Christ washes her sins in the Jordan; the Magi hasten with gifts to the regal nuptials; and the guests are gladdened with water made wine, alleluia.

Canticle of Zachary

Luke 1.68-79

P: "Blessed be the Lord, the God of Israel!* He has visited His people and brought about its redemption.

All: He has raised for us a stronghold of salvation* in the house of David His servant,

P: And redeemed the promise He had made * through the mouth of His holy prophets of old--

All: To grant salvation from our foes * and from the hand of all that hate us;

P: To deal in mercy with our fathers * and be mindful of His holy covenant,

All: Of the oath he had sworn to our father Abraham, * that He would enable us--

P: Rescued from the clutches of our foes--* to worship Him without fear,

All: In holiness and observance of the Law, * in His presence, all our days.

P: And you, my little one, will be hailed 'Prophet of the Most High'; * for the Lord's precursor you will be to prepare His ways;

All: You are to impart to His people knowledge of salvation * through forgiveness of their sins.

P: Thanks be to the merciful heart of our God! * a dawning Light from on high will visit us

All: To shine upon those who sit in darkness and in the shadowland of death, * and guide our feet into the path of peace."

P: Glory be to the Father.

All: As it was in the beginning.

Or instead of the "Benedictus" the "Magnificat" may be chosen (for the Magnificat see Blessing of Homes). At the end of the canticle the antiphon given above is repeated. Then the celebrant sings:

P: The Lord be with you.

All: May He also be with you.

Let us pray.
God, who on this day revealed your only-begotten Son to all nations by the guidance of a star, grant that we who now know you by faith may finally behold you in your heavenly majesty; through Christ our Lord.
All: Amen.

Next he blesses the water:

P: Our help is in the name of the Lord.
All: Who made heaven and earth.

From here on the exorcism of salt and the prayer that follows it, the exorcism of water and the two prayers that follow it, the mixing of the salt and water and then the concluding prayer
At the end of the blessing the priest sprinkles the people with the blessed water.

Lastly the "Te Deum" is sung (for the "Te Deum" and its oration see Renewal of the Marriage Vows).

6. BLESSING OF GOLD, INCENSE, MYRRH

On Epiphany

P: Our help is in the name of the Lord.
All: Who made heaven and earth.
P: The Lord be with you.
All: May He also be with you.

Let us pray.

Accept, holy Father, from me, your unworthy servant, these gifts which I humbly offer to the honor of your holy name and in recognition of your peerless majesty, as you once accepted the sacrifice of the just Abel and the same kind of gifts from the three Magi.

God's creatures, gold, incense, and myrrh, I cast out the demon from you by the Father almighty, by Jesus Christ, His only-begotten Son, and by the Holy Spirit, the Advocate, so that you may be freed from all deceit, evil, and cunning of the devil, and become a saving remedy to mankind against the snares of the enemy. May those who use you, with confidence in the divine power, in their lodgings, homes, or on their persons, be delivered from all perils to body and soul, and enjoy all good things. We ask this through the power and merits of our Lord and Savior, the intercession of the blessed Virgin Mary, Mother of God, and of all the saints, in particular the godly men who on this day venerated Christ the Lord with the very same gifts.
All: Amen.

God, the invisible and endless One, in the holy and awesome name of your Son, be pleased to endow with your blessing and power these creatures of gold, incense, and myrrh. Protect those who will have them in their possession from every kind of illness, injury, and danger, anything that would interfere with the well-being of body and soul, and so be enabled to serve you joyously and confidently in your Church; you who live and reign in perfect Trinity, God, forever and ever.
All: Amen.

And may the blessing of almighty God, Father, Son, and Holy Spirit, come upon these creatures of gold, incense, and myrrh, and remain always.
All: Amen.

They are sprinkled with holy water.

7. BLESSING OF CHALK

On Epiphany

P: Our help is in the name of the Lord.
All: Who made heaven and earth.
P: The Lord be with you.
All: May He also be with you.

Bless, O Lord God, this creature, chalk, and let it be a help to mankind. Grant that those who will use it with faith in your most holy name, and with it inscribe on the doors of their homes the names of your saints, Casper, Melchior, and Baltassar, may through their merits and intercession enjoy health in body and protection of soul; through Christ our Lord.
All: Amen.

It is sprinkled with holy water.

8. BLESSING OF HOMES

On Epiphany

As the priest comes into the home he says:

P: God's peace be in this home.

All: And in all who live here.

P. Ant.: Magi from the East came to Bethlehem to adore the Lord; and opening their treasure chests they presented Him with precious gifts: gold for the great King, incense for the true God, and myrrh in symbol of His burial. Alleluia.

Canticle of the Magnificat

Luke 1.46-55

P: "My soul * extols the Lord;

All: And my spirit leaps for joy in God my Savior.

P: How graciously He looked upon His lowly maid! * Oh, see, from this hour onward age after age will call me blessed!

All: How sublime is what He has done for me, * the Mighty One, whose name is 'Holy'!

P: From age to age He visits those * who worship Him in reverence.

All: His arm achieves the mastery: * He routs the haughty and proud of heart.

P: He puts down princes from their thrones, * and exalts the lowly;

All: He fills the hungry with blessings, * and sends away the rich with empty hands.

P: He has taken by the hand His servant Israel, * and mercifully kept His faith,

All: As He had promised our fathers * with Abraham and his posterity forever and evermore."

P: Glory be to the Father.

All: As it was in the beginning.

Meanwhile the home is sprinkled with holy water and incensed. At the end of the Magnificat the antiphon is repeated. Then the priest says Our Father (the rest inaudibly until:)

P: And lead us not into temptation.

All: But deliver us from evil.

P: Many shall come from Saba.

All: Bearing gold and incense.

P: Lord, heed my prayer.

All: And let my cry be heard by you.

P: The Lord be with you.

All: May he also be with you.

Let us pray.
God, who on this day revealed your only-begotten Son to all nations by the guidance of a star, grant that we who now know you by faith may finally behold you in your heavenly majesty; through Christ our Lord.
All: Amen.

Responsory: Be enlightened and shine forth, O Jerusalem, for your light is come; and upon you is risen the glory of the Lord Jesus Christ born of the Virgin Mary.

P: Nations shall walk in your light, and kings in the splendor of-your birth.

All: And the glory of the Lord is risen upon you.

Let us pray.
Lord God almighty, bless   this home, and under its shelter let there be health, chastity, self-conquest, humility, goodness, mildness, obedience to your commandments, and thanksgiving to God the Father, Son, and Holy Spirit. May your blessing remain always in this home and on those who live here; through Christ our Lord.
All: Amen.

9. BLESSING OF CANDLES

On the Feast of St. Blaise, Bishop and Martyr

P: Our help is in the name of the Lord.
All: Who made heaven and earth.
P: The Lord be with you.
All: May He also be with you.

Let us pray.
God, almighty and all-mild, by your Word alone you created the manifold things in the world, and willed that that same Word by whom all things were made take flesh in order to redeem mankind; you are great and immeasurable, awesome and praiseworthy, a worker of marvels. Hence in professing his faith in you the glorious martyr and bishop, Blaise, did not fear any manner of torment but gladly accepted the palm of martyrdom. In virtue of which you bestowed on him, among other gifts, the power to heal all ailments of the throat. And now we implore your majesty that, overlooking our guilt and considering only his merits and intercession, it may please you to bless and sanctify and impart your grace to these candles. Let all men of faith whose necks are touched with them be healed of every malady of the throat, and being restored in health and good spirits let them return thanks to you in your holy Church, and praise your glorious name which is blessed forever; through Christ our Lord.
All: Amen.

They are sprinkled with holy water.

10. BLESSING OF THROATS

On the Feast of St. Blaise

{This is one of the most popular blessings. St. Blaise was bishop of Sebaste in Cappadocia, and was martyred by beheading about A.D.

316. Not much more can be affirmed of him with any degree of historical accuracy, but legends about him are numerous. One day--so goes the legend-Blaise met a poor woman whose only pig had been snatched up in the fangs of a wolf but at the command of the bishop the wolf restored the pig alive to its owner. The woman did not forget the favor, for later, when the bishop was languishing in prison, she brought him tapers to dispel the darkness and gloom. To this story may be attributed the practice of using lighted candles in bestowing the blessing of St. Blaise. While in prison he performed a wonderful cure on a boy who had a fishbone lodged in his throat and who was in danger of choking to death. From this account we have the longtime custom of invoking the Saint for all kinds of throat trouble.}

After blessing the candles on the feast of St. Blaise, the priest holds two candles fastened like a cross to the throat of the person kneeling before him, and says:

By the intercession of St. Blaise, bishop and martyr, may God deliver you from every malady of the throat, and from every possible mishap; in the name of the Father, and of the Son, and of the Holy Spirit.
R. Amen.

11. BLESSING OF BREAD, WINE, WATER, FRUIT

For the Relief of Throat Ailments

On the Feast of St. Blaise

(Approved by the Congregation of Sacred Rites on Sept. 25, 1883)

P: Our help is in the name of the Lord.
All: Who made heaven and earth.
P: The Lord be with you.
All: May He also be with you.

Let us pray.

God, Savior of the world, who consecrated this day by the martyrdom of blessed Blaise, granting him among other gifts the power of healing all who are afflicted with ailments of the throat; we humbly appeal to your boundless mercy, begging that these fruits, bread, wine, and water brought by your devoted people be blessed   and sanctified by your goodness. May those whoeat and drink these gifts be fully healed of all ailments of the throat and of all maladies of body and soul, through the prayers and merits of St. Blaise, bishop and martyr. We ask this of you who live and reign, God, forever and ever.

All: Amen.

They are sprinkled with holy water.

12. IMPOSING BLESSED ASHES

On Ash Wednesday

The priest says, as he sprinkles the blessed ashes on the head of the person:

Gen. 3.19: Remember, man, that you are dust, and into dust you will return.

13. BLESSING OF HOMES

On Holy Saturday and during Eastertime

1. The parish priest (or a priest who has his permission), vested in surplice and white stole, visits the homes of his parishioners on Holy Saturday or another day during Eastertime, in order to bless the homes and their occupants with the Easter water. He should be assisted by a server who carries a vessel containing blessed water taken from the baptismal font before the holy oils were added. As he enters the home he says:

P: God's peace be in this home.
All: And in all who live here.

2. Then he sprinkles the dwelling's main room and the occupants, saying the antiphon:

I saw water flowing out from beneath the threshold of the temple, alleluia; and all to whom this water came were saved, and they shall say, alleluia, alleluia. Give thanks to the Lord, for He is good, for His mercy endures forever. V. Glory be to the Father, and to the Son, and to the Holy Spirit. As it was in the beginning, is now, and ever shall be, world without end. Amen. I saw water flowing out from beneath the threshold of the temple, alleluia; and all to whom this water came were saved, and they shall say, alleluia, alleluia.

Next he says:

P: Lord, show us your mercy, alleluia.
All: And grant us your salvation, alleluia.
P: Lord, heed my prayer.
All: And let my cry be heard by you.
P: The Lord be with you.
All: May He also be with you.

Let us pray.
Hear us, holy Lord and Father, almighty everlasting God; and as you guarded the homes of the Israelites from the avenging angel on their flight from Egypt, if their homes were signed with the blood of a lamb--therein prefiguring our Easter sacrifice in which Christ is the victim—so likewise in your goodness send your holy angel to watch over and protect all who live in this home, to be with them and give them comfort and encouragement; through Christ our Lord.

All: Amen.

3. The rite described above is used also when the blessing of homes is carried out on another day in Eastertime, in accord with

local custom.

14. THE EASTER BLESSINGS OF FOOD

{The Easter blessings of food owe their origin to the fact that these particular foods, namely, fleshmeat and milk products, including eggs, were forbidden in the Middle Ages during the Lenten fast and abstinence. When the feast of Easter brought the rigorous fast to an end, and these foods were again allowed at table, the people showed their joy and gratitude by first taking
the food to church for a blessing. Moreover, they hoped that the Church's blessing on such edibles would prove a remedy for whatever harmful effects the body might have suffered from the long period of self-denial. Today the Easter blessings of food are still held in many churches in the U. S., especially in those of the Slavic peoples.}

A. Blessing of Lamb

P: Our help is in the name of the Lord.
All: Who made heaven and earth.
P: The Lord be with you.
All: May He also be with you.

Let us pray.
God, who by your servant Moses commanded your people in their deliverance from Egypt to kill a lamb as a type of our Lord Jesus Christ, and prescribed that its blood be used to sign the two door-posts of their homes; may it please you to bless   and sanctify this creature-flesh which we, your servants, desire to eat in praise of you. We ask this in virtue of the resurrection of our Lord Jesus Christ, who lives and reigns with you forever and ever.
All: Amen.

It is sprinkled with holy water.

B. Blessing of Eggs

P: Our help is in the name of the Lord.
All: Who made heaven and earth.
P: The Lord be with you.
All: May He also be with you.

Let us pray.
Lord, let the grace of your blessing   come upon these eggs, that they be healthful food for your faithful who eat them in thanksgiving for the resurrection of our Lord Jesus Christ, who lives and reigns with you forever and ever.
All: Amen.

They are sprinkled with holy water.

C. Blessing of Bread

P: Our help is in the name of the Lord.
All: Who made heaven and earth.
P: The Lord be with you.
All: May He also be with you.

Let us pray.
Lord Jesus Christ, bread of angels, true bread of everlasting life, be pleased to bless   this bread, as you once blessed the five loaves in the wilderness, so that all who eat of it may derive health in body and soul. We ask this of you who live and reign forever and ever.
All: Amen.

It is sprinkled with holy water.

D. Another Blessing of Bread

P: Our help is in the name of the Lord.
All: Who made heaven and earth.
P: The Lord be with you.

All: May He also be with you.

Let us pray.
Holy Lord and Father, almighty everlasting God, be pleased to bless this bread, imparting to it your hallowed favor from on high. May it be for all who eat of it a healthful food for body and soul, as well as a safeguard against every disease and all assaults of the enemy. We ask this of our Lord Jesus Christ, your Son, the bread of life who came down from heaven and gives life and salvation to the world; who lives and reigns with you, in the unity of the Holy Spirit, God, forever and ever.
All: Amen.

It is sprinkled with holy water.

E. Blessing of New Produce

P: Our help is in the name of the Lord.
All: Who made heaven and earth.
P: The Lord be with you.
All: May He also be with you.

Let us pray.
Lord, bless this new produce, N., and grant that those who eat of it in praise of your holy name may be nourished in body and soul; through Christ our Lord.
All: Amen.

15. BLESSING OF CROSSES

Which are to be set in vineyards, fields, etc.,
on or about May 3

(Approved by the Congregation of Sacred Rites, Feb. 10, 1888)

P: Our help is in the name of the Lord.
All: Who made heaven and earth.

P: The Lord be with you.
All: May He also be with you.

Let us pray.
Almighty everlasting God, merciful Father and our unalloyed
comfort, in virtue of the bitter suffering that your only-begotten
Son, our Lord Jesus Christ, endured for us sinners on the wood of
the cross, bless these crosses which your faithful will set up in their
vineyards, gardens, fields, and other places. Shield the land where
they are placed from hail, tornado, storm, and every onslaught of
the enemy, so that the produce, ripened for the harvest, may be
gathered to your honor by those who put their trust in the holy
cross of our Lord Jesus Christ, your Son, who lives and reigns with
you forever and ever.
All: Amen.

They are sprinkled with holy water.

16. BLESSING OF A BONFIRE

On the Vigil of the Birthday of St. John the Baptist

conferred by the clergy outside of church

In the Church's veneration of her saints the cult of John the Baptist
had from earliest times and continues to have a most prominent
and honored place. John gave testimony of the true light that shines
in the darkness, although he proclaimed in utter humility: "He must
increase, but I must decrease." And the Master also spoke in
highest praise of His precursor: "I say to you, among those born of
women there is not a greater prophet than John the Baptist."
Attuned to the words of the Gospel the Christians of former times
were filled with love and enthusiasm for this saint, and expressed a
justifiable conviviality at the approach of his feastday by lighting a
bonfire the night before in front of their churches, in the market-
place, on the hilltops, and in the valleys. The custom of St. John
bonfires, indicative of a people with unabashed and childlike faith,
continues in some places to this day.

P: Our help is in the name of the Lord.
All: Who made heaven and earth.
P: The Lord be with you.
All: May He also be with you.

Let us pray.
Lord God, almighty Father, the light that never fails and the source of all light, sanctify   this new fire, and grant that after the darkness of this life we may come unsullied to you who are light eternal; through Christ our Lord.
All: Amen.

The fire is sprinkled with holy water; after which the clergy and the people sing the following hymn (for the music see the music supplement):

Hymn: Ut queant laxis

O for your spirit, holy John, to chasten
Lips sin-polluted, fettered tongues to loosen;
So by your children might your deeds of wonder
Meetly be chanted.

Lo! a swift herald, from the skies descending,
Bears to your father promise of your greatness;
How he shall name you, what your future story,
Duly revealing.

Scarcely believing message so transcendent,
Him for a season power of speech forsaketh,
Till, at your wondrous birth, again returneth,
Voice to the voiceless.

You, in your mother's womb all darkly cradled,
Knew your great Monarch, biding in His chamber,
Whence the two parents, through their offspring's merits,
Mysteries uttered.

Praise to the Father, to the Son begotten,
And to the Spirit, equal power possessing,
One God whose glory, through the lapse of ages,
Ever resounding.

P: There was a man sent from God.
All Whose name was John.

Let us pray.
God, who by reason of the birth of blessed John have made this
day praiseworthy, give your people the grace of spiritual joy,
and keep the hearts of your faithful fixed on the way that leads
to everlasting salvation; through Christ our Lord.
All: Amen.

17. BLESSING OF HERBS

On the Assumption of the Blessed Virgin Mary

{This blessing comes from Germany, and formulas for it are found
as early as the tenth century. The blessing of herbs was reserved
only to the feast of the Assumption. Herbs had not our restricted
English meaning but included all kinds of cultivated and wild
flowers, especially those which in some way had a symbolic
relation to our Lady. The people brought herbs to church on her
feast not only to secure for themselves another blessed object, but
also to make of the occasion a harvest festival of thanksgiving to
God for His great bounty manifested in the abundant fruits of the
earth. The herbs were placed on the altar, and even beneath the
altar-cloths, so that from this close contact with the Eucharist they
might receive a special consecration, over and above the ordinary
sacramental blessing of the Church.}

After the Asperges if it is a Sunday, otherwise immediately before
Mass, the priest, standing before the altar and facing the people

who hold the herbs and fruits in their hands, says in a
clear voice:

P: Our help is in the name of the Lord.
All: Who made heaven and earth.

Psalm 64

P: To you we owe our hymn of praise, O God, in Sion; to you must
vows be fulfilled, you who hear prayers.

All: To you all flesh must come* because of wicked deeds.

P: We are overcome by our sins; * it is you who pardon them.

All: Happy the man you choose, * and bring to dwell in your
courts.

P: May we be filled with the good things of your house, * the holy
things of your temple.

All: With awe-inspiring deeds of justice you answer us, * O God
our Savior,

P: The hope of all the ends of the earth * and of the distant seas.

All: You set the mountains in place by your power, * you who are
girt with might;

P: You still the roaring of the seas, * the roaring of their waves and
the tumult of the peoples.

All: And the dwellers at the earth's ends are in fear at your
marvels; * the farthest east and west you make resound with joy.

P: You have visited the land and watered it; * greatly have you
enriched it.

All: God's watercourses are filled; you have prepared the grain. * Thus have you prepared the land:

P: Drenching its furrows, * breaking up its clods,

All: Softening it with showers, * blessing its yield.

P: You have crowned the year with your bounty, * and your paths overflow with a rich harvest;

All: The untilled meadows overflow with it, * and rejoicing clothes the hills.

P: The fields are garmented with flocks and the valleys blanketed with grain. * They shout and sing for joy.

All: Glory be to the Father.

P: As it was in the beginning.

P: The Lord will be gracious.

All: And our land will bring forth its fruit.

P: You water the mountains from the clouds.

All: The earth is replenished from your rains.

P: Giving grass for cattle.

All: And plants for the benefit of man.

P: You bring wheat from the earth.

All: And wine to cheer man's heart.

P: Oil to make his face lustrous.

All: And bread to strengthen his heart.

P: He utters a command and heals their suffering.

All: And snatches them from distressing want.

P: Lord, heed my prayer.
All: And let my cry be heard by you.
P: The Lord be with you.
All: May He also be with you.

Let us pray.
Almighty everlasting God, who by your word alone brought into being the heavens, earth, sea, things seen and things unseen, and garnished the earth with plants and trees for the use of man and beast; who appointed each species to bring forth fruit in its kind, not only for the food of living creatures, but for the healing of sick bodies as well; with mind and word we urgently call on you in your great kindness to bless these various herbs and fruits, thus increasing their natural powers with the newly given grace of your blessing. May they keep away disease and adversity from men and beasts who use them in your name; through Christ our Lord.
All: Amen.

Let us pray.
God, who through Moses, your servant, directed the children of Israel to carry their sheaves of new grain to the priests for a blessing, to pluck the finest fruits of the orchard, and to make merry before you, the Lord their God; hear our supplications, and shower blessings in abundance upon us and upon these bundles of new grain, new herbs, and this assortment of produce which we gratefully present to you on this festival, blessing them in your name. Grant that men, cattle, flocks, and beasts of burden find in them a remedy against sickness, pestilence, sores, injuries, spells, against the fangs of serpents or poisonous creatures. May these blessed objects be a protection against diabolical mockery, cunning, and deception wherever they are kept, carried, or otherwise used. Lastly, through the merits of the Blessed Virgin Mary, whose Assumption we are celebrating, may we all, laden

with the sheaves of good works, deserve to be taken up to heaven; through Christ our Lord.
All: Amen.

Let us pray.
God, who on this day raised up to highest heaven the rod of Jesse, the Mother of your Son, our Lord Jesus Christ, that by her prayers and patronage you might communicate to our mortal nature the fruit of her womb, your very Son; we humbly implore you to help us use these fruits of the soil for our temporal and everlasting welfare, aided by the power of your Son and the prayers of His glorious Mother; through Christ our Lord.
All: Amen.

And may the blessing of almighty God, Father, Son, and Holy Spirit, come upon these creatures and remain always.
All: Amen.

They are sprinkled with holy water and incensed.

18. BLESSING OF SEED AND SEEDLINGS

on the Birthday of the Blessed Virgin Mary

P: Our help is in the name of the Lord.
All: Who made heaven and earth.
P: The Lord be with you.
All: May He also be with you.

Let us pray.
Holy Lord and Father, almighty everlasting God, we ask and beseech you to look with merry countenance and fair eyes on these seeds and seedlings. And as you proclaimed to Moses, your servant, in the land of Egypt, saying: "Tell the children of Israel that when they enter the land of promise which I shall give them, they are to offer the first-fruits to the priests, and they shall be blessed"; so too at our request, O Lord, be merciful and pour out the blessing of your right hand upon these seeds, which you in

your benevolence bring forth to sustain life. Let neither drought nor flood destroy them, but keep them unharmed until they reach their full growth and produce an abundant harvest for the service of body and soul. We ask this of you who live and reign in perfect Trinity forever and ever.

All: Amen.

Let us pray.

Almighty everlasting God, sower and tiller of the heavenly word, who cultivate the field of our hearts with heavenly tools, hear our prayers and pour out abundant blessings upon the fields in which these seeds are to be sown. By your protecting hand turn away the fury of the elements, so that this entire fruit may be filled with your blessing,   and may be gathered unharmed and stored up in the granary; through Christ our Lord.

All: Amen.

They are sprinkled with holy water and may be incensed.

3

BLESSINGS OF PERSONS

1. BLESSING OF AN EXPECTANT MOTHER

At the approach of confinement

{In the Middle Ages it was customary for a pastor to announce from the pulpit on Sundays the names of women whose time of childbirth was close at hand, and to ask the people's prayers for them. But his solicitude did not stop there. He also visited the homes of such women, first said prayers outside the home, and then entered and administered the sacraments and the sacramentals of the Church. Without going quite to these lengths today, an occasional word of instruction about this very fine blessing would encourage some women to present themselves for it.}

P: Our help is in the name of the Lord.

All: Who made heaven and earth.

P: Save your servant.

All: Who trusts in you, my God.

P: Let her find in you, Lord, a tower of strength.

All: In the face of the enemy.

P: Let the enemy have no power over her.

All: And the son of iniquity be powerless to harm her.

P: Lord, send her aid from your holy place.

All: And watch over her from Sion.

P: Lord, heed my prayer.

All: And let my cry be heard by you.

P: The Lord be with you.

All: May He also be with you.

Let us pray.
Almighty everlasting God, who enable us, your servants, in our profession of the true faith, to acknowledge the glory of the three Persons in the eternal Godhead, and to adore their oneness of nature, their co-equal majesty; grant, we pray, that by steadfastness in that faith this servant of yours, N., may ever be guarded against all adversity; through Christ our Lord.
All: Amen.

Let us pray.
Lord God, Creator of all things, mighty and awesome, just and forgiving, you alone are good and kind. You saved Israel from all manner of plagues, making our forefathers your chosen people, and hallowing them by the touch of your Spirit. You, by the co-operation of the Holy Spirit, prepared the body and soul of the glorious Virgin Mary to be a worthy dwelling for your Son. You filled John the Baptist with the Holy Spirit, causing him to leap with joy in his mother's womb. Accept the offering of a humble spirit, and grant the heartfelt desire of your servant, N. who pleads

for the safety of the child you allowed her to conceive. Guard the life that is yours; defend it from all the craft and spite of the pitiless foe. Let your gentle hand, like that of a skilled physician, aid her delivery, bringing her offspring safe and sound to the light of day. May her child live to be reborn in holy baptism, and continuing always in your service, be found worthy of attaining everlasting life; through Christ our Lord.

All: Amen.

The priest sprinkles the woman with holy water and then adds the following:

Psalm 66

P: May God have pity on us and bless us; * may He let His face shine upon us.

All: So may His way be known upon earth; * among all nations, His salvation.

P: May the peoples praise you, O God; * may all the peoples praise you.

All: May all the nations be glad and exult because you rule the peoples in equity; * you guide the nations on earth.

P: May the peoples praise you, O God; * may all the peoples praise you.

All: The earth has yielded its fruits; * God, our God, has blessed us.

P: May God bless us, * and may all the ends of the earth fear him.

All: Glory be to the Father.

P: As it was in the beginning.

P: Let us bless the Father, the Son, and the Holy Spirit.

All: Let us praise and glorify Him forever.

P: God has given His angels charge over you.

All: To guard you in all your paths.

P: Lord, heed my prayer.

All: And let my cry be heard by you.

P: The Lord be with you.

All: May He also be with you.

Let us pray.
Lord, we beg you to visit this dwelling, and to drive away from it and from this servant of yours, N, all the enemy's wiles. Let your holy angels be appointed here to keep her and her offspring in peace; and let your blessing ever rest upon her. Save them, almighty God, and grant them your everlasting light; through Christ our Lord.
All: Amen.

May the blessing of almighty God, Father, Son, and Holy Spirit, come on you and your child, and remain with you forever.
All: Amen.

2. BLESSING OF A MOTHER AFTER CHILDBIRTH

{This blessing is often referred to as the churching of women, but the Roman Ritual more appropriately calls it simply the blessing of a woman after childbirth. The practice of "churching a woman" developed out of a related practice in the Old Testament (cf. Lev 12.1-8). According to the Mosaic Law a woman incurred

47

legal uncleanness in childbirth and remained unclean until her legal purification. This view, that a woman incurs some kind of defilement in childbirth, persisted even in Christian times, especially in the East, but in the West too, despite the opposition of Pope Gregory the Great (d. 604). The sufferings of childbirth were looked upon as part of the penalty imposed on Eve and on all her daughters. Yet it must be understood clearly that the Jews did not say there was actually any stain of sin on the mother in consequence of giving birth to a child, but merely a restriction imposed by law. With Christ's coming womankind was elevated and ennobled, and motherhood too was more clearly seen as something honorable, deserving a blessing rather than a purification. The exact time of origin of this sacramental is not known, except that it is very ancient, and dates possibly from the first half of the fourth century.}

1. After giving birth to a child a mother may wish to give thanks to God in church for a safe delivery, and to obtain the Church's blessing. This has long been a devout and praiseworthy practice. The priest, vested in surplice and white stole (assisted by a server who carries the aspersory), goes to the threshold of the church. The woman kneels there, holding a lighted candle.

{The very fact that the priest goes to meet her and escort her into the church is in itself a mark of respect for the mother, and puts one in mind of a bishop who meets a royal personage or anyone of high rank when the latter comes to a cathedral to attend a solemn function. The rest of the rite speaks for itself; but it may be pointed out that psalm 23, which the priest recites over the woman, is a psalm of majesty, praise, and gratitude.}

The priest sprinkles her with holy water, saying:

P: Our help is in the name of the Lord.

All: Who made heaven and earth.

He then says the following antiphon and psalm 23:

Antiphon: This woman shall receive a blessing from the Lord and mercy from God, her Savior; for she is one of the people who seek the Lord.

Psalm 23

(for this psalm see Rite for Burial of Children)

After psalm 23 the above antiphon is repeated.

{In the "Collectio Rituum," both for Germany and the U. S. A., the antiphon and the psalm are omitted; and according to the same ritual the priest says first "Peace be with you"; then "Come into the temple of God"; and then the "Magnificat." If the priest wishes he may substitute the "Magnificat" for psalm 23.}

2. Then the priest places the end of the stole hanging from his left shoulder in the hand of the woman and leads her into the church, saying:
Come into God's house. Adore the Son of the blessed Virgin Mary, and thank God who has given you the grace of motherhood.

3. The woman kneels before the altar, giving thanks to God for the benefits He has bestowed on her. The priest continues:

Lord, have mercy. Christ, have mercy. Lord, have mercy. Our Father (the rest inaudibly until:)

P: And lead us not into temptation.

All: But deliver us from evil.

P: Save your servant.

All: Who trusts in you, my God.

P: Lord, send her aid from your holy place.

All: And watch over her from Sion.

P: Let the enemy have no power over her.

All: And the son of iniquity be powerless to harm her.

P: Lord, heed my prayer.
All: And let my cry be heard by you.
P: The Lord be with you.
All: May He also be with you.

Let us pray.
Almighty everlasting God, who by means of the blessed Virgin
Mary's childbearing has given every Christian mother joy, even in
her pains of bringing forth her child; look kindly on this servant of
yours who has come in gladness to your holy dwelling to offer her
thanks. And grant that after this life, through the merits and prayers
of that same blessed Mary, she and her child may be deemed
worthy of attaining the happiness of everlasting life; through Christ
our Lord.
All: Amen.

The "Collectio Rituum," both for Germany and the U. S. A.,
provide the following blessing for the child:

Let us pray.
Lord Jesus Christ, Son of the living God, begotten before time was,
yet willing to be an infant within time; who love childhood
innocence; who deigned to tenderly embrace and to bless the
little ones when they were brought to you; be ready with your
dearest blessings for this child as he (she) journeys through life,
and let no evil ways corrupt his (her) understanding. May
he (she) advance in wisdom and grace with the years, and be
enabled ever to please you, who are God, living and reigning with
the Father, in the unity of the Holy Spirit, forever and ever.

All: Amen.

4. The priest again sprinkles her with holy water, saying:

May the peace and blessing of almighty God, Father, Son, and Holy Spirit, come upon you and remain with you forever.
All: Amen.

5. The blessing of a woman after childbirth ought to be given by the pastor, if he is requested to do so. But any priest may impart it in any church or public oratory, in which case he should notify the superior.

3. BLESSING OF A WOMAN AFTER CHILDBIRTH

In a case where the child was stillborn or died after birth

{The "Collectio Rituum," both of Germany and the U. S., give the following blessing of a mother whose child was stillborn or died after birth.}

The priest meets the woman at the threshold of the church, sprinkles her with holy water, and says:

God's peace be with you.
Come into God's house. Adore the Son of the blessed Virgin Mary, and ask God to console and comfort you.

Then he leads her and those who accompany her to the altar. They kneel before the altar; whereas the priest goes up to the altar predella, turns to them, and says the following:

Psalm 120

P: I lift up my eyes toward the mountains; * whence shall help come to me?

All: My help is from the Lord, * who made heaven and earth.

P: May He not suffer your foot to slip; * may He who guards you not slumber;

All: Indeed He neither slumbers nor sleeps, * the guardian of Israel.

P: The Lord is your guardian; * the Lord is your shade; He is beside you at your right hand.

All: The sun shall not harm you by day, * nor the moon by night.

P: The Lord will guard you from all evil; * He will guard your life.

All: The Lord will guard your coming and your going, * both now and forever.

P: Glory be to the Father.

All: As it was in the beginning.

After the psalm the priest continues:

Lord, have mercy. Christ, have mercy. Lord, have mercy. Our Father (the rest inaudibly until:)

P: And lead us not into temptation.

All: But deliver us from evil.

P: Lord, heed my prayer.

All: And let my cry be heard by you.

P: The Lord be with you.

All: May He also be with you.

Let us pray.
Almighty everlasting God, lover of holy purity, who chose in your
wisdom and goodness to call this woman's child to your heavenly
kingdom; be pleased also, O Lord, to show your mercy to this
servant of yours, comforting her with your love, helping her to
accept bravely your holy will. Thus comforted by the merits of
your sacred passion, and aided by the intercession of blessed Mary,
ever a Virgin, and of all the saints, may she be united at last with
her child for all eternity in the kingdom of heaven. We ask this of
you who live and reign forever and ever.
All: Amen.

As he sprinkles her with holy water in the form of a cross, the
priest concludes:

May the peace and blessing of almighty God, Father, Son, and
Holy Spirit, come upon you and remain with you forever.
All: Amen.

4. BLESSING OF AN INFANT OR LITTLE CHILD

P: Our help is in the name of the Lord.
All: Who made heaven and earth.
P: Our God is merciful.
All: He is the Lord who watches over little children.
P: Lord, heed my prayer.
All: And let my cry be heard by you.
P: The Lord be with you.
All: May He also be with you.

Let us pray.
Lord Jesus Christ, Son of the living God, begotten before time was,
yet willing to be an infant within time; who love childhood
innocence; who deigned to tenderly embrace and to bless the
little ones when they were brought to you; be ready with your
dearest blessings for this child (these children) as he (she) (they)

journey(s) through life, and let no evil ways corrupt his (her) (their) understanding. May he (she) (they) advance in wisdom and grace with the years, and be enabled ever to please you, who are God, living and reigning with the Father, in the unity of the Holy Spirit, forever and ever.
All: Amen.

Then the priest sprinkles the infant (or infants) with holy water, saying:

May the peace and blessing of almighty God, Father, Son, and Holy Spirit, come upon you and remain with you forever.

All: Amen.

5. BLESSING OF A CHILD

P: Our help is in the name of the Lord.
All: Who made heaven and earth.
P: The Lord be with you.
All: May He also be with you.

Let us pray.
Lord Jesus Christ, Son of the living God, who said: "Let the little children come to me, and do not stop them. The kingdom of God belongs to such as these," pour out the power of your blessing   on this child, and consider the faith and devotion of the Church and of its parents. Advancing in virtue and wisdom before God and men, may he (she) reach a blessed old age and
finally attain everlasting salvation. We ask this of you who live and reign forever and ever.
All: Amen.

Psalm 112

After the psalm the priest continues:

Lord, have mercy. Christ, have mercy. Lord, have mercy. Our Father (the rest inaudibly until:)

P: And lead us not into temptation.

All: But deliver us from evil.

May the blessing of almighty God, Father, Son, and Holy Spirit, come upon you and remain with you forever.
All: Amen.

6. BLESSING OF CHILDREN

When on some special occasion they are assembled in church for this purpose

At the appointed time the children assemble in church under the tutelage of parents or teachers to ensure quiet and order. When they are properly placed, boys and girls separate, the priest approaches and speaks to them very briefly and simply on a suitable topic. Then standing and facing them he says:

P: Our help is in the name of the Lord.
All: Who made heaven and earth.

After this the following antiphon and psalm are sung (for the music see the music supplement):

Antiphon: Praise, you children of the Lord, * praise the name of the Lord.

Psalm 112

(For this psalm see Rite for Burial of Children)

At the end of the psalm the antiphon is repeated. This psalm and its antiphon may be omitted if the blessing is imparted less solemnly or only to a few. Next the priest says:

P: Let the little children come to me.

All: The kingdom of God belongs to such as these.

P: Their angels.

All: Ever see the face of the heavenly Father.

P: Let the enemy have no power over them.

All: And the son of iniquity be powerless to harm them.

P: Lord, heed my prayer.
All: And let my cry be heard by you.
P: The Lord be with you.
All: May He also be with you.

Let us pray.
Lord Jesus Christ, who embraced the little children when they came or were brought to you, and laying your hands on them blessed them and said: "Let the little children come to me, and do not stop them. The kingdom of heaven belongs to such as these; and their angels ever see the face of my Father;" we beg you to look with favor on the innocence of these children here present and on the devotion of their parents, and to bless them today through our ministry. Let them ever advance in your grace and goodness, the better to know you, love you, fear you, and serve you, and happily reach their blessed destiny. We ask this of you, Savior of the world, who live and reign with the Father and the Holy Spirit, God, forever and ever.
All: Amen.

Let us pray.
We beg you, Lord, through the intercession of the blessed Mary, ever a Virgin, to defend this family of yours from every kind of adversity; and as they offer their hearts to you, protect them in your kindness and mercy from all wiles of the enemy; through Christ our Lord.

All: Amen.

Let us pray.
God, who by your wondrous providence gave us your holy angels
as our guardians, grant that we, your suppliants, may ever be
shielded by their protection, and finally enjoy their fellowship in
heaven; through Christ our Lord.
All: Amen.

Making the sign of the cross over them, he blesses them, saying:

May God bless you, and may He be the guardian of your hearts
and your understanding, the Father, Son,   and Holy Spirit.
All: Amen.

He then sprinkles the children with holy water.

7. BLESSING OF CHILDREN

On Feastdays of the Holy Childhood Association

P: Our help is in the name of the Lord.
All: Who made heaven and earth.
P: The Lord be with you.
All: May He also be with you.

Let us pray.
We implore you, almighty God, to bless these children, and we
ask that you keep them in your love. Strengthen their hearts by the
power of the Holy Spirit, sanctify their lives, foster their
innocence. Keep their minds intent on good, help them to prosper,
give them peace, health, and charity. By your might and protection
shield them always from every temptation of men or demons. And
in your mercy may they finally attain the happiness and rest of
Paradise; through Christ our Lord.
All: Amen.

Let us pray.

Lord Jesus Christ, who embraced the little children when they came or were brought to you (here the priest extends his hands over them), and laying your hands on them blessed them and said: "Let the little children come to me, and do not stop them. The kingdom of heaven belongs to such as these; and their angels ever see the face of my Father;" we beg you to look with favor on the devotion of these boys and girls here present, and let your blessing come on them in fullest measure. Let them ever advance in your grace and goodness, the better to know you, love you, fear you, and serve you, and happily reach their blessed destiny. We ask this of you, Savior of the world, who live and reign with the Father and the Holy Spirit, God, forever and ever.
All: Amen.

May the blessing of almighty God, Father, Son,   and Holy Spirit, come upon you, keep and direct you, and remain with you forever.
All: Amen.

They are sprinkled with holy water.

8. BLESSING OF PILGRIMS

Before they set out for the holy shrines

In accord with ancient ecclesiastical discipline, pilgrims who are to visit the holy shrines should obtain a letter of recommendation from their Ordinary or pastor before they set out. Having put their affairs in order, they prepare themselves with sacramental confession, assist at Mass and receive holy communion. In this Mass the Collect for pilgrims (pro re gravi) is said. After Mass they kneel before the priest who says the following (for the music see the music supplement):

Antiphon: May the almighty and merciful Lord lead you in the way of peace and prosperity. May the Angel Raphael be your companion on the journey and bring you back to your homes in peace, health, and happiness.

Then the Canticle of Zachary is said; and after the canticle the above antiphon is repeated. Then the priest continues:

Lord, have mercy. Christ, have mercy. Lord, have mercy. Our Father (the rest inaudibly until:)

P: And lead us not into temptation.

All: But deliver us from evil.

P: Save your servants.

All: Who trust in you, my God.

P: Lord, send them aid from your holy place.

All: And watch over them from Sion.

P: Let them find in you, Lord, a fortified tower.

All: In the face of the enemy.

P: Let the enemy have no power over them.

All: And the son of iniquity be powerless to harm them.

P: May the Lord be praised at all times.

All: May God, our helper, grant us a happy journey.

P: Lord, shows us your ways.

All: And lead us along your paths.

P: Oh, that our life be bent.

All: On keeping your precepts.

P: For the crooked ways will be made straight.

All: And the rough places plain.

P: God has given His angels charge over you.

All: To guard you in all your undertakings.

P: Lord, heed my prayer.
All: And let my cry be heard by you.
P: The Lord be with you.
All: May He also be with you.

Let us pray.
God, who led the children of Israel dry-shod through the sea, and showed the way to the three Magi by the guidance of a star; grant these pilgrims, we pray, a happy journey and peaceful days, so that, with your holy angel as a guide, they may safely reach their destination and finally come to the haven of everlasting salvation.

God, who led your servant, Abraham out of Ur of the Chaldeans, and kept him safe in all his wanderings; may it please you, we pray, also to watch over these servants of yours. Be to them, Lord, a help in their preparations, comfort on the way, shade in the heat, shelter in the rain and cold, a carriage in tiredness, a shield in adversity, a staff in insecurity, a haven in shipwreck; so that under your guidance they may happily reach their destination, and finally return safe to their homes.

Lord, we beg you to hear our request that you guide the steps of your servants along the path of well-being that comes from you and that in the midst of this fickle world they may always live under your protection.

Grant, we pray, O almighty God, that your family of pilgrims find a safe route; and heeding the admonitions of blessed John, the precursor, come finally to Him whom John foretold, your Son, Jesus Christ our Lord.

Hear, Lord, our prayers, and kindly accompany your servants on

their journey; and as you are present everywhere lend them your aid at all times, so that with you as their shield they will be defended from all dangers and pay you their homage of gratitude; through Christ our Lord.
All: Amen.

May the peace and blessing of almighty God, Father, Son, and Holy Spirit, come upon you and remain with you forever.
All: Amen.

They are sprinkled with holy water.

If there is only one pilgrim the prayers are said in the singular; but if the priest who bestows the blessing is a member of the pilgrimage they are said in the plural.

9. BLESSING OF PILGRIMS

On their return

P: Our help is in the name of the Lord.
All: Who made heaven and earth.

Next the following antiphon and psalm are sung (for the music see the music supplement):

Antiphon: See, thus is the man blessed who fears the Lord.

Psalm 127

(For this psalm see Rite for Marriage within Mass)

After the psalm the above antiphon is repeated. Then the priest continues:

Lord, have mercy. Christ, have mercy. Lord, have mercy. Our Father (the rest inaudibly until:)

P: And lead us not into temptation.

All: But deliver us from evil.

P: Blessed are they who come in the name of the Lord.

All: Blessed be you by the Lord who made heaven and earth.

P: Look with favor, Lord, on your servants and their works.

All: And keep them in the way of your precepts.

P: Lord, heed my prayer.
All: And let my cry be heard by you.
P: The Lord be with you.
All: May He also be with you.

Let us pray.
We beg you, Lord, be appeased, and lavish on your servants pardon and peace, so that being cleansed of all their transgressions they may serve you with tranquil hearts.

Almighty everlasting God, the ruler of our lives and destinies, grant to your servants continual and abundant peace, so that those whom you have brought back safely to their various occupations may bask in the security of your protection.

God, the support of the lowly, you who console us by the love of our brethren; bestow your grace on our brotherhood, so that we may always see your presence in those in whom you live by your grace; through Christ our Lord.
All: Amen.

May the peace and blessing of almighty God, Father, Son, and Holy Spirit, come upon you and remain with you forever.
All: Amen.

They are sprinkled with holy water.

10.PRAYER OF POPE PAUL VI FOR PRISONERS

{This prayer was composed by Pope Paul VI for the inmates of Rome's Regina Coeli prison, which he visited on April 9, 1964. It deserves a place in the Ritual; and I am grateful to the N.C.W.C. News Service for its permission to print it.}

Lord, they tell me I must pray; but how can I pray when I am so unhappy? How can I speak to you in the conditions in which I find myself? I am sad; I am angry. Sometimes I am desperate. I would like to curse rather than pray. I suffer deeply because everyone is against me and criticizes me because I am here, away from my own family and from my activities. I am without peace, and how can I pray, O Lord?

I know you were good, you were wise, you were innocent. Yet they slandered you, they dishonored you, they tried you, they beat you, they crucified you, they put you to death? But why? Where is justice? And you were able to forgive those who treated you so unjustly and so cruelly. You were able to pray for them. Indeed, they tell me that you allowed yourself to be put to death in that manner in order to save your executioners, to save all us sinful men. And also to save me?

If this is so, Lord, it means that one may be good at heart even though the condemnation of the courts of men weighs on one's shoulders. I too, Lord, feel at the bottom of my heart that I am better than others would believe. I know what justice is, what honesty is, what honor is, and what goodness is. Before you, these thoughts stir in me. Do you see them? Do you see how disgusted I am with my miseries? Do you see that I would like to cry out and weep? Do you understand me, Lord? Is this my prayer?

Yes, this is my prayer. From the depths of my bitterness I raise my voice to you. Do not reject it. You at least, who have suffered as I have, more than I have, you at least, Lord, listen to me. I have so many things to ask of you. Give me, Lord, peace of heart. Give me a tranquil conscience, a new conscience capable of good thoughts.

Indeed, Lord, to you I say it. If I have been remiss, forgive me. We all have need of forgiveness and mercy. I am praying to you for myself. And then, Lord, I pray to you for my loved ones, who are still so dear to me. Lord, assist them. Lord, console them. Lord, tell them to remember me and to love me still. I have so much need to know that somebody is still thinking of me and loves me. And also on these companions in misfortune and affliction, together here in this prison, Lord, have mercy. Mercy on everyone. Yes, also on those who make me suffer, on all. We are all men of this unhappy world. But we are, Lord, your creatures, your likeness, your brothers, O Christ. Have pity on us.

To our poor voice we add the sweet and innocent voice of the Madonna, of the most blessed Mary, who is your Mother, and who is for us also a Mother of intercession and consolation. Lord, give us your peace; give us hope. Amen.

11. BLESSING OF SICK PILGRIMS

The priest, vested in surplice and white stole, places the end of the stole on the head of the sick person, and reads the following passage from the Gospel. If he blesses more than one he holds the stole above them with his right hand.

P: The Lord be with you.
All: May He also be with you.
P: A reading from the holy Gospel according to St. Matthew.
All: Glory be to you, O Lord.

Matthew 13.44-52

At that time Jesus said to His disciples: "The kingdom of heaven reminds me of a treasure buried in the field; as soon as a person discovers it, he hides it again, and off he goes in his joy and sells all his possessions and buys that field.

Again, the kingdom of heaven reminds me of a merchant in quest of beautiful pearls; as soon as he discovers one pearl of great value, off he goes and promptly sells all his possessions and buys it.

Again, the kingdom of heaven reminds me of a dragnet thrown into the sea and taking in fish of every description; when it is filled, the crew haul it on the beach and settle down to sorting what is usable into receptacles, and throwing away what is worthless. So it will be at the end of the world. The angels will go forth and separate the sinners from among the saints and consign them to the blazing furnace. There it is that weeping and gnashing of teeth will really be heard.

"Do you understand all these lessons?" "Yes," they replied. "Therefore," He continued, "every teacher initiated in the mysteries of the kingdom of heaven is like the head of a household who produces from his store new things and old."

After the Gospel he blesses the sick person, saying:

May the blessing of almighty God, Father, Son, and Holy Spirit, come upon you and remain with you forever.
All: Amen.

Then he presents the end of the stole to the sick to be kissed, and sprinkles him with holy water, saying:

May God sprinkle you with the dew of His grace and bring you to everlasting life.
All: Amen.

12. BLESSING OF A SICK ADULT

The priest on entering the sick-room says:

P: God's peace be in this home.

All: And in all who live here.

Then he goes up to the sick person and continues:

P: Our help is in the name of the Lord.
All: Who made heaven and earth.
P: Lord, heed my prayer.
All: And let my cry be heard by you.
P: The Lord be with you.
All: May He also be with you.

Let us pray.
Lord Jesus Christ, as I, in all humility, enter this home, let there enter with me your peace and your mercy. Let all wiles of the devil be driven far from here, and let your angels of peace take over and put down all wicked strife. Teach us, O Lord, to recognize the majesty of your holy name, and bless what we are about to do; you who are holy, you who are kind, you who abide with the Father and the Holy Spirit forever and ever.
All: Amen.

Let us pray.
We entreat you, Lord, to look with favor on your servant who is weak and failing, and revive the soul you have created. Chastened by suffering may he (she) know that he (she) has been saved by your healing; through Christ our Lord.
All: Amen.

Let us pray.
Merciful Lord, consoler of all who believe in you, we appeal to your boundless compassion that at my humble visit you will also visit this servant of yours, lying on his (her) bed of pain, as you visited the mother-in-law of Simon Peter. Graciously stand by him (her), Lord, so that he (she) may recover his (her) lost strength, and join with your Church in returning thanks to you, who are God, living and reigning forever and ever.
All: Amen.

Then he holds his hand outstretched over the sick person and says:

May our Lord Jesus Christ be with you to guard you, within you to preserve you, before you to lead you, behind you to protect you, above you to bless you; He who lives and reigns with the Father and the Holy Spirit forever and ever.
All: Amen.

May the blessing of almighty God, Father, Son, and Holy Spirit, come upon you and remain with you forever.
All: Amen.

He sprinkles the sick person with holy water.

13. BLESSING OF SICK CHILDREN

If children who are ill are old enough to receive the sacrament of anointing of the sick, the same prayers and ceremonies are used as given in the chapter dealing with the visitation and care of the sick, depending on circumstances of time and illness. But for younger children the following can be used:

On entering the room of the sick child the priest says:

P: God's peace be in this home.
All: And in all who live here.

Next he sprinkles the sick child, the bed, and the room without saying anything. Then he says psalm 112; and after the psalm he continues:

Lord, have mercy. Christ, have mercy. Lord, have mercy. Our Father (the rest inaudibly until:)

P: And lead us not into temptation.

All: But deliver us from evil.

P: Our God is merciful.

All: He is the Lord who watches over little children.

P: Let the little children come to me.

All: The kingdom of God belongs to such as these.

P: Lord, heed my prayer.
All: And let my cry be heard by you.
P: The Lord be with you.
All: May He also be with you.

Let us pray.
God, by whose power all things grow to maturity, and once mature retain their strength, reach out your right hand to this boy (girl) who is afflicted at this tender age. Let him (her) regain health, grow up to manhood (womanhood), and serve you in gratitude and fidelity all the days of his (her) life; through Christ our Lord.
All: Amen.

Let us pray.
Merciful God and Father, our unalloyed comfort, who, having the interests of your creatures at heart, are inclined in your goodness to bestow the grace of healing not only on the soul but on the body as well; be pleased to raise up this sick child from his (her) bed of suffering, and to return him (her) in full health to your Church and to his (her) parents. May he (she) then throughout the days of his (her) life, as he (she) advances in favor and knowledge in your sight and that of men, serve you in righteousness and holiness, and render you due thanks for your goodness; through Christ our Lord.
All: Amen.

Let us pray.
God, who in a marvelous way have disposed the ministries of angels and of men, mercifully grant that the life on earth of this boy (girl) may be under the protection of those who minister to you in heaven; through Christ our Lord.
All: Amen.

After this prayer the priest puts his right hand on the head of the child and says:

They shall lay their hands upon the sick and all will be well with them. May Jesus, Son of Mary, Lord and Savior of the world, through the merits and intercession of His holy apostles Peter and Paul and all His saints, show you favor and mercy.

If he wishes, the priest may add the following passage from the Gospel, depending on the child's condition and the desire of the parents:

P: The Lord be with you.
All: May He also be with you.
P: The beginning of the holy Gospel according to St. John.
All: Glory be to you, O Lord.

As the priest says "The beginning," etc., he signs himself on the brow, mouth, and breast in the usual way; and signs the sick child in the same way, if the child cannot do so himself.

For this passage from the Gospel see John 1.1-14.

Lastly he blesses the child, saying:

May the blessing of almighty God, Father, Son, and Holy Spirit, come upon you and remain with you forever.
All: Amen.

He sprinkles him (her) (them) with holy water.

If there are several sick children in the room the prayers given above are said in the plural.

14. RITE FOR IMPARTING THE PAPAL BLESSING TO THE PEOPLE

The rite to be used by those priests to whom this faculty has been granted by the Holy See

(According to a decree of the Congregation of Sacred Rites, March 12, 1940)

1. The people are to be informed of the day, the time, and the church where the papal blessing will be given. When they are assembled in church a short and edifying instruction should be delivered to them in order to arouse a spirit of devotion and compunction. After this the priest, vested in surplice and white stole, kneels at the altar and implores God's help as follows (he is not assisted by anyone):

P: Our help is in the name of the Lord.
All: Who made heaven and earth.
P: Lord, save your people.
All: And bless your inheritance.
P: The Lord be with you.
All: May He also be with you.

Then he stands and says this oration:

Let us pray.
Almighty and merciful God, grant us your aid from your holy place, and graciously hear the prayers of these people who humbly ask for pardon of their sins, and look for your blessing and your grace. Kindly reach out your right hand over them, and pour out your blessing in fullest measure, that fortified with your gifts they may come to everlasting life and happiness; through Christ our Lord.
All: Amen.

2. He then goes to the corner of the altar-steps at the epistle side, and blesses the people with one sign of the cross, saying in a clear voice:

May the almighty God bless you, Father, Son, and Holy Spirit.
All: Amen.

3. Priests who enjoy the faculty of imparting the papal blessing are obliged to observe the prescribed form, and may use this faculty only in the church designated. They may not use it on the same day or in the same city or place on and in which a bishop imparts it.

15. THE PAPAL BLESSING

With Plenary Indulgence at the end of a Sermon, Mission, or Retreat

(Approved by the Congregation of Sacred Rites, May 11, 1911)

If the Brief states that the papal blessing with plenary indulgence at the end of a sermon is to be given with a crucifix-i.e., according to the rite prescribed here--a single sign of the cross is made with a crucifix, using the form:

May the blessing of almighty God, Father, Son, and Holy Spirit, come upon you and remain with you forever.
All: Amen.

4
BLESSINGS OF ANIMALS

1. BLESSING OF CATTLE, HERDS, FLOCKS

(Cattle, oxen, sheep, goats, swine, etc.)

P: Our help is in the name of the Lord.
All: Who made heaven and earth.
P: The Lord be with you.
All: May He also be with you.

Let us pray.
Lord God, King of heaven and earth, Word of the Father by whom were made all creatures destined for our sustenance; we beg you to look with favor on our lowly condition; and as you have given us assistance in our work and in our needs, so may you bless,   shield, and watch over these animals (this animal) with your mercy and heavenly care. And to us, your servants, be pleased to give everlasting grace together with creature needs, thus enabling us to praise and glorify and offer thanks to your holy name; through Christ our Lord.
All: Amen.

They are sprinkled with holy water:

2. BLESSING OF HORSES AND OTHER ANIMALS

P: Our help is in the name of the Lord.
All: Who made heaven and earth.
P: The Lord be with you.
All: May He also be with you.

Let us pray.
God, our refuge and our strength and source of all goodness, heed the holy prayers of your Church, and grant that we fully obtain whatever we ask for in faith; through Christ our Lord.
All: Amen.

Let us pray.
Almighty everlasting God, who helped the illustrious St. Antony to emerge unscathed from the many temptations that beset him in this world; help also your servants to grow in virtue by his noble example, and to be delivered from the ever-present dangers of this life by his merits and intercession; through Christ our Lord.
All: Amen.

Let us pray.
Lord, let these animals have your blessing   to the benefit of their being, and by the intercession of St. Antony deliver them from all evil; through Christ our Lord.
All: Amen.

They are sprinkled with holy water.

3. BLESSING OF SICK ANIMALS

The priest, vested in surplice and purple stole, says:

P: Our help is in the name of the Lord.

All: Who made heaven and earth.

P: Deal not with us, Lord, as our sins deserve.

All: Nor take vengeance on us for our transgressions.

P: You, O Lord, will save both men and beasts.

All: Just as you, O God, show mercy again and again.

P: You open your hand.

All: And fill every living creature with your blessing.

P: Lord, heed my prayer.
All: And let my cry be heard by you.
P: The Lord be with you.
All: May He also be with you.

Let us pray.
God, who supplied even dumb animals to lighten man's toil, we humbly entreat you to preserve these creatures for our use, since without them mankind cannot subsist; through Christ our Lord.
All: Amen.

Let us pray.
We humbly entreat your mercy, O Lord, praying that in your name and by the power of your blessing   these animals may be cured of the dire sickness that afflicts them. Let the devil's power over them be utterly abolished, and do you, Lord, protect their life and health against recurrent sickness; through Christ our Lord.
All: Amen.

Let us pray.
Have pity on us, Lord, we beg you, and turn away every scourge from your faithful. Rid our beasts of the dread sickness that is destroying them, so that we who are justly punished when we go astray may feel your gracious mercy when we repent; through Christ our Lord.
All: Amen.

They are sprinkled with holy water.

4. BLESSING OF FOWL OR ANY KIND OF BIRD

P: Our help is in the name of the Lord.

All: Who made heaven and earth.
P: The Lord be with you.
All: May He also be with you.

Let us pray.
God, author of all nature, who, among the many created species, also brought forth winged creatures from the primeval waters for the use of mankind; from which Noe, on coming out of the Ark, offered you a pleasing holocaust; who commanded your people, delivered from Egypt through Moses, your servant, to eat these winged creatures, separating the clean from the unclean; we humbly entreat you to bless   and to sanctify this flesh of clean birds, so that all who eat thereof may be filled with your bounteous blessing, and may deserve to come to the feast of everlasting life; through Christ our Lord.
All: Amen.

They are sprinkled with holy water.

5. BLESSING OF BEES

P: Our help is in the name of the Lord.
All: Who made heaven and earth.
P: The Lord be with you.
All: May He also be with you.

Let us pray.
Lord God almighty, who made the heavens and the earth, and all living things in the air and on land for the use of mankind; who ordered, through the ministers of holy Church, that candles made from the industry of bees should be lighted during the solemn mystery in which the most sacred body and blood of Jesus Christ, your Son, is confected and consumed; send your holy blessing upon these bees and these beehives, causing them to multiply and to produce and to be kept from harm, so that their yield of wax can be turned to your honor, to that of the Son and Holy Spirit, and to the veneration of the blessed Virgin Mary; through Christ our Lord.

All: Amen.

They are sprinkled with holy water.

6. BLESSING OF SILKWORMS

P: Our help is in the name of the Lord.
All: Who made heaven and earth.
P: The Lord be with you.
All: May He also be with you.

Let us pray.
God, Creator and King of the universe, who in creating living
things endowed each with the power of propagating its kind; we
pray that in your kindness you bless these silkworms, thus
fostering them and increasing their numbers. Let your holy altars
be adorned with the fruit of their industry. And let your faithful
people, resplendent in silken apparel, acknowledge you
with heartfelt praise as the donor of every good. We ask this of you
who, with your only-begotten Son and the Holy Spirit, live and
reign forever and ever.
All: Amen.

They are sprinkled with holy water.

7. DEPRECATORY BLESSING AGAINST PESTS

(Mice and rats, locusts, worms, etc.)

The priest vests in surplice and purple stole, and coming to the
field or place infested with these creatures, says:

Antiphon: Arise, Lord, help us; and deliver us for your kindness'
sake.

Ps 43.1: O God, our ears have heard, our fathers have declared to
us.

All: Glory be to the Father.

P: As it was in the beginning.

All Ant.: Arise, Lord, help us; and deliver us for your kindness' sake.

P: Our help is in the name of the Lord.
All: Who made heaven and earth.
P: Lord, heed my prayer.
All: And let my cry be heard by you.
P: The Lord be with you.
All: May He also be with you.

Let us pray.
We entreat you, Lord, be pleased to hear our prayers; and even though we rightly deserve, on account of our sins, this plague of mice (or locusts, worms, etc.), yet mercifully deliver us for your kindness' sake. Let this plague be expelled by your power, and our land and fields be left fertile, so that all it produces redound to your glory and serve our necessities; through Christ our Lord.
All: Amen.

Let us pray.
Almighty everlasting God, the donor of all good things, and the most merciful pardoner of our sins; before whom all creatures bow down in adoration, those in heaven, on earth, and below the earth; preserve us sinners by your might, that whatever we undertake with trust in your protection may meet with success by your grace. And now as we utter a curse on these noxious pests, may they be cursed by you; as we seek to destroy them, may they be destroyed by you; as we seek to exterminate them, may they be exterminated by you; so that delivered from this plague by your goodness, we may freely offer thanks to your majesty; through Christ our Lord.
All: Amen.

Exorcism

I cast out you noxious vermin, by God   the Father almighty, by Jesus Christ, His only-begotten Son, and by the Holy Spirit. May you speedily be banished from our land and fields, lingering here no longer, but passing on to places where you can do no harm. In the name of the almighty God and the entire heavenly court, as well as in the name of the holy Church of God, we pronounce a curse on you, that wherever you go you may be cursed, decreasing from day to day until you are obliterated. Let no remnant of you remain anywhere, except what might be necessary for the welfare and use of mankind. Be pleased to grant our request, you who are coming to judge both the living and the dead and the world by fire. All: Amen.

The places infested are sprinkled with holy water.

5
BLESSINGS OF HOMES, BUILDINGS, OR PLACES

Not designated for sacred functions

1. BLESSING OF A CORNERSTONE

P: Our help is in the name of the Lord.
All: Who made heaven and earth.
P: The Lord be with you.
All: May He also be with you.

Let us pray. God, from whom every good thing takes its start and receives its steady and full growth; grant, we beg of you, that what we commence for the glory of your name may be carried to completion by the ever-present aid of your fatherly wisdom; through Christ our Lord.
All: Amen.

It is sprinkled with holy water.

2. BLESSING OF A PRIVATE OR DOMESTIC ORATORY

P: Our help is in the name of the Lord.
All: Who made heaven and earth.
P: The Lord be with you.
All: May He also be with you.

Let us pray.
God, who sanctify the places dedicated to your name, pour out your grace on this house of prayer, that all who here call on your name may experience your kind assistance; through Christ our Lord.
All: Amen.

It is sprinkled with holy water.

3. BLESSING OF AN APARTMENT OR A HOME

P: Our help is in the name of the Lord.
All: Who made heaven and earth.
P: The Lord be with you.
All: May He also be with you.

Let us pray.
Lord God almighty, bless this apartment (or home), that it be the shelter of health, purity, and self-control; that there prevail here a spirit of humility, goodness, mildness, obedience to the commandments, and gratitude to God the Father, Son, and Holy Spirit. May this blessing remain on this place and on those who live here now and always.
All: Amen.

It is sprinkled with holy water.

4. BLESSING OF HOMES

Outside of Eastertime

A pastor or another priest may wish to sprinkle with holy water a particular home or the homes of the faithful in general. On entering the home he says:

P: God's peace be in this home.

All: And in all who live here.

As he sprinkles the principal room he says:

Antiphon: Purify me with hyssop, Lord, and I shall be clean of sin. Wash me, and I shall be whiter than snow. (Ps. 50.1) Have mercy on me, God, in your great kindness.

V. Glory be to the Father, and to the Son, and to the Holy Spirit.

All: As it was in the beginning, is now, and ever shall be, world without end. Amen.

P: Ant. Purify me with hyssop, Lord, and I shall be clean of sin. Wash me, and I shall be whiter than snow.

P: Lord, heed my prayer.
All: And let my cry be heard by you.
P: The Lord be with you.
All: May He also be with you.

Let us pray.
Hear us, holy Lord and Father, almighty everlasting God, and in your goodness send your holy angel from heaven to watch over and protect all who live in this home, to be with them and give them comfort and encouragement; through Christ our Lord.
All: Amen.

5. ANOTHER BLESSING OF A HOME

P: Our help is in the name of the Lord.

All: Who made heaven and earth.
P: The Lord be with you.
All: May He also be with you.

Let us pray.
God the Father almighty, we fervently implore you for the sake of
this home and its occupants and possessions, that you may bless
and sanctify   them, enriching them by your kindness in every way
possible. Pour out on them, Lord, heavenly dew in good measure,
as well as an abundance of earthly needs. Mercifully listen to their
prayers, and grant that their desires be fulfilled. At our lowly
coming be pleased to bless and sanctify this home, as you once
were pleased to bless the home of Abraham, Isaac, and Jacob.
Within these walls let your angels of light preside and stand watch
over those who live here; through Christ our Lord.
All: Amen.

It is sprinkled with holy water.

6. BLESSING OF A BRIDAL CHAMBER

P: Our help is in the name of the Lord.
All: Who made heaven and earth.
P: The Lord be with you.
All: May He also be with you.

Let us pray.
Lord, bless   this bridal chamber, that those who share it may abide
in your peace and conform themselves to your will. And as they
grow older may they know many happy years together, and come
finally to your heavenly kingdom; through Christ our Lord.
All: Amen.

It is sprinkled with holy water.

7. BLESSING OF A SCHOOL

On entering the school the priest sprinkles the rooms with holy water saying:

P: God's peace be in this school.

All: And in all who assemble here.

P: Our help is in the name of the Lord.

All: Who made heaven and earth.

P: The Lord be with you.

All: May He also be with you.

Let us pray.
Lord Jesus Christ, who bade your apostles to pray that peace might come on any house they entered, we entreat you to bless by our ministry this building destined for the education of the young. Bestow your peace and blessing on it in full measure, so that its teachers and pupils may experience your saving grace, as did Zaccheus when you came into his home. Bid your angels to keep guard here and to drive away all power of the enemy. Inspire the teachers with knowledge, wisdom, and holy fear. Foster their pupils with grace from on high, so that they may grasp, retain, and put into practice the lessons they are taught. May teachers and pupils alike so please you by a truly virtuous life that they may finally deserve to be received into your everlasting home in heaven; through you, Jesus Christ, our Savior and our God, who live and reign forever and ever.
All: Amen.

8. SOLEMN BLESSING OF A SCHOOL

On a Sunday or feastday chosen by the pastor and the patron and duly announced, the celebrant and the clergy and other assistants assemble in the rectory or other suitable place, where they vest in white vestments. At the appointed time--everything being in order-

-they march in solemn procession to the church, singing the Litany of the Saints or other sacred hymns; and the church bells are rung. The procession proceeds in the following order: schoolchildren (with one of them carrying their banner), the choir, the subdeacon with the processional cross, the patron or his representative, the rest of the faithful, and lastly the clergy and the ministrants. Having come into church the celebrant kneels on the lowest step of the main altar and intones the "Veni Creator" in the usual way (for the music see the music supplement). If there is no church at the place, the first part of the service is held in the room of assembly and vesting.

Hymn: Veni Creator
(for the text of this hymn see Veni Creator)

At the end of the hymn the celebrant chants:

Lord, have mercy. Christ, have mercy. Lord, have mercy. Our Father (the rest inaudibly until:)

P: And lead us not into temptation.
All: But deliver us from evil.
P: Lord, heed my prayer.
All: And let my cry be heard by you.
P: The Lord be with you.
All: May He also be with you.

Let us pray.
God, who instructed the hearts of the faithful by the light of the Holy Spirit, guide us by your Spirit to desire only what is good and so always to find joy in His comfort.

God, who know the secrets of man's heart and will, from whom nothing is hidden; chasten our innermost thoughts by the outpouring of the Holy Spirit, so that we may perform this blessing in a worthy manner, and thus obtain for your faithful the welfare they seek.

We beg you, Lord, let a breath of your grace prompt our undertakings and guide them along their course, so that our least prayer and work may ever begin in you and end in you; through Christ our Lord.
All: Amen.

P: Let the little children come to me.

All: The kingdom of God belongs to such as these.

Let us pray.
Almighty everlasting God, we humbly beg you to look with favor on your children. Pour out on their hearts the grace of the Holy Spirit, that through Him they may ever be enlightened and instructed in whatever is pleasing to you, and so make progress in wisdom, age, and grace; through Christ our Lord.
All: Amen.

P: Our help is in the name of the Lord.
All: Who made heaven and earth.
Deacon: Let us go forth in peace.
All: In Christ's name. Amen.

Now the celebrant goes in solemn procession to bless the school. Arriving there he stands outside before the door and chants:

P: May God's peace be in this school.
All: And in all who assemble here.

He intones the following antiphon. The choir continues with it and the psalm verse and repeats the antiphon at the end. For the music see the music supplement.

Purify me with hyssop, * Lord, and I shall be clean of sin. Wash me, and I shall be whiter than snow. (Ps. 50.1) Have mercy on me, God, * in your great kindness. V. Glory be to the Father, and to the Son, and to the Holy Spirit. * As it was in the beginning, is now, and ever shall be, world without end. Amen. Purify me with hyssop, Lord, and I shall be clean of sin. Wash me, and I shall be whiter than snow.

While this is being sung he sprinkles the outer walls with holy water at least the front. After this he chants:

P: The Lord be with you.
All: May He also be with you.

Let us pray.
Almighty and merciful God, who conferred on your priests above all others so great a grace, that whatever they do worthily and exactly in your name is regarded as being done by you; we pray that in your kindness you may be present wherever we are present and may bless   whatever we bless. And at our lowly coming, through the merits of your saints, may demons flee and the angel of peace be at hand.

Holy Lord, almighty Father, through the intercession of St. Ignatius and St. Aloysius, bless   this building, bless our coming, bless our entering here, as you were pleased to bless the home of the patriarchs Abraham, Isaac, and Jacob; through Christ our Lord.
All: Amen.

Now all enter the school. The celebrant goes into the main room and there chants:

P: May God's peace be in this school.
All: And in all who assemble here.

Accompanied by the choir and clergy the celebrant goes up to the table which is covered with a linen cloth and on which is placed a crucifix and two lighted candles. There he chants the following:

P: Lord, heed my prayer.
All: And let my cry be heard by you.
P: The Lord be with you.
All: May He also be with you.

Let us pray.

Hear us, holy Lord and Father, almighty everlasting God, and in your goodness send your holy angel from heaven to watch over and protect all who assemble in this school, teachers and pupils, to be with them and give them comfort and encouragement; through Christ our Lord.
All: Amen.

Let us pray.
Lord Jesus Christ, who said to your disciples: "In whatever home you enter, greet it, saying, 'Peace be in this home'"; let this same peace, we pray, abide in this school and in all who assemble here, teachers and pupils. Shield them, Lord, from all sickness. Inspire the teachers with knowledge, wisdom, and holy fear. Foster their pupils with your grace, so that they may grasp, retain, and put into practice the many salutary and useful lessons they are taught. May it please you, through our lowly ministry, to bless   and to sanctify this school. Let your angels of light dwell within its walls and stand guard over the teachers and pupils; you who live and reign forever and ever.
All: Amen.

Then the celebrant again intones the antiphon of the "Asperges" as above; and while the choir sings the rest of it he walks around the room and sprinkles it with holy water. Coming back to the table he puts incense in the thurible and blesses it with the words:

Through the intercession of St. Michael the Archangel, who stands at the right of the altar of incense, and that of all the angels, be pleased, Lord, to bless   this incense and to accept it as a fragrant offering; through Christ our Lord.
All: Amen.

After this he takes the thurible and incenses the room. During the incensation the choir sings the following antiphon and psalm verses (for the music see the music supplement):

Antiphon: May this incense blessed by you ascend to you, O Lord, and may your kindness descend upon us.

Psalm 140.2-4

Let my prayer come like incense before you; * the lifting up of my hands, like the evening sacrifice.Lord, set a watch before my mouth, * a guard at the door of my lips. Let not my heart incline to the evil * of engaging in deeds of violence. Glory be to the Father. As it was in the beginning.

After the incensation the celebrant stands before the crucifix and chants:

P: The Lord be with you.
All: May He also be with you.

Let us pray.
We beg you, O Lord, to visit this school and to drive out all wiles of the enemy. Let your holy angels dwell here and keep a peaceful watch over all who assemble here, teachers and pupils, and let your blessing be with them at all times.

Lord, bless   this school, and let there be found here health and holiness, virtue and glory. Let there prevail here a spirit of humility, goodness, mildness, gentleness, docility, fidelity and obedience to your law, and gratitude to God, the Father, Son, and Holy Spirit. Let this blessing remain here for all time, and let the seven-fold gifts of the Holy Spirit come upon the teachers and pupils; through Christ our Lord.
All: Amen.

The celebrant hangs the cross in a prominent place in the room saying as he does so:

Lord, let the sign of our salvation dominate this building, and forbid entrance here to the avenging angel; in the name of the Father, and of the Son,   and of the Holy Spirit.
All: Amen.

Then standing before the cross he says:

Let us pray.
Almighty everlasting God, who are in full command of all places
under your dominion, and without whose leave nothing occurs;
shield this school from all harm, and let no evil power work
havoc here. By the power of the holy cross and by the operation of
the Holy Spirit may a worthy service be rendered to you in this
place, and may a holy freedom abound; through Christ our
Lord.
All: Amen.

Let us pray.
Abide with us, O Lord our God, and be a constant help to those
who take refuge in your holy cross; through Christ our Lord.
All: Amen.

Making the sign of the cross with his right hand, the celebrant
blesses I the room and all who are present, saying:

May the blessing of almighty God, Father, Son, and Holy Spirit,
come on this school, on all who assemble here, teachers and pupils,
and on us all, and remain forever.
All: Amen.

After this all go in solemn procession to the church, where the
Mass proper to the day's office is celebrated. During the procession
the children sing hymns and the church bells are rung.

9. BLESSING OF A LIBRARY
(Approved by the Congregation of Sacred Rites, July 23, 1924)

P: Our help is in the name of the Lord.
All: Who made heaven and earth.
P: The Lord be with you.
All: May He also be with you.

Let us pray.

God, Lord of all wisdom, pour out your blessing on this library. Let it safely withstand fire and every peril, and let it increase its volumes day by day. May all who come here for work or for study grow in knowledge of things human and divine, and grow likewise in their love of you; through Christ our Lord.
All: Amen.

It is sprinkled with holy water.

10. BLESSING OF AN ARCHIVE
(Approved by the Congregation of Sacred Rites, July 23, 1924)

P: Our help is in the name of the Lord.
All: Who made heaven and earth.
P: The Lord be with you.
All: May He also be with you.

Let us pray.
God, who love truth and justice, pour out your blessing on this archive constructed to preserve the records of past events and legal documents from destruction by man or time. Let it safely withstand fire and every peril. And let all who come here for research be intent on truth and justice, and grow in their love of you; through Christ our Lord.
All: Amen.

It is sprinkled with holy water

11. BLESSING OF A SEMINARY

{This blessing is not to be found in the latest edition of the Roman Ritual of 1952, for its composition is of later origin, and was approved by the Congregation of Sacred Rites on May 12, 1953}

The rector of the seminary, or another priest appointed by the

Ordinary to bless new seminary buildings (unless the Ordinary himself wishes to perform the rite), goes at the appointed time to the chapel of the seminary and vests there in surplice and white stole. He is assisted by two clerics, both wearing surplices, one of whom carries the aspersory, the other the Ritual. Kneeling at the altar he intones the "Veni Creator," which is then sung by the seminarians (for the music of this hymn see the music supplement). At the conclusion of the hymn the priest says:

P: Send forth your Spirit and all things shall be recreated.

All: And you shall renew the face of the earth.

Let us pray.
God, who instructed the hearts of the faithful by the light of the Holy Spirit, guide us by your Spirit to desire only what is good and so always to find joy in His comfort.

We beg you, Lord, let a breath of your grace prompt our undertakings and guide them along their course, so that our least prayer and work may ever begin in you and end in you; through Christ our Lord.
All: Amen.

Then he receives the aspersory from the assistant and intones the Asperges (see The Sunday Blessing with Holy Water). The antiphon is continued by the seminarians (for the music see the music supplement), and is followed by psalm 50; and if time allows by part of psalm 118.

Meanwhile the priest, assisted by the cleric who carries the holy water stoup, goes around to all the rooms and other places of the seminary, sprinkling them with holy water in the usual way.

He then returns to the chapel and stands before the altar. Glory be to the Father is sung now, even though the psalm may not be finished. After this the priest says:

P: Lord, heed my prayer.

All: And let my cry be heard by you.
P: The Lord be with you.
All: May He also be with you.

Let us pray.
Hear us, holy Lord and Father, almighty everlasting God, and in your goodness send your holy angel from heaven to watch over and protect all who live in this seminary, to be with them and give them comfort and encouragement; through Christ our Lord.
All: Amen.

Let us pray.
God, who for the glory of your majesty and the salvation of mankind appointed your only-begotten Son as the eternal High Priest; grant that those whom you are pleased to select as the ministers and dispensers of your mysteries may be filled with the spirit of wisdom, knowledge, and holy fear. Help them to put on Christ and to accept their sacred ministry with a pure heart and blameless conduct, and to persevere in it faithful until death.

God, who gave the Holy Spirit to the apostles while they were at prayer together with Mary, the Mother of Jesus; grant that, while we are preparing for our future ministry in this holy cenacle, we may render a faithful service to your majesty under the protection of our Mother, Queen of the apostles, and thus be made ready to extend the glory of your name by word and by example.

God, who made your Church illustrious by the renowned learning of blessed Thomas, your confessor, and extended her kingdom by his holy life; help us, we pray, to gain a higher understanding of his teaching and a fuller imitation of his integrity; through Christ our Lord.
All: Amen.

Then the priest takes a crucifix and hangs it in a suitable place, the seminary, one previously selected for this purpose. If the place is some distance from the chapel, the participants may go there in procession, singing the hymn, "Vexilla Regis".

As the priest hangs the crucifix in its place he says:

Lord, let the sign of our salvation dominate this building, and forbid entrance here to the avenging angel; in the name of the Father, and of the Son,   and of the Holy Spirit.
All: Amen.

Then standing before the cross he says:

Almighty everlasting God, who are in full command of all places under your dominion, and without whose leave nothing occurs; shield this seminary from all harm, and let no evil power work havoc here. By the power of the holy cross and by the operation of the Holy Spirit may a worthy service be rendered to you in this place, and may a holy freedom abound; through Christ our Lord.
All: Amen.

Let us pray.
Abide with us, O Lord our God, and be a constant help to those who take refuge in your holy cross; through Christ our Lord.
All: Amen.

Making the sign of the cross with his right hand, the priest blesses the building and all who are present, saying:

May the blessing of almighty God, Father, Son,   and Holy Spirit, come on this seminary, on all who live here, teachers and students, and on us all, and remain forever.
All: Amen.

12. BLESSING OF A PRINTING-OFFICE AND PRINTING-PRESS

(Approved by the Congregation of Sacred Rites, May 12, 1909)

Standing at the entrance the priest says:

We beg you, Lord, let a breath of your grace prompt our

undertakings and guide them along their course, so that our least prayer and work may ever begin in you and end in you; through Christ our Lord.

All: Amen.

As he goes into the building he says:

P: God's peace be in this establishment.

All: And in all who are employed here.

Then he says the antiphon "Purify me with hyssop," etc. (see The Sunday Blessing with Holy Water) as he sprinkles with holy water the various rooms of the printing-office, until he comes to the main part. He stops here and says:

P: Our help is in the name of the Lord.
All: Who made heaven and earth.
P: The Lord be with you.
All: May He also be with you.

Let us pray.
Lord Jesus Christ, who said to your apostles: "In whatever home you enter, greet it, saying, 'Peace be in this home'"; let this same peace, we pray, abide in this printing establishment and in all who transact business here. Be pleased, O Lord, to shield and to free all those who work here from every injury of body and soul. Fill the writers, managers, and employees with the spirit of wisdom, prudence, and strength, and instill in them a holy fear, so that they may faithfully observe the precepts of the Church, and thus use their vocation for your glory and for the benefit of their fellowmen. Good Jesus, who are the way, the truth, and the life, bless this place, and grant, through the intercession of the glorious and immaculate Virgin Mary, your Mother, that all who are employed here may happily attain the imperishable crown of glory. We ask this of you who are God, living and reigning forever and ever.

All: Amen.

Then he blesses the machines and instruments, saying: Let us pray. Lord God, the only source of knowledge, who were pleased so to enlighten men's resourcefulness that they have succeeded in inventing new kinds of printing-presses; put your blessing, we beg you, on these presses (this press). By your gracious help may we learn from the books here produced only such wisdom that comes from you and leads to you; through Christ our Lord.
All: Amen.

They are sprinkled with holy water; after which the priest adds:

P: The Lord be with you.
All: May He also be with you.

Let us pray.
Hear us, holy Lord and Father, almighty everlasting God, and in your goodness send your holy angel from heaven to watch over and protect all who are employed here, to be with them and give them comfort and encouragement; through Christ our Lord.
All: Amen.

If only the printing-office is to be blessed, one omits the second prayer along with the sprinkling of the machines and instruments. But if only the latter are to be blessed, one begins at the versicle "Our help," etc., says the second prayer, and sprinkles the instruments with holy water.

13. BLESSING OF A HOSPITAL OR SANATORIUM

(Approved by the Congregation of Sacred Rites, July 18, 1939)

The priest, vested in surplice and white stole, recites the following antiphon and psalm alternately with the bystanders:

P: Ant.: Christ cured all the sick. He took on Himself our infirmities and lightened the burden of our illnesses.

Psalm 6

After the psalm the above antiphon is repeated. Then the priest says:

P: Our help is in the name of the Lord.
All: Who made heaven and earth.
P: The Lord be with you.
All: May He also be with you.

Let us pray.
God, who in a wonderful way created man and still more wonderfully renewed him; who were pleased to aid with many healing remedies the various infirmities that beset the human condition; mercifully pour out your holy   blessing on this hospital, so that the sick who come here may find in you a physician of body and soul, a kind and fatherly helper, and may be taken by you, after the course of this life, to the unending joys of the life to come; through Christ our Lord.
All: Amen.

Let us pray.
Lord Jesus Christ, Savior and consoler of our weakness, who delivered Peter's mother-in-law and the ruler's son from a high fever; who restored strength to the paralytic, cleansed the lepers, healed the centurion's servant; who saved the woman suffering from hemorrhage, raised up the man lying helpless on his pallet at the pool of Bethsaida, went about the towns and villages healing all kinds of ailments; we entreat you to bless and sanctify   this hospital, so that the sick confined here may be freed from their illness and restored in body and mind, and may rightly see fit to praise your power until the end of their days; you who live and reign forever and ever.
All: Amen.

The priest sprinkles with holy water the main parts of the hospital after which he continues:

P: Lord, show us your mercy.
All: And grant us your salvation.
P: Lord, heed my prayer.
All: And let my cry be heard by you.
P: The Lord be with you.
All: May He also be with you.

Let us pray.
Almighty everlasting God, who drive out all sickness of body and soul, manifest your mighty help to the sick, that by the work of your mercy they may be restored to their duty of serving you.

We entreat you, Lord God, grant us, your servants, the enjoyment of lasting health of body and mind; and by the glorious intercession of blessed Mary, ever a virgin, free us from present sorrow and give us everlasting joy.

God, who by the wondrous ministry of angels guard and govern us, appoint your angel to stand watch over this hospital and to drive afar all the powers of evil. Let the sick confined here be shielded from fear and anxiety, and let them recover their former good health.

God, who in your wondrous providence chose blessed Joseph as the spouse of your holy Mother; grant, we pray, that we may deserve to have him for our advocate in heaven whom we venerate as our defender here on earth.

God, most merciful Father, who raised up St. Camillus and St. John of God, men imbued with deep compassion, to be comforters and nurses of the sick; by their merits and prayers be pleased to be present with your healing power to the sick confined here. Free them of bodily ailments and relieve them of mental distress, so that, once restored to their former good health, they may always show you due gratitude for your loving mercy; through Christ our Lord.
All: Amen.

14. BLESSING OF A RADIO STATION

{This blessing is not to be found in the latest edition of the Roman Ritual of 1952, for its composition is of later origin, and was approved by the Congregation of Sacred Rites on October 24, 1957}

From the nearest church or from another place designated for the purpose the priest proceeds to the radio-station, chanting or reciting the Canticle of Zachary or the Canticle of the ThreeYouths. On arriving at the radio-station he intones the following antiphon and then says psalm 18:

P: Ant.: Through all the earth their voice resounds, * and to the ends of the world their message.

Psalm 18

P: The heavens declare the glory of God, * and the firmament proclaims His handiwork.

All: Day pours out the word to day, * and night to night imparts knowledge;

P: Not a word nor a discourse * whose voice is not heard;

All: Through all the earth their voice resounds, * and to the ends of the world, their message.

P: He has pitched a tent there for the sun, which comes forth like the groom from his bridal chamber * and, like a giant, joyfully runs its course.

All: At one end of the heavens it comes forth, and its course is to their other end; * nothing escapes its heat.

P: The law of the Lord is perfect, refreshing the soul; * the decree of the Lord is trustworthy, giving wisdom to the simple.

All: The precepts of the Lord are right, rejoicing the heart; * the command of the Lord is clear, enlightening the eye;

P: The fear of the Lord is pure, enduring forever; * the ordinances of the Lord are true, all of them just;

All: They are more precious than gold, than a heap of purest gold; * sweeter also than syrup or honey from the comb.

P: Though your servant is careful of them, * very diligent in keeping them.

All: Yet who can detect failings? * Cleanse me from my unknown faults!

P: From wanton sin especially, restrain your servant; * Let it not rule over me.

All: Then shall I be blameless and innocent * of serious sin.

P: Let the words of my mouth and the thought of my heart find favor * before you, O Lord, my rock and my Redeemer.

All: Glory is to the Father.

P: As it was in the beginning.

All: Ant.: Through all the earth their voice resounds, * and to the ends of the world their message.

Then the priest says:

P: Our help is in the name of the Lord.
All: Who made heaven and earth.
P: The Lord be with you.
All: May He also be with you.

Let us pray.
God, who ordered all things in creation in a marvelous way, determining even their measure, number, and weight; and who gave man a share in your knowledge, thus enabling him to detect and control the latent forces with which you endowed the things of the universe; be pleased, we pray, to bless these instruments made for transmitting wavelengths of sound through the air, spreading out in all directions as instantaneously as lightning. Let them carry messages of aid in times of crises, of solace in times of distress, of advice in times of doubt, of light in times of darkness, and thus make known the glory of your name more widely throughout the world that all its peoples may be gathered into the fellowship of your love; through Christ our Lord.
All: Amen.

Let us pray.
Almighty everlasting God, who created the world by your Word, and decreed that all things be brought to a head in Him who was made flesh and who suffered for us; graciously grant that His Gospel may be preached to every creature on the wavelengths of sound, so that, aided by the prayers of the blessed Mary, Mother of God and ever a Virgin, and of St. Gabriel the Archangel, messenger of the heavenly mysteries, all peoples may be united in the body of Christ and be gladdened with the gift of His peace; through Christ our Lord.
All: Amen.

The radio-station is sprinkled with holy water. And after the blessing the "Te Deum" is sung or recited, together with its versicles and oration (see Renewal of the Marriage Vows).

15. BLESSING OF THE SEA

{This blessing is not to be found in the latest edition of the Roman Ritual of 1952, for its composition is of later origin, and was approved by the Congregation of Rites on April 27, 1955. In the city of Chioggia-Venezia, in Italy, it has been the custom for many years to bless the Adriatic Sea, in accord with a very ancient custom prevailing for centuries in the onetime flourishing Republic of Venice. In composing this blessing the Holy See has acceded to a request that has come in from many quarters of the globe. After the splendid psalm 28, which tells of God's glory manifested in the mighty seas, there follow three prayers, the first of which asks that, in view of the magnitude of the waters, we may become enraptured with contemplating the "secrets" of God; the second, which is directed to Christ, begs that all ocean-voyagers may be saved from the dangers of the tempestuous waters; the third asks God's blessing and success on fishermen who earn their daily sustenance from the sea.}

The priest intones the following antiphon, which is then followed by psalm 28:

P: Ant.: The voice of the Lord is over the waters, * the God of glory thunders, the Lord, over vast waters.

Psalm 28

After the psalm the above antiphon is repeated. Then the priest continues:

Lord, have mercy. Christ, have mercy. Lord, have mercy. Our Father (the rest inaudibly until:)

P: And lead us not into temptation.

All: But deliver us from evil.

P: All you fountains of waters, bless the Lord.

All: All you seas and waves, bless the Lord.

P: Our help is in the name of the Lord.
All: Who made heaven and earth.

P: Lord, heed my prayer.
All: And let my cry be heard by you.
P: The Lord be with you.
All: May He also be with you.

Let us pray.
Almighty everlasting God, Father of incomprehensible majesty, whose invisible power can be glimpsed from your visible creation; O God, whose Spirit hovered over the waters in the beginning of the world, grant to us, your servants, that as often as we behold with our bodily eyes the mighty waters swelling out in billows on the heavenly horizon, we may be enraptured in contemplation of your hidden mysteries. Let such a sight and the thoughts it arouses prompt us to invoke and to glorify with due praise your holy name, and to render to you, to whose empire all creatures are subject, the homage of our minds in true humility and devotion; through Christ our Lord.
All: Amen.

Let us pray.
Lord Jesus Christ, who once walked upon the waters, who uttered a word of command to the raging tempest of wind and sea and there came a great calm; let your piteous glance fall on us, your servants, who find ourselves surrounded by the many perils of this life; and grant that by the power of your blessing poured out on these waters all wicked spirits may be repelled, the danger of the tempestuous winds may subside, and that all who are at voyage on the seas, through the intercession of the Immaculate Virgin, your Mother, may safely reach their destination, and finally return unharmed to their homes. We ask this of you who live and reign forever and ever.
All: Amen.

Let us pray.
Lord, who said: "In the sweat of your brow you shall eat your bread"; kindly heed our prayers and bestow your blessing on this sea, so that all who are obliged to earn their daily bread for themselves and their families by traversing these waters may be enriched with your bounty and offer you due gratitude for your

goodness; through Christ our Lord.
All: Amen.

The sea is sprinkled with holy water.

16. BLESSING OF FIELDS, MOUNTAIN-MEADOWS OR PASTURES

(Approved by the Congregation of Sacred Rites, Dec. 1, 1886)

P: Our help is in the name of the Lord.
All: Who made heaven and earth.
P: The Lord be with you.
All: May He also be with you.

Let us pray.
God, from whom every good has its beginning and from whom it receives its increase, we beg you to hear our prayers, so that what we begin for your honor and glory may be brought to a happy ending by the gift of your eternal wisdom; through Christ our Lord.
All: Amen.

Let us pray.
Almighty everlasting God, who conferred on your priests above all others so great a grace, that whatever they do worthily and exactly in your name, is regarded as being done by you; we pray that in your kindness you may be present wherever we are present and may bless   whatever we bless. And at our lowly coming, through the merits and prayers of your saints, may demons flee and the angel of peace be at hand; through Christ our Lord.
All: Amen.

Now the Litany of the Saints is said; all kneel during the litany. After the following invocation has been said: That you deliver our souls and the souls of our brethren, relatives, and benefactors from everlasting damnation, etc., the priest rises and says:

P: That you bless   these fields (or acres, or these mountain-meadows, or pastures, or meadows).

All: We beg you to hear us.

P: That you bless and consecrate these fields (or acres, or these mountain-meadows, or pastures, or meadows).

All: We beg you to hear us.

P: That you bless and consecrate and protect from diabolical destruction these fields (or acres, or these mountain-meadows, or pastures, or meadows).

All: We beg you to hear us.

P: That you mercifully ward off and dispel from this place all lightning, hail-storm, destructive tempests, and harmful floods.

All: We beg you to hear us.

Then the litany is resumed to the end; after which the priest says Our Father (the rest inaudibly until:)

P: And lead us not into temptation.

All: But deliver us from evil.

P: Send forth your Spirit and all things shall be recreated.

All: And you shall renew the face of the earth.

P: The Lord shall manifest His goodness.

All: And the earth shall yield her fruit.

P: Lord, heed my prayer.
All: And let my cry be heard by you.
P: The Lord be with you.
All: May He also be with you.

Let us pray.
Almighty God, we humbly appeal to your kindness, asking that
you pour out the dew of your blessing   on these fields (or acres, or
mountain-meadows, or pastures, or meadows), which it has
pleased you to nurture with favorable weather. Grant to your
people a spirit of constant gratitude for your gifts. Wipe out any
infertility from this land, thus filling the hungry with an abundance
of good things, so that the poor and the needy may praise your
wondrous name forever and ever.
All: Amen.

The fields are sprinkled with holy water.

17. BLESSING OF ORCHARDS AND VINEYARDS

P: Our help is in the name of the Lord.
All: Who made heaven and earth.
P: The Lord be with you.
All: May He also be with you.

Let us pray.
Almighty God, we appeal to your kindness, asking that you pour
out the dew of your blessing   on these budding creatures of yours,
which it has pleased you to nurture with rain and mild breezes, and
that you bring the fruits of your earth to a ripe harvest. Grant to
your people a spirit of constant gratitude for your gifts. And from a
fertile earth all the hungry with an abundance of good things, so
that the poor and needy may praise your wondrous name forever
and ever.
All: Amen.

They are sprinkled with holy water.

18. BLESSING OF A GRANARY OR THE HARVEST

P: Our help is in the name of the Lord.

All: Who made heaven and earth.
P: The Lord be with you.
All: May He also be with you.

Let us pray.
Lord God almighty, who never fail to bestow on men an abundance of heavenly gifts, as well as the rich fruits of the earth; we give thanks to you in your glory for this harvest of grain, and beg you again to bless   the harvest which we have received from your bounty, to preserve it and to shield it from harm. Grant also that, having had our desire for earthly needs filled, we may bask under your protection; praise your kindness and mercy without ceasing, and make use of temporal goods in such a way as not to lose everlasting goods; through Christ our Lord.
All: Amen.

They are sprinkled with holy water.

19. BLESSING OF A MILL

P: Our help is in the name of the Lord.
All: Who made heaven and earth.
P: The Lord be with you.
All: May He also be with you.

Let us pray.
Almighty everlasting God, who in punishment for sin declared to man: "In the sweat of your brow you shall eat your bread"; bestow your blessing   on this mill which has been built to produce flour, and thus supply bread for our nourishment. May it please you to appoint your angel of light to stand watch over it; through Christ our Lord.
All: Amen.

It is sprinkled with holy water.

20. BLESSING OF A STABLE

For horses, cattle, etc.

P: Our help is in the name of the Lord.
All: Who made heaven and earth.
P: The Lord be with you.
All: May He also be with you.

Let us pray.
Lord God almighty, who willed that your only-begotten Son, our
Redeemer, be born in a stable, and lie in a manger between two
beasts of burden; we beg you to bless this stable and to defend
it from all spite and wickedness of the devil. Let it be a healthful
shelter for horses, cattle, and other animals, safe from every kind
of assault. And as the ox knows his master and
the ass the manger of his lord, so grant that your servants, made in
your image and only a little lower than the angels, to whom you
have subjected all sheep and oxen and cattle of the fields,
may not be like senseless beasts, like the horse or the mule who are
without understanding. But let them acknowledge you alone as
God and the source of all good. Let them faithfully persevere in
your service, show you gratitude for favors received, and thus
merit greater benefits in future; through Christ our Lord.
All: Amen.

Then if the animals are kept in the stable the priest may add some
of the prayers from the blessings for animals given above. The
stable and animals are sprinkled with holy water.

21. BLESSING OF A FOUNTAIN

P: Our help is in the name of the Lord.
All: Who made heaven and earth.
P: The Lord be with you.
All: May He also be with you.

Let us pray.
Lord, we humbly appeal to your kindness, asking that you sanctify

this fountain of water with a blessing from on high, thus making it a wholesome water for our daily use. May it please you to keep it pure and free of every diabolical defilement, so that all who draw water from it or drink of it may delight in its strengthening and health-giving quality, and give thanks to you, the Lord and Savior of all; through Christ our Lord.
All: Amen.

It is sprinkled with holy water.

22. BLESSING OF A WELL

P: Our help is in the name of the Lord.
All: Who made heaven and earth.
P: The Lord be with you.
All: May He also be with you.

Let us pray.
Lord God almighty, who so disposed matters that water comes forth from the depths of this well by means of its pipes; grant, we pray, that with your help and by this blessing imparted through our ministry all diabolical wiles and cunning may be dispelled, and the water of this well may always remain pure and wholesome; through Christ our Lord.
All: Amen.

It is sprinkled with holy water.

23. BLESSING OF A BRIDGE

P: Our help is in the name of the Lord.
All: Who made heaven and earth.
P: The Lord be with you.
All: May He also be with you.

Let us pray.
Lord, heed our prayers, and be pleased to bless this bridge and all

who pass over it, that they may ever find in you a safeguard amidst the joys and sorrows of this fickle world; through Christ our Lord. All: Amen.

Let us pray.
Hear us, holy Lord and Father, almighty everlasting God, and in your goodness send your holy angel from heaven to watch over, protect, and support this bridge and all who pass over it; through Christ our Lord.
All: Amen.

It is sprinkled with holy water.

24. BLESSING OF A LIME-KILN

P: Our help is in the name of the Lord.
All: Who made heaven and earth.
P: The Lord be with you.
All: May He also be with you.

Let us pray.
Almighty everlasting God, to whom all creatures owe their origin and are made subject to man's use by an admirable arrangement of your kindness; who in times past prescribed that your altar be made of stones and smoothly joined together with lime, so that the words of Deuteronomy could be inscribed thereon as a reminder of your commandments; we humbly beg you to bless   this lime-kiln, and to dispel from it all harmful tricks of the devil. Let it be productive and serve its purpose well, with its fires exerting their full force, so that the workmen may receive by
your bounty a good quality of lime. And let them in turn likewise receive an increase of your saving grace; through Christ our Lord.
All: Amen.

It is sprinkled with holy water.

25. BLESSING OF A BLAST-FURNACE

or of a Brick-Kiln

P: Our help is in the name of the Lord.
All: Who made heaven and earth.
P: The Lord be with you.
All: May He also be with you.

Let us pray.
Almighty everlasting God, to whom all creatures owe their origin
and are made subject to man's use by an admirable arrangement of
your kindness; who in one moment shielded the three youths in the
fiery furnace by mitigating the heat of its flames, and in another
moment again enkindled them to destroy those evil men who had
cast the saintly youths therein; we humbly beg you to bless this
furnace, and to dispel from it all harmful tricks of the devil. Let it
be productive and serve its purpose well, with its fires exerting
their full force, so that the workmen may receive
a good quality of metal (or a goodly number of brick). And let
them in turn likewise receive an increase of your saving grace;
through Christ our Lord.
All: Amen.

It is sprinkled with holy water.

26. BLESSING OF STONE-QUARRIES

{This blessing and the following one are not to be found in the
latest edition of the Roman Ritual of 1952, for their composition is
of later origin, and they were approved by the Congregation of
Sacred Rites on October 31, 1956.}

P: Our help is in the name of the Lord.
All: Who made heaven and earth.
P: The Lord be with you.
All: May He also be with you.

Let us pray.
Almighty everlasting God, the Creator and dispenser of all good things, who for our use planted innumerable riches in the bowels of the earth, to be dug out by the industry of man; be pleased, we pray, to pour out your blessing   on these stone-quarries, so that they may not be ruined, and that all who work in them may be safeguarded from accidents; through Christ our Lord.

The place is sprinkled with holy water.

27. BLESSING OF A MARBLE-FACTORY

P: Our help is in the name of the Lord.
All: Who made heaven and earth.
P: The Lord be with you.
All: May He also be with you.

Let us pray.
Lord God almighty, who by the coming of your only begotten Son sanctified all things for your faithful, we beg you to bless and prosper this marble-factory, and to protect your servants who work here from every kind of adversity. Grant also that they may so pursue their work as to have it be a means of their salvation, meriting to be living and chosen stones in the everlasting dwelling of your majesty; through Christ our Lord.
All: Amen.

It is sprinkled with holy water.

28. BLESSING TO WARD OFF FLOODS

{Approved by the Congregation of Sacred Rites, Dec. 1, 1886}

The priest, vested in surplice and stole, accompanied by the people, carries a relic of the True Cross to the river or stream, and there devoutly reads at each of four different spots one of the introductions to the four Gospels. After each Gospel he adds the following verses and prayers:

P: Help us, O God, our Savior.

All: And deliver us for your name's sake.

P: Save your servants.

All: Who trust in you, my God.

P: Deal not with us, Lord, as our sins deserve.

All: Nor take vengeance on us for our transgressions.

P: Lord, send us aid from your holy place.

All: And watch over us from Sion.

P: Lord, heed my prayer.
All: And let my cry be heard by you.
P: The Lord be with you.
All: May He also be with you.

Let us pray.
God, who give saving grace even to the wicked land who do not will the death of the sinner, we humbly appeal to you in glory, asking that you protect with your heavenly aid your trusting servants from all perils of flood. Let them find in you a constant safeguard, so that they may always serve you and never be separated from you through any temptation; through Christ our Lord.
All: Amen.

And may the blessing of almighty God, Father, Son, and Holy Spirit, come upon these waters and keep them always under control.
All: Amen.

6

BLESSINGS OF PLACES DESIGNATED FOR SACRED PURPOSES

1. BLESSING AND LAYING THE CORNER-STONE OF A CHURCH

{This blessing is reserved to the Ordinary or to a priest delegated by him. The rite given here is revised in accordance with the new Pontifical of 1962.}

1. The blessing and laying of the corner-stone of a church may take place on any day and at any hour.

2. The foundations of the church should be evident or at least delineated.

3. A wooden cross of convenient size should be fixed on the spot where the main altar is to be.

4. The following things are prepared for the sacred action:

(a) the corner-stone which should be quadrangular, and mortar and tools for fixing it in the foundations; a mason should be at hand to set the stone in the foundations;

(b) a vessel of ordinary holy water and an aspersory made of hyssop if available

(c) two torches for the acolytes and the processional cross;

(d) amice, alb, cincture, and a white stole and cope; a gold-embroidered mitre and crozier (if a bishop is to preside); an amice, alb and cincture for the deacon and subdeacon, as well as a white stole for the deacon;

(e) an ornamented faldstool set on a carpet before the wooden cross;

(f) provision should be made that the foundations of the church are so ordered that the ministrants can easily walk around them.

5. The pastor or others concerned should see to it that the faithful, for whose use the church will be erected, are imbued with proper devotion for their church, and they should not only be given a timely announcement of the blessing and laying of the corner-stone, but should also be properly instructed on the rites and their signification. Lastly the faithful should be encouraged to lend their free and spontaneous support to the building of the church and to its ornamentation.

Part I

Blessing the Site for the Church

6. At the proper time the bishop (or the delegated priest) goes to the place where the church is to be built and vests with the assistance of the deacon and subdeacon in the aforementioned

vestments.

7. Preceded by the acolytes with lighted torches, the cross-bearer, and the clergy, he goes with his ministers to the cross erected on the spot where the altar is to be (a bishop wears the mitre and carries the crozier but removes them when he comes to the place for the blessing). He then sings the following with all present making the responses (for the music see the music supplement):

Celebrant: God, come to my rescue.
All: Lord, make haste to help me.
C: Glory be to the Father, etc.
All: As it was in the beginning, etc.

8. He then sprinkles the spot where the cross stands without saying anything (a bishop wears the mitre); after which, preceded by crossbearer, acolytes, and clergy, he walks around the foundations sprinkling them with holy water without saying anything. He starts behind the cross and then encircles the foundations clockwise. During this time the choir sings the following (Music):

C: Ant. Lord Jesus Christ, * raise up the sign of salvation in this place; and forbid entry here to the avenging angel.

Psalm 47

During this psalm the choir, if necessary (i.e., depending on the time element), repeats the antiphon after every two verses:

C: Great is the Lord and wholly to be praised * in the city of our God.

All: His holy mountain, fairest of heights, * is the joy of all the earth;

C: Mount Sion, "the recesses of the North," * is the city of the great King.

All: God is with her castles; renowned is He as a stronghold.

C: For lo! the kings assemble, * they come on together;

All: They also see, and at once are stunned, * terrified, routed;

C: Quaking seizes them there; * anguish, like a woman's in labor,

All: As though a wind from the east * were shattering ships of Tharsis.

C: As we had heard, so have we seen * in the city of the Lord of hosts,

All: In the city of our God; * God makes it firm forever.

C: O God, we ponder your kindness * within your temple.

All: As your name, O God, so also your praise * reaches to the ends of the earth.

C: Of justice your right hand is full; * let Mount Sion be glad,

All: Let the cities of Juda rejoice, * because of your judgments.

C: Go about Sion, make the round; * count her towers.

All: Consider her ramparts, * examine her castles,

C: That you may tell a future generation * that such is God,

All: Our God forever and ever; * He will guide us.

The usual doxology is omitted, but the above antiphon is repeated. If necessary the verses of the psalm may be repeated until the sprinkling of the foundations is finished; but if it is finished earlier the psalm is broken off and the antiphon repeated as a conclusion.

9. After this the celebrant, standing before the cross and facing the site for the church that is to be built, hands over the aspersory and

with hands folded sings the following in the ferial tone (a bishop removes the mitre):

C: The Lord be with you.

All: May He also be with you.

Let us pray.
Almighty and merciful God, who conferred on your priests above all others so great a grace, that whatever they do worthily and exactly in your name, is regarded as being done by you; we pray that in your kindness you may be present wherever we are present and may bless whatever we bless. And at our lowly coming, through the merits of your saints, may demons flee and the angel of peace be at hand; through Christ our Lord.
All: Amen.

Part II

Blessing of the Corner-stone

10. The celebrant goes to the place where the corner-stone is located. and standing there with hands joined blesses the stone, singing the following in the ferial tone. A bishop uses the mitre and crozier as he walks to the place, but gives them up before he begins the blessing.

C: Our help is in the name of the Lord.
All: Who made heaven and earth.
C: The Lord be with you.
All: May He also be with you.

Let us pray.
Lord Jesus Christ, Son of the living God, who are the corner-stone hewn from the mountain-side not by the hand of man, and the foundation which cannot be moved; make firm this stone which is to be laid in your name. You who are the beginning and the end, be likewise, we pray, the beginning, the increase, and the end of this

work, which is fittingly begun for your praise and glory. We ask this of you who live and reign forever and ever.
All: Amen.

He sprinkles the stone with holy water without saying anything.

11. According to local custom the document concerning the blessing of the corner-stone and the beginning of the church may be read; after which the bishop as well as the others, clergy and laity (who should also be invited), may add their signatures. The document is then sealed within the stone which is later to be laid in the foundations. After the reading of the document a popular hymn may be sung.

Part III

Laying of the Corner-stone

12. The celebrant places his hand on the corner-stone as it is lowered into place, saying (a bishop wears the mitre and holds the crozier):

In the faith of Jesus Christ, we lay this corner-stone on this foundation; in the name of the Father, and of the Son, and of the Holy Spirit. May the true faith flourish here, along with fear of God and brotherly love. May this place finally be devoted to prayer, to the adoration and praise of the name of Jesus Christ our Lord, who lives and reigns with the Father and the Holy Spirit, God, forever and ever.
All: Amen.

13. The assisting mason fixes the stone in place with mortar; after which the celebrant sprinkles it with holy water without saying anything, and then returns to the place where the cross is (a bishop takes the faldstool). In the meantime the choir sings the following (for the music see the music supplement):

C: Ant.: May the Lord build us a dwelling, * and keep a watch over the city.

Psalm 126

C: Unless the Lord build the house, * they labor in vain who build it.

All: Unless the Lord guard the city, * in vain does the guard keep vigil.

C: It is vain for you to rise early, * or put off your rest.

All: You that eat hard-earned bread, * for He gives to His beloved in sleep.

C: See, sons are a gift from the Lord; * the fruit of the womb is a reward.

All: Like arrows in the hand of a warrior * are the sons of one's youth.

C: Happy the man whose quiver is filled with them; * they shall not be put to shame when they contend with enemies at the gate.

The usual doxology is not said, but the above antiphon is repeated.

14. When the psalm and antiphon are finished, the celebrant, standing before the cross with hands joined and facing the site where the church is to be built, sings the following in the ferial tone (a bishop removes the mitre):

C: The Lord be with you.
All: May He also be with you.

In this oration the name of the saint in whose name and honor the church is founded is mentioned at the letter N. However, the words "by the prayers and merits of blessed N." are omitted if the church is erected in honor of some mystery.

Let us pray.
Lord God, whom the heavens and the earth cannot contain, but who condescended to have a dwelling-place here on earth where your name may constantly be invoked; we entreat you, by the prayers and merits of blessed N., to be present in this place, to cleanse it from all stains by an outpouring of your grace, and to preserve it in its purified state. And as you let the vow of David, your beloved, be fulfilled in the work of Solomon, his son, so may you graciously fulfill our desires in this work; through Christ our Lord.
All: Amen.

C: The Lord be with you.
All: May He also be with you.
Deacon: Let us bless the Lord.
All: Thanks be to God.

If a bishop presides he gives the solemn blessing, grants the indulgences, and having removed his vestments departs in peace.

2. BLESSING OF A NEW CHURCH OR A PUBLIC ORATORY*

{This blessing is reserved to the Ordinary or to a priest delegated by him. The rite given here is revised in accordance with the new Pontifical of 1962.}

1. Every church that is to be solemnly blessed must have a title. It may be named in honor of the Holy Trinity; or our Lord Jesus Christ with mention of a mystery of His life or an appellation already introduced into the sacred liturgy; of the Holy Spirit; or the blessed Virgin Mary and also with mention of a mystery or an appellation already used in the sacred liturgy; or the holy angels; or after a saint inscribed in the Roman Martyrology, but not a blessed. The local Ordinary should never allow unusual titles, those savoring of novelty, or in general those foreign to the approved tradition of the Church. In case of doubt one should have recourse to the Congregation of Sacred Rites.

2. The blessing of churches, although it may lawfully take place on almost any day, is more fittingly done on Sundays or feast days. But it is prohibited on the vigil and feast of Christmas, on the feasts of Epiphany, Ascension, and Corpus Christi, on the days beginning with Palm Sunday until Easter inclusive, on Pentecost, and on All Souls. The blessing of a church should ordinarily take place in the morning, unless the good of a notable part of the faithful urges that it be done in the afternoon.

3. The water for the sprinkling of the church, as well as the altar linens and other appurtenances for the altar and church, may be blessed before this sacred rite, by the bishop or by another priest delegated by him, using the forms given in their proper place. The following things are to be prepared for the blessing of a church:

(a) a vessel of ordinary holy water and an aspersory made of hyssop if available; the fonts for holy water should be empty and well cleaned;

(b) two torches for the acolytes and the processional cross;

(c) altar-linens and vessels and ornaments for the altar and church;

(d) amice, alb, cincture, and a white stole and cope; a gold-embroidered mitre and crozier (if a bishop is to preside); an amice, alb, and cincture for the deacon and subdeacon, as well as a white stole for the deacon;

(e) an ornamented faldstool set on a carpet, one in front of the main door of the church, another in the sanctuary; if two are not available the one is carried to the sanctuary at the proper time; all this, of course, only if a bishop is presiding;

(f) the interior of the church should be empty and the altars bare;

(g) provision should be made that the ministrants can easily walk around the exterior of the church;

(h) it should also be provided that the celebrant and his ministers, after they have entered the church, have ready access from the altar to the main door; also that they can walk around the side aisles, in order to carry out the prescribed rites properly.

4. The pastor or others concerned should see to it that the faithful for whom the church was built, should not only be given a timely announcement of the solemn blessing, but should also be properly instructed on the rites and their signification. Lastly the faithful should be imbued with proper devotion for their church, so that also in future they will lend, as far as they can, their free and spontaneous support to its proper ornamentation and upkeep.

5. The doors of the church should be closed, and no one should remain inside. At the proper time the bishop (or the delegated priest) goes to the sacristy, where he vests with the assistance of the deacon and subdeacon in the aforementioned vestments. If a bishop presides he wears the gold-embroidered mitre and carries the crozier in his left hand.

6. Then, preceded by the acolytes with lighted torches, the crossbearer, and the clergy, he goes with his ministers to the doors of the church to be blessed. Arriving there (a bishop removes the mitre and the crozier) he sings the following with all present making the responses (for the music see the music supplement):

Celebrant: God, come to my rescue.
All: Lord, make haste to help me.
C: Glory be to the Father, etc.
All: As it was in the beginning, etc.

7. After this the celebrant (a bishop wears the mitre), preceded by cross-bearer, acolytes, clergy, and the people, walks around the outside of the church sprinkling the walls with holy water. He starts at the right of the church. During this time the choir sings the following (for the music see the music supplement):

C: Ant.: The Lord's dwelling is well founded on a firm rock.

Psalm 86

During this psalm the choir, if the time element requires it, repeats the antiphon after every two verses:

C: The Lord loves His foundation * upon the holy mountain;

All: The gates of Sion * more than any dwelling of Jacob.

C: Glorious things are said of you, * O city of God.

All: I tell of Egypt and Babylon * among those that know the Lord;

C: Of Philistia, Tyre, Ethiopia: * "This man was born there."

All: And of Sion they shall say: * "One and all were born in her;

C: And He who has established her * is the Most High Lord."

All: They shall note, when the peoples are enrolled: * "This man was born there."

C: And all shall sing in their festive dance: * "My home is within you."

The usual doxology is omitted but the above antiphon is repeated. If necessary the verses of the psalm may be repeated until the sprinkling of the walls is finished; but if it is finished earlier the psalm is broken off and the antiphon repeated as a conclusion.

8. After this the celebrant, standing before and facing the door of the church, hands over the aspersory and with hands folded sings the following in the ferial tone (a bishop removes the mitre):

C: The Lord be with you.
All: May He also be with you.

Let us pray.
Almighty everlasting God, who are wholly present and wholly active in every place under your dominion; hearken to our humble prayers, and be the protector of this dwelling as you are its founder. Let no vileness of hostile powers prevail here, but by the working of the Holy Spirit may a faultless service always be rendered to you in this place, and a holy liberty abound; through Christ our Lord.
All: Amen.

9. Led by the cross-bearer the celebrant, along with the clergy and people, go in procession into the church; a bishop wears the mitre and carries the crozier. The chanters begin the Litany of the Saints, the invocations of which are not doubled. In the litany there is a threefold invocation of the saint in whose honor the church is blessed. When the celebrant arrives at the altar (a bishop kneels at the faldstool), all kneel in their place and make the responses. When the invocation "That you grant eternal rest to all the faithful departed. We beg you to hear
us" has been said, the celebrant rises (a bishop takes the crozier in his left hand), and facing the nave of the church sings in the same tone:

C: That you graciously visit this place.
All: We beg you to hear us.
C: That you appoint your angels to guard it.
All: We beg you to hear us.

Then raising up his right hand he makes the sign of the cross over the church, saying:

C: That you bless   this church for the honor of your name and that of St. N.

All: We beg you to hear us.

After this he kneels again (a bishop kneels at the faldstool), and the chanters resume the litany to the end.

10. At the end of the litany the celebrant rises (a bishop removes the mitre), and standing with hands joined and facing the altar sings the following in the ferial tone:

Let us pray.
O Lord our God, manifest your glory to your saints, and show yourself present in this sanctuary built in your honor; and as you work great marvels in the children you have adopted, may your praises ever resound among the people who belong to you; through Christ our Lord.
All: Amen.

11. Then the celebrant walks around the interior of the church sprinkling its walls with holy water, using an aspersory made of hyssop. Leaving the main altar he begins at the gospel side and completes the circuit. In the meantime the choir sings the following antiphon and psalm (for the music see the music supplement):

C: Ant.: This is the house of the Lord built with a compact unity; * it is well founded upon a firm rock.

Psalm 121

During this psalm the choir, if the time element requires it, repeats the antiphon after every two verses:

C: I rejoiced because they said to me, * "We will go up to the house of the Lord."And now we have set foot * within our gates, O Jerusalem;

C: Jerusalem, built as a city * with compact unity.

All: To it the tribes go up, the tribes of the Lord, * according to the decree for Israel, to give thanks to the name of the Lord.

C: In it are set up judgment seats, * seats for the house of David.

All: Pray for the peace of Jerusalem. * May those who love you prosper;

C: May peace be within your walls, * prosperity in your buildings.

All: Because of my relatives and friends * I will pray for your good.

The usual doxology is omitted, but the antiphon is repeated. If necessary the verses of the psalm may be repeated until the sprinkling of the walls is finished; but if it is finished earlier the psalm is broken off and the above antiphon repeated as a conclusion.

12. Next the celebrant (a bishop retains the mitre) sprinkles with holy water the floor of the church, first in the middle from the altar to the main door, and then in the transept, from one wall to the other, starting on the gospel side. In the meantime the choir sings the following antiphon and psalm (for the music see the music supplement):

C: Ant.: This is none other * than the house of God and the gate of heaven.

Psalm 83

During this psalm the choir, if the time element requires it, repeats the antiphon after every two verses:

C: How lovely is your dwelling place, * O Lord of hosts!

All: My soul yearns and pines * for the courts of the Lord.

C: My heart and my flesh * cry out for the living God.

All: Even the sparrow finds a home, * and the swallow a nest in which she puts her young.

All: Your altars, O Lord of hosts, * my King and my God.

C: Happy they who dwell in your house. * Continually they praise you.

All: Happy the men whose strength you are; * their hearts are set upon the pilgrimage;

C: When they pass through the arid valley, * they make a spring of it; the early rain clothes it with generous growth.

All: They go from strength to strength; * they shall see the God of gods in Sion.

C: O Lord of hosts, hear my prayer; * hearken, O God of Jacob.

All: O God, behold our shield, * and look upon the face of your anointed.

C: I had rather one day in your courts * than a thousand elsewhere;

All: I had rather lie at the threshold of the house of my God * than dwell in the tents of the wicked.

C: For a sun and a shield is the Lord God; * grace and glory He bestows;

All: The Lord withholds no good thing * from those who walk in sincerity.

C: O Lord of hosts, * happy the men who trust in you.

The usual doxology is omitted, but the antiphon is repeated. If necessary the verses of the psalm may be repeated until the sprinkling of the floor is finished: but if it is finished earlier the psalm is broken off and the above antiphon is repeated as a conclusion.

13. After the sprinkling of the floor the celebrant returns to the altar and facing the nave of the church and with hands joined sings

the following in the ferial tone (a bishop removes the mitre):

C: The Lord be with you.
All: May He also be with you.

Let us pray.
God, who sanctify the places dedicated to your name, pour out your grace on this house of prayer, so that all   who here invoke you may experience the help of your mercy; through Christ our Lord.

All: Amen.

C: The Lord be with you.

All: May He also be with you.

Deacon: Let us bless the Lord.

All: Thanks be to God.

14. Then the celebrant (a bishop wears the mitre and carries the crozier) goes with his ministers to the sacristy, where, having removed the cope, he vests for the celebration of Mass. A bishop, however, may depute another priest to offer the Mass. In the meantime the clergy or ministers prepare the altar for the celebration of Mass. While this is happening the choir and the people sing the following (for the music see the music supplement):

C: Ant.: Confirm, O God, * the work you have begun in us from your heavenly sanctuary, the new Jerusalem, alleluia, alleluia (omit the alleluias after Sept.).

Psalm 95

During the singing of this psalm the above antiphon is repeated after every two verses:

C: Sing to the Lord a new song; * sing to the Lord, all you lands.

All: Sing to the Lord; bless His name; * announce His salvation, day after day.

C: Tell His glory among the nations; * among all peoples, His wondrous deeds.

All: For great is the Lord and highly to be praised; * awesome is He, beyond all gods.

C: For all the gods of the nations are things of nought, * but the Lord made the heavens.

All: Splendor and majesty go before Him; * praise and grandeur are in His sanctuary.

C: Give to the Lord, you families of nations, give to the Lord glory and praise; * give to the Lord the glory due His name.

All: Bring gifts, and enter His courts; * worship the Lord in holy attire.

C: Tremble before Him, all the earth; * say among the nations: the Lord is King.

All: He has made the world firm, not to be moved; * He governs the peoples with equity.

C: Let the heavens be glad and the earth rejoice; let the sea and what fills it resound; * let the plains be joyful and all that is in them.

All: Then shall all the trees of the forest exult before the Lord, for He comes; * for He comes to rule the earth.

C: He shall rule the world with justice * and the peoples with His constancy.

The usual doxology is omitted, but the above antiphon is repeated.

15. Mass is said as a votive of the II class, of the mystery or saint in whose honor the church was dedicated.

16. As the celebrant approaches the altar the introit antiphon is sung with its psalm as the length of time requires.

17. When the celebrant comes to the altar and has made the reverence, he omits the psalm and confiteor and at once ascends the altar saying the usual prayers and then kissing the altar at the middle.

18. At the end of Mass the bishop gives the solemn blessing and announces the indulgences. The last Gospel is omitted, and all return to the sacristy.

3. RITE FOR RECONCILING A PROFANED CHURCH

Which previously was only blessed

1. If a church is profaned, a cemetery which is contiguous is not thereby to be considered profaned, or vice versa. But if both are profaned their reconciliation is performed together.

If a church that was blessed is profaned, it may be reconciled by the pastor or by any priest who has his permission, expressed or presumed. The altar should be entirely bare. It should be prearranged that the officiants can conveniently go around the building, both outside and inside. At hand there should be a vessel of holy water and an aspersory made of hyssop. The priest, vested in amice, alb, cincture, white stole and cope, goes with his assistants to the main entrance of the church, and standing outside facing the door, he intones the following antiphon which is continued by the clergy:

Purify me with hyssop, * Lord, and I shall be clean of sin. Wash me, and I shall be whiter than snow.

Then the entire psalm 50 is said with the doxology, and the above antiphon is repeated. Meanwhile the priest goes around the exterior of the church, alternately sprinkling the walls of the church and the cemetery grounds. But the cemetery is not sprinkled if it has not been desecrated. On coming back to the entrance the priest says:

Let us pray.
Almighty and merciful God, who conferred on your priests above all others this great grace, that whatever they do worthily and exactly in your name, is regarded as being done by you; we pray that in your kindness you may be present wherever we are present and may bless   whatever we bless. And at our lowly coming, through the merits of your saints, may demons flee and the angel of peace be at hand; through Christ our Lord.
All: Amen.

2. After this prayer all go into church, two by two, and the ministrants proceed to the altar. During this procession the Litany of the Saints is chanted. The priest kneels at the altar until the following versicle has been chanted: "That you grant eternal rest to all the faithful departed," etc.; after which he rises and sings in a clear voice:

That you purify and reconcile this church and this altar (and cemetery). R. We beg you to hear us.

3. However, if the cemetery has not been profaned, omit the words "and cemetery."

Then he kneels again until the litany is concluded. After this he stands, and facing the altar he says:

P: Let us pray.

Ministers: Let us kneel. R. Arise.

The priest:

We beseech you, Lord, let your mercy precede the execution of our plans, and by the intercession of all your saints, let your forgiveness and kindness anticipate our requests; through Christ our Lord.
All: Amen.

4. Then the priest kneels at the altar, and signing himself with the cross, says:

P: God, come to my rescue.

All: Lord, make haste to help me.

P (standing): Glory be to the Father, and to the Son, and to the Holy Spirit.

All: As it was in the beginning, is now, and ever shall be, world without end. Amen.

5. Then the priest intones the following antiphon, which is continued by the clergy or choir. Psalm 67 follows, with the chanters singing the verses of the psalm; after each verse the antiphon is repeated by all (for the music of the antiphon and psalm see the music supplement).

Psalm 67

P: God arises; * His enemies are scattered; * and those who hate Him flee before Him.

C: In your churches bless God; * bless the Lord, you of Israel's well-spring.

All: God arises; His enemies are scattered; * and those who hate Him flee before Him.

C: There is Benjamin, the youngest, * leading them.

All: God arises; His enemies are scattered; * and those who hate Him flee before Him.

C: The princes of Juda in a body, * the princes of Zabulon, the princes of Nephthali.

All: God arises; His enemies are scattered; * and those who hate Him flee before Him.

C: Show forth, O God, your power, * the power, O God, with which you took our part.

All: God arises; His enemies are scattered; * and those who hate Him flee before Him.

C: Let the kings bring you gifts * for your temple in Jerusalem.

All: God arises; His enemies are scattered; * and those who hate Him flee before Him.

C: Rebuke the wild beast of the reeds, * the herd of strong bulls and the bullocks, the nations.

All: God arises; His enemies are scattered; * and those who hate Him flee before Him.

C: Let them fall prostrate with bars of silver; * scatter the peoples who delight in war.

All: God arises; His enemies are scattered; * and those who hate Him flee before Him.

C: Let nobles come from Egypt; * let Ethiopia extend its hands to God.

All: God arises; His enemies are scattered; * and those who hate Him flee before Him.

C: You kingdoms of the earth, sing to God, chant praise to the Lord, * who rides on the heights of the ancient heavens.

All: God arises; His enemies are scattered; * and those who hate Him flee before Him.

C: See, His voice resounds, the voice of power: * "Confess the power of God."

All: God arises; His enemies are scattered; * and those who hate Him flee before Him.

C: Over Israel is His majesty; * His power is in the skies.

All: God arises; His enemies are scattered; * and those who hate Him flee before Him.

C: Awesome in His sanctuary is God, the God of Israel; * He gives power and strength to His people. Blessed be God.

All: God arises; His enemies are scattered; * and those who hate Him flee before Him.

The usual doxology is omitted at the end of the above psalm.

6. While the foregoing antiphon and psalm are sung, the priest goes around the interior of the church sprinkling it, especially the place where the desecration took place. Then he returns to the middle of the sanctuary, faces the altar, and says:

God, who lovingly and benignly defend the purity of every place which is under your dominion, hear us, we pray, and grant that in future this place be preserved inviolably hallowed, and that the whole Christian community who here invoke you may be the recipients of your bounty; through Christ our Lord.
All: Amen.

7. Lastly the Mass of the day is celebrated, adding to the collect of the day under one conclusion the "ritual collect," which is No. 10

among the "Missae Votivae ad diversa" in the new Missal.

8. In the case of a church which was consecrated, a priest may reconcile it only if he has the permission of the Ordinary, and then he uses the rite given in the Roman Pontifical. He vests in the manner noted above and is assisted by a number of clerics vested in surplices.

If, in a real and urgent emergency, the Ordinary cannot be reached the pastor of a church which previously had been consecrated may reconcile it without delay, and later inform his superior of the fact.

4. RITE FOR BLESSING A NEW CEMETERY*

* This blessing is reserved to the Ordinary or to a priest delegated by him. The rite given here is revised in accordance with the new Pontifical of 1962.

1. The blessing of a cemetery may take place on any day and at any hour, excepting only those days on which the consecration of a church is prohibited. It is permitted, however, on November 2, All Souls Day.

2. A wooden cross of convenient height is erected at the end of the cemetery opposite the entrance, unless there happens to be one there already.

3. The following things are prepared for the sacred action:

(a) A vessel of ordinary holy water and an aspersory made of hyssop if available;

(b) Two torches for the acolytes and the processional cross;

(c) Amice, alb, cincture, and a purple stole and cope; a gold-embroidered mitre and crozier (if a bishop is to preside); an amice, alb, and cincture for the deacon and subdeacon, as well as a purple stole for the deacon;

(d) An ornamented faldstool set on a carpet before the wooden cross;

(e) provision should be made so that the celebrant and his Ministers have an open path to perform easily the ceremony of sprinkling.

4. The pastor or others concerned should see to it that the faithful not only are given a timely announcement of the blessing of the cemetery, but are also to be properly instructed on the rites and their signification. Moreover, they should be instructed that a cemetery is a sacred place, and be admonished to give it the respect due it.

5. At the proper time the bishop (or the delegated priest) goes to the cemetery which is to be blessed, and in a suitable place vests in the aforementioned vestments, being assisted by the deacon and subdeacon who are already vested.

6. Then, preceded by the acolytes with lighted torches, the crossbearer, and the clergy, he goes with his ministers to the place where the cross is erected. A bishop wears the mitre and carries the crozier, but gives them up when he comes to the cross. Next he says the following with all present making the responses:

Celebrant: God, come to my rescue.
All: Lord, make haste to help me.
C: Glory be to the Father, etc.
All: As it was in the beginning, etc.

7. After this, preceded by cross-bearer, acolytes, and the clergy, he walks around the cemetery grounds sprinkling them with holy water without saying anything. He starts behind the cross and goes around counterclockwise. During this time the choir sings (music):

C: Ant.: Purify me with hyssop, * Lord, and I shall be clean of sin. Wash me, and I shall be whiter than snow.

Psalm 50

During this psalm the choir, if necessary, repeats the antiphon after every two verses. At the end of the psalm the usual doxology is omitted but the above antiphon is repeated. If the sprinkling is finished earlier the psalm is broken off and the antiphon repeated as a conclusion.

8. After this the celebrant, having handed over the aspersory and mitre, and standing before the cross and looking out over the cemetery sings with hands folded the following in the ferial tone:

C: The Lord be with you.
All: May He also be with you.

Let us pray.
Lord God, Father of everlasting glory, solace of the sorrowing, life of the just, glory of the lowly, we humbly importune you to keep this cemetery free from any vileness of unclean spirits, to cleanse and to bless it, and finally to give lasting wholeness to the bodies brought here for burial. And at the end of time, when the angels sound their trumpets, let all who have received the sacrament of baptism, who have persevered in the Catholic faith until death, and who have had their remains laid to rest in this cemetery, be rewarded in body and in soul with the unending joys of heaven; through Christ our Lord.
All: Amen.

9. Then again, preceded by cross-bearer, acolytes, and clergy, the celebrant (a bishop wears the mitre) sprinkles the cemetery without saying anything. In doing so he walks down the middle from the cross to the entrance, and then transversely in front of the cross, from the left side to the right. During this time the choir sings the following antiphon and psalm:

C: Ant. For your name's sake, O Lord, * preserve me in your justice.

Psalm 142

During this psalm the choir, if necessary, repeats the antiphon after every two verses. At the end of the psalm the usual doxology is omitted, but the above antiphon is repeated. If the sprinkling is finished earlier the psalm is broken off and the antiphon repeated as a conclusion.

10. After this the celebrant, having handed over the aspersory and mitre, and standing before the cross and looking out over the cemetery, sings with hands folded the following in the ferial tone:

C: The Lord be with you.
All: May He also be with you.

Let us pray.
God, Creator of the world and Redeemer of mankind, who wondrously dispose the destinies of all creatures, visible and invisible; we humbly and sincerely beseech you to hallow, purify, and bless this cemetery, where the bodies of your servants are duly laid to rest, after the labor and fatigue of this life come to an end. Pardon, in your great mercy, the sins of those who put their trust in you, and graciously grant unending consolation to their bodies that will lie at rest in this cemetery, awaiting the trumpet-call of the Archangel Michael. We ask this through our Lord Jesus Christ, your Son, who lives and reigns with you, in the unity of the Holy Spirit, God,

C: Forever and ever.
All: Amen.

C: The Lord be with you.

All: May He also be with you.

C: Lift up your hearts.

All: We have lifted them up to the Lord.

C: Let us give thanks to the Lord our God.

All: It is fitting and right to do so.

It is indeed fitting and right, worthy and salutary that we should
always and everywhere give thanks to you, O Lord, holy Father,
almighty everlasting God, through Christ our Lord. For He is
eternal day, unfailing light, and everlasting splendor, who
commanded His followers to so walk in the light as to escape the
darkness of never ending night, and happily come to the abode of
light. He is the One who in His humanity wept over Lazarus, and
in His divine power raised up the dead, restoring life to that man
four days consigned to the tomb. Through Him, then, we humbly
entreat you, O Lord, that on the last day, at the angels' trumpet-
call, you would loose from the fetters of sin those who are buried
in this cemetery, granting them everlasting happiness
and numbering them in the ranks of the blessed. Thus may they
come to know that you, our everlasting life, are merciful and
benign, and may have cause to exalt you as the author of life and to
sing your praises with the saints forevermore. Through our Lord
Jesus Christ, your Son, who lives and reigns with you, in the unity
of the Holy Spirit, God, forever and ever.
All: Amen.

C: The Lord be with you.
All: May He also be with you.
Deacon: Let us bless the Lord.
All: Thanks be to God.

11. After the blessing of the cemetery, if circumstances allow, the
bishop or another priest celebrates Mass, which will conform to the
day's office; and in this Mass there is added under one conclusion
the proper ritual collect (see no. 447 f of the new rubrics in the
Missal), excluding all other non-privileged commemorations.

12. As the celebrant approaches the altar the introit antiphon is
sung with its psalm as the length of time requires.

13. When the celebrant comes to the altar and has made the
reverence, he omits the psalm and confiteor and at once ascends

the altar, saying the usual prayers and then kissing the altar at the middle.

14. At the end of Mass the bishop gives the solemn blessing and announces the indulgences. The last Gospel is omitted, and all depart in peace.

5. RITE FOR RECONCILING A PROFANED CEMETERY

1. If a cemetery contiguous to a profaned church has likewise been profaned, it is reconciled along with the church (see above, Rite for Reconciling a Profaned Church). Otherwise, the reconciling of a cemetery takes place as follows:

In the morning the rector of the cemetery, or another priest who has at least the presumed permission of the former, vested as described above, comes with his assistants to the middle of the cemetery. Here he and the other ministrants kneel on a carpet; and all others present kneel in their places. The Litany of the Saints is chanted in the usual way. At the words "That you grant eternal rest to all the faithful departed," etc., the priest rises, and making the sign of the cross over the cemetery, says:

That you reconcile and hallow this cemetery. R:. We beg you to hear us.

2. He kneels again and the litany is concluded.

3. Then all rise, and the celebrant, taking the aspersory, intones the following antiphon, which is continued by the clergy:

Purify me with hyssop, * Lord, and I shall be clean of sin. Wash me, and I shall be whiter than snow.

The entire psalm 50 is said, but without the doxology, and the above antiphon is repeated.

4. During the psalmody the celebrant, beginning at the right, goes

around the entire cemetery, sprinkling it with holy water, above all the place where the profanation occurred. On returning to his place he stands and says:

P: Let us pray.

Ministers: Let us kneel. R. Arise.

The priest:

Merciful Lord, who willed that the potter's field priced with your blood should be bought as a burial place for strangers, be pleased to remember this mystery of your goodness. For you, Lord, are also our potter, the field of our rest, the price of this field. You gave it even as you accepted it. At the cost of your life-giving blood you gave us peaceful rest. Therefore, Lord, you who are the most merciful pardoner of our guilt, the most considerate judge, the most lavish dispenser of clement judgment, hear our entreaties and be to us an advocate and reconciler, forgetting the harsh judgment that we rightly deserve, and remembering only the mercy of your loving redemption. Deign to purify and to reconcile this resting place of your pilgrims, who look for a haven in your heavenly kingdom. And may you finally awaken the bodies of those who are or who will be buried here, by the power and the glory of your resurrection, to incorruptible glory, calling them forth not to condemnation but to unending happiness. We ask this of you who are coming to judge both the living and the dead and the world by fire.
All: Amen.

{The new code of rubrics for the Missal, no. 447 h, seems to take for granted that Mass will be offered after the reconciliation of a cemetery.}

6. RITE OR SHORTER FORM FOR CONSECRATING A FIXED ALTAR

Which has lost its consecration if the table or mensa was separated from its support, even if only for a moment. See the Code of Canon Law, 1200.

After the altar has been repaired the bishop, vested in rochet and white stole (or a delegated priest vested in surplice and white stole) goes to the altar and anoints with chrism in the form of a cross the four points of contact of the table with the base. At each anointing he says:

In the name of the Father, and of the Son, and of the Holy Spirit.

Then he says the following prayers:

Let us pray.
Lord, we humbly appeal to your sovereignty, asking that it please you to effectually bless   and to sanctify this altar anointed with a libation of holy oil to receive the offerings of your people; that having been anointed by us, your unworthy servants, with holy chrism and in the power of your name, to the honor of the blessed Virgin Mary and of all the saints, and in memory of your servant, N., this altar may be well-pleasing to you, and may remain a permanent altar. May you regard as a worthy holocaust whatever henceforth is offered or consecrated thereon. May you graciously accept, merciful Lord, the sacrifices offered here by all your servants. May the bonds of our sins be thereby loosed, our stains blotted out, pardon obtained, and graces acquired, so that together with your saints and your elect we may merit the joys of everlasting life; through Christ our Lord.
All: Amen.

Let us pray.
Almighty everlasting God, we humbly implore you, through your only-begotten Son, our Lord Jesus Christ, to hallow with a blessing from on high this altar devoted to holy purposes. And as you once accepted with wondrous favor the offering of your High Priest Melchisedech, so also be pleased ever to accept the gifts laid on this new altar. May the people who assemble in this holy

dwelling of your Church be ransomed and sanctified by these offerings, and their souls be rewarded with everlasting life; through Christ our Lord.

All: Amen.

Without delay the officiate should declare and testify in writing that this altar has been duly consecrated by him, with ordinary or delegated authority as the case may be, and that it is to be regarded as such, and under the same title it enjoyed before it was desecrated.

7. ANOTHER RITE OR SHORTER FORM FOR CONSECRATING A FIXED ALTAR

Which has lost consecration by serious breakage or by the reliquary tomb having been broken or opened: Code of Canon Law, 1200.[1]-2

The bishop, vested in rochet and white stole (or a delegated priest vested in surplice and white stole), goes to the altar, and at some distance from it blesses water, salt, ashes, and wine, beginning with the exorcism of salt:

God's creature, salt, I cast out the demon from you in the name of our Lord Jesus Christ, who said to His apostles: "You are the salt of the earth"; and through the Apostle says: "Let your speech be at all times pleasing, seasoned with salt." May you become a sacred thing for the consecration of this altar, to drive away all temptations of the devil. May you be a shield for body and soul, health, protection, and a safeguard for all who use you; through Christ our Lord.

All: Amen.

P: The Lord be with you.
All: May He also be with you.

Let us pray.
Lord God, almighty Father, who from on high bestowed on salt the

gift of seasoning all food created for man, bless this creature, salt, to banish the foe, and endow it with healing properties for the welfare of both body and soul of those who use it; through Christ our Lord.
All: Amen.

Next he exorcizes the water:

God's creature, water, I cast out the demon from you in the name of God the Father,   and of the Son, and of the Holy Spirit. May you drive out Satan from the borders of the just, lest he lurk within the shadows of this church and this altar. And you, Lord Jesus Christ, pour out your Holy Spirit on this your church and altar, that those who worship you here may be rewarded in body and soul, that your name may be glorified among all nations, and the hearts of unbelievers be converted to you, and have no other God but you, the only true Lord, who is coming to judge both the living and the dead and the world by fire.
All: Amen.

P: Lord, heed my prayer.
All: And let my cry be heard by you.
P: The Lord be with you.
All: May He also be with you.

Let us pray.
Lord God, almighty Father, Creator of all the elements, who by Jesus Christ, your Son, our Lord, willed that this element, water, should serve in the salvation of mankind; we humbly beg you to hearken to our prayers, and to hallow this water by your benign glance. Let it be freed from the power of all unclean spirits, so that wherever it is sprinkled in your name the gift of your blessing may descend, and by your mercy all evils may be driven away; through Christ our Lord.
All: Amen.

Next he blesses the ashes:

P: Lord, heed my prayer.

All: And let my cry be heard by you.
P: The Lord be with you.
All: May He also be with you.

Let us pray.
Almighty everlasting God, spare those who repent, show mercy to those who call upon you, and be pleased to send your holy angel from on high to bless and hallow these ashes. Let them be a wholesome remedy to all who invoke your holy name, and who, conscious of their transgressions, accuse themselves; to all who mourn over their offenses before your divine mercy, or humbly and earnestly ask your loving pardon. Grant that in calling on your holy name those who sprinkle these ashes on themselves to redeem their sins may receive health in body and protection for soul; through Christ our Lord.
All: Amen.

Then he takes salt and sprinkles it on the ashes in the form of a cross, saying:

May this salt and ashes be mingled together; in the name of the Father, and of the Son, and of the Holy Spirit.
All: Amen.

Then taking a handful of the mixed salt and ashes, he drops it into the water in the form of a cross, saying:

May this salt, ashes, and water be mingled together; in the name of the Father,   and of the Son,   and of the Holy   Spirit.
All: Amen.

Then he blesses the wine:

P: Lord, heed my prayer.
All: And let my cry be heard by you.
P: The Lord be with you.
All: May He also be with you.

Let us pray.

Lord Jesus Christ, who are the true vine, who in Cana of Galilee changed water into wine, show us your mercy again and again, and be pleased to bless   and to hallow this creature, wine. Wherever it is poured out or sprinkled, may that place be filled and hallowed with the bounty of your heavenly blessing. We ask this of you who are God, living and reigning with the Father and the Holy Spirit forever and ever.
All: Amen.

Then he pours the wine into the water in the form of a cross, saying:

May this wine, salt, ashes, and water be mingled together; in the name of the Father,   and of the Son, and of the Holy Spirit.
All: Amen.

P: Lord, heed my prayer.
All: And let my cry be heard by you.
P: The Lord be with you.
All: May He also be with you.

Let us pray.
Almighty everlasting God, maker and preserver of mankind, the giver of spiritual gifts and the lavish dispenser of everlasting salvation, send forth your Holy Spirit upon this wine mixed with water, salt, and ashes. Endow it with power from above that it may serve for the consecration of this your altar; through Christ our Lord.
All: Amen.

Then using this blessed water he makes a plaster or cement. which he blesses, saying:

Let us pray.
Most High God, who guard all things from the highest to the lowest, whose solicitude embraces every creature; hallow and bless these creatures of lime and cement; through Christ our Lord.
All: Amen.

This mortar thus blessed is kept, but what remains of the blessed water is poured into the sacrarium.

Then the consecrator goes to the altar and anoints with chrism the sepulchre of the altar from which the relics have been removed. He anoints each of the four corners, making at each the sign of the cross and saying:

May this sepulchre be consecrated and hallowed; in the name of the Father, and of the Son, and of the Holy Spirit. Peace be to this house.

Then he reverently places the case containing the relics and other things therein; and taking the stone or cover, he anoints the bottom side in the middle with chrism, saying:

May this cover (or this stone) be consecrated and hallowed by this anointing and God's blessing; in the name of the Father, and of the Son, and of the Holy Spirit. Peace be to you.

Using the blessed cement, he fits the cover to the sepulchre (being assisted if required by a mason); after which he says:

Let us pray.
God, who are preparing from the community of the saints an everlasting dwelling for your glory, let this dwelling for you on earth also prosper, so that what has been started with your approval may be brought to completion by your grace; through Christ our Lord.
All: Amen.

Then with the help of a mason he seals the cover with cement, and signs the top with chrism, saying:

May this altar be sealed and hallowed; in the name of the Father, and of the Son, and of the Holy Spirit. Peace be to you.

8. RITE FOR CONSECRATING A PORTABLE ALTAR

(From the new Roman Pontifical of 1962)

{The new Pontifical contains the very elaborate form for consecrating an altar when this is done simultaneously with the dedication of a church; another elaborate form when done apart from the dedication of a church; and two more forms for the consecration of a "portable altar" (altare portatile), one a solemn form and the other a simple form. This simple form, according to "Ephemerides Liturgicae" 77 (1963), is to be used, among other instances, instead of the shorter form for consecrating a portable altar granted to bishops only a few years ago; in other words, the last-mentioned is now abrogated. The first two elaborate forms are to be used, except by special indult, only when a bishop consecrates an altar. The new faculties conceded to bishops by Pope Paul VI permit them to delegate priests to consecrate portable altars. It must be clearly noted, however, as is evident in the rubrics below, that the term "portable altar" does not have its usual restricted meaning in the new Pontifical, but can mean either the entire table of an altar which is already erected in a church, or else an altar-stone which is to be inserted later in another altar. If all this seems hopelessly confusing, one had better consult the SCR for clarification.}

1. The consecration of a portable altar can be done with the solemn or simple form as indicated below. The solemn form is used when the table of an altar already erected in a church is to be solemnly consecrated: "altar portatile"; the simple form when one (Or more) altarstone later to be inserted in an altar is to be consecrated "tabula." The letters printed in italics in the rubrics below refer to the simple form.

2. The solemn consecration of a portable altar is prohibited on the same days that the consecration of a fixed altar is prohibited. But the consecration with the simple form of one or several altarstones can be done on any convenient day and at any hour.

3. The following things are prepared at the place where the consecration takes place: (a) the relics of holy martyrs and the three grains of incense that are to be sealed into the altar should be resting on a white-linen-covered table, between two lighted candles;

(b) Holy chrism

(c) A vessel of blessed "gregorian" water and an aspersory; this particular water may be blessed at a more convenient time before this sacred action, by the bishop or by another priest delegated by him, using the form given in the Pontifical:

(d) A thurible with lighted charcoal and the incense-boat and spoon,

(e) Towels for wiping the altar or altar-stone;

(f) Mortar for sealing the sepulchre for the relics; there should also be at hand a mason, who at the proper time will assist the celebrant in sealing the sepulchre;

(g) A vessel of water for washing the celebrant's hands, as well as particles of bread and towels;

(h) Amice, alb, cincture, and a white stole and cope; a gold-embroidered mitre for a bishop; an amice, alb, and cincture for the deacon and subdeacon, as well as a white stole for the deacon, if the consecration takes place with the solemn form; if the consecration takes place with the simple form, the bishop wears the rochet, white stole, and gold-embroidered mitre; the ministers wear surplices;

(i) Moreover, if the consecration of a portable altar is done with the solemn form, the following are prepared: five small crosses made of fine candle-wax and grains of incense (these may be blessed before the sacred action) which are to be burned with them; several wooden spatulas for removing this burnt matter from the altar;

(j) When the consecration takes place with the simple form, the altar-stone or altar-stones should be resting on a white-linen-cover on the altar table.

Part I

Blessing of the Altar

4. At the proper time the bishop (or the delegated priest) goes to the sacristy, where he vests with the assistance of the deacon and subdeacon in the aforementioned vestments. If a bishop presides he wears the gold-embroidered mitre and carries the crozier in his left hand.

5. Then, preceded by the acolytes with lighted torches, the cross-bearer, and the clergy, he goes with his ministers to the altar which is to be consecrated. Arriving there (a bishop removes themitre and the crozier) he sings the following with all present making the responses (for the music see the music supplement):

6. The bishop, wearing the rochet and white stole, stands (without mitre) before the altar-stone to be consecrated, which is resting on table, and says:

Celebrant: God, come to my rescue.

All: Lord, make haste to help me.

C: Glory be to the Father, etc.

All: As it was in the beginning, etc.

{Then the bishop blesses "gregorian" water, unless it was already blessed before the sacred action by the bishop or another priest delegated by him, with the form given in the Pontifical.}

6. The bishop, having put on the mitre, walks around the altar, sprinkling it with "gregorian" water, using an aspersory made of hyssop, and without saying anything. Then, having returned the aspersory, he ascends the altar, and standing on the predella, dips his right thumb in the blessed "gregorian" water and traces five crosses on the altar-table in the manner given in the graph below. While tracing the crosses he says in each instance:

6a. The bishop, standing with the mitre on, dips his right thumb in the blessed "gregorian" water and traces five crosses on the altar-stone, in the manner given in the graph below. While tracing the crosses he says in each instance:

May this stone be hallowed; in the name of the Father, and of the Son, and of the Holy Spirit.
Ministers: Amen.

7. If several altars, or several altar-stones, are being consecrated at the same time, the bishop carries out the same actions and words at each of the altars, or altar-stones, successively, the same as he did at the first.

8. In the meantime the choir sings, or the ministers recite, the following antiphon and psalm (for the music see the music supplement):

C: Ant.: I will go to the altar of God, * the God of my gladness and joy.

Psalm 42

During this psalm the choir, if necessary, repeats the antiphon after every two verses:

C: Do me justice, O God, and fight my fight against a faithless people; * from the deceitful and impious man rescue me.

All: For you, O God, are my strength. Why do you keep me so far away? * Why must I go about in mourning, with the enemy oppressing me?

C: Send forth your light and your fidelity; * they shall lead me on and bring me to your holy mountain, to your dwelling-place.

All: Then will I go in to the altar of God, * the God of my gladness and joy.

C: Then will I give you thanks upon the harp, O God, my God! * Why are you so downcast, O my soul? Why do you sigh within me?

All: Hope in God, for I shall again be thanking Him, * in the presence of my Savior and my God.

The usual doxology is omitted, but the above antiphon is repeated.

The psalm is broken off as soon as the celebrant finishes the sprinkling and the above antiphon is repeated as a conclusion.

9. After this the celebrant, standing before the altar, or the altar stone (without mitre), sings the following in the ferial tone:

C: The Lord be with you.
All: May He also be with you.

Let us pray.
God, the Creator of all things visible and invisible, and the consecrator of all that is holy, be pleased to assist at the dedication of this altar of the Lord, and to pour out on it your consecratory and sanctifying power, as we, all unworthy, anoint it with holy chrism. Grant that all who approach this altar in order to pay homage to you may experience your merciful aid; through Christ our Lord.
All: Amen.

Part II

Burial of the Relics

10. Then the bishop or celebrant (without mitre) reverently places the relics along with the three grains of incense in the sepulchre of the altar or altar-stone. While this is done the choir, as time allows, sings the following antiphons (for the music see the music supplement), or the ministers recite them:

Antiphon 1: You have been favored with places at God's altar, O saints of God, intercede for us to the Lord Jesus Christ.

Antiphon 2: I saw under the altar of God the souls of those who had been slain, and they cried out: "Why do you not avenge our blood?" And they received the reply from God: "Wait patiently a little longer until the number of your fellow servants is complete."

Antiphon 3: The bodies of the saints are buried in peace, and their names shall live forevermore.

These antiphons may be repeated if necessary.

11. Meanwhile the mason makes a mortar with the "gregorian" water, which the bishop blesses, saying in a low voice:

C: The Lord be with you.
All: May He also be with you.

Let us pray.
Most High God, the keeper of all things from the highest to the lowest, who encompass all creatures in their inmost being, bless this mortar; through Christ our Lord.
All: Amen.

12. With the help of the mason the bishop smears the lid with mortar, puts it in place, and seals it on the sepulchre.

13. Then with hands joined the bishop sings the following in the ferial tone:

C: The Lord be with you.
All: May He also be with you.

Let us pray.
God, who fashion an everlasting dwelling-place for yourself out of the chosen saints, bestow heavenly increase on this work done in your name; and grant that we may always be aided by the merits of the saints whose relics we reverently enclose in this altar; through Christ our Lord.
All: Amen.

Part III

Consecration of the Altar

14. Having put on the mitre the bishop stands on the altar-predella, or before the altar-stone, and dipping his right thumb in holy chrism traces the sign of the cross on the surface of the altar, or on the altar-stone, in the manner indicated in the graph given above. He says in tracing each cross:

May this stone be sealed, hallowed, and consecrated; in the name of the Father, and of the Son, and of the Holy Spirit.
Ministers: Amen.

15. While this is being done the choir sings (Music), or the ministers recite:

C: Ant.: God, your God, has anointed you with the oil of gladness above your fellow kings.

During this psalm the choir, if necessary, repeats the antiphon after every two verses:

Psalm 44

C: My heart overflows with a goodly theme; * as I sing my ode to the king, my tongue is nimble as the pen of a skillful scribe.

All: Fairer in beauty are you than the sons of men; grace is poured out upon your lips; * thus God has blessed you forever.

C: Gird your sword upon your thigh, * O mighty one!

All: In your splendor and your majesty * ride on triumphant;

C: In the cause of truth and for the sake of justice; * and may your right hand show you wondrous deeds.

All: Your arrows are sharp; peoples are subject to you; * the king's enemies lose heart.

C: Your throne, O God, stands forever and ever; * a tempered rod is your royal scepter.

All: You love justice and hate wickedness; * therefore God, your God, has anointed you with the oil of gladness above your fellow kings.

C: With myrrh and aloes and cassia your robes are fragrant; from ivory palaces string music brings you joy.* The daughters of kings come to meet you;

All: The queen takes her place at your right hand * in gold of Ophir.

C: Hear, O daughter, and see; turn your ear, * forget your people and your father's house.

All: So shall the king desire your beauty; * for he is your lord, and you must worship him.

C: And the city of Tyre is here with gifts; * the rich among the people seek your favor.

All: All glorious is the king's daughter as she enters; * her raiment is threaded with spun gold.

C: In embroidered apparel she is borne in to the king; * behind her the virgins of her train are brought to you.

All: They are borne in with gladness and joy; * they enter the palace of the king.

C: The place of your fathers your sons shall have; * you shall make them princes through all the land.

All: I will make your name memorable * through all generations.

C: Therefore shall nations praise you * forever and ever.

The usual doxology is omitted, but the above antiphon is repeated. If the consecration is finished first the psalm is broken off and the antiphon repeated as a conclusion.

16. The bishop puts incense into the thurible and blesses it: then he incenses the altar, or the altar-stone, while the choir sings (see the music supplement), or the ministers recite, one or several of the following antiphons:

Antiphon 1: The angel came and stood at the altar of the temple, carrying a golden censer.

Antiphon 2: A great quantity of incense was given to him that he might offer it on the golden altar before the throne of the Lord.

Antiphon 3: The smoke of the incense ascended from the angel's hand to the presence of God.

17. When the antiphons are finished the bishop (without mitre) with hands joined sings the following:

C: The Lord be with you.

All: May He also be with you.

Let us pray.

{The following (i.e., all contained within the brackets) are omitted if the consecration of the altar is done with the simple form.}

We beg you, Lord, let our prayer rise like incense in your sight, and let your Christian people be the recipients of copious favors. Let all who will devoutly offer to you bread and wine for hallowing on this altar or receive the hallowed elements in return experience your help in this life, along with remission of all sins, and finally the grace of everlasting salvation; through Christ our Lord.
All: Amen.

Here the bishop blesses the incense that is to be burned on the altar, unless it was already blessed before the sacred action by the bishop or another priest delegated by him. With the form in the Pontifical.

18. The bishop, having put on the mitre, forms five crosses out of grains of incense on the same five spots where earlier he traced the crosses with the blessed water and the holy chrism. On each one of these he puts one of the crosses made of fine candle-was. The latter are then lighted so that they burn the incense. After this all kneel and the bishop, who is also kneeling (without mitre), intones the following antiphon which is taken up by the choir (for the music see the music supplement):

Antiphon: Come, Holy Spirit,   fill the hearts of your faithful, and enkindle in them the fire of your love.

19. After the singing all rise, and the bishop (with mitre), facing the people with hands joined, says in a loud voice:

My dear brethren, let us appeal to the mercy of God, the Father almighty, that in the solemn prayer we are about to utter during the present rite, He would sanctify this altar, which is to be dedicated to spiritual sacrifices. May He be pleased ever to bless and to hallow the offerings that will be placed on it by His servants in pledge of their devotion. May He find favor in the incense of the spirit and be ready to hear the petitions of His people.

Then turning back toward the altar and removing the mitre he adds at once:

Let us pray.
Deacon: Let us kneel.

And all, including the bishop, kneel and spend a little time in silent prayer, until the deacon says:

Arise.

Hereupon all rise, and the bishop with hands joined sings the following oration in the ferial tone:

Lord our God, we pray that your Holy Spirit may descend upon this altar, that He may sanctify thereon our and your people's gifts, and that it may please Him to cleanse the hearts of all who partake of them. We ask this through our Lord Jesus Christ, your Son, who lives and reigns with you, in the unity of the Holy Spirit, God,

C: Forever and ever.

All: Amen.

C: The Lord be with you.

All: May He also be with you.

C: Lift up your hearts.

All: We have lifted them up to the Lord.

C: Let us give thanks to the Lord our God.

All: It is fitting and right to do so.

It is indeed fitting and right, worthy and salutary that we should always and everywhere give thanks to you, O Lord, holy Father, almighty everlasting God. For after the offenses that came in the wake of the first fallen man, you instituted figurative sacrifices to be offered in propitiation to you, so that the fault engendered by pride might be expiated by the gifts of a future time, for which purpose altars are consecrated and a temple is dedicated. Hence be present in your inexpressible kindness and mercy, and pour out your precious blessing on this stone, so that by your bounty all who offer sacrifice on it may receive your reward. Through our Lord Jesus Christ, your Son, who lives and reigns with you, in the unity of the Holy Spirit, God, forever and ever.
All: Amen.

20. And the bishop immediately adds:

C: The Lord be with you.

All: May He also be with you.

Deacon: Let us bless the Lord.

All: Thanks be to God.

21. After the altar or altar-stone has been thoroughly cleansed by the clergy or the ministers, the bishop celebrates Mass on it or he commissions another priest to do so, as convenience dictates.

But if the consecration takes place with the simple form, the bishop gives the blessing and departs.

7

BLESSINGS OF THINGS DESIGNATED FOR SACRED FUNCTIONS OR OTHER SACRED PURPOSES

1. BLESSING OF AN ANTIMENSION*
Reserved to a bishop but may be delegated to a priest.

Which by a special Apostolic indult may be used in the celebration of Mass in mission territories, in place of an altar-stone or portable altar

(Approved by the Congregation of Sacred Rites, March 12, 1947)

The bishop (or a priest delegated for this), having ascertained the authenticity of the relics of holy martyrs to be used here, encloses them in a tiny sack which is sewn in the right corner of the antimension. Then he blesses the antimension, saying:

P: Our help is in the name of the Lord.
All: Who made heaven and earth.
P: The Lord be with you.
All: May He also be with you.

Let us pray.
Lord, we humbly appeal to your sovereignty, asking that it please you to bless this antimension, made ready by our lowly ministry to receive the offerings of your people. For on it we are to offer the holy Sacrifice to you, to the honor of the blessed Virgin Mary and all the saints, and in particular to the honor of Saints N. and N., whose relics we have enclosed therein. Grant that by these sacred mysteries the bonds of our sins be loosed, our stains blotted out, pardon obtained and graces acquired, so that together with your holy elect we may merit the joys of everlasting life through Christ our Lord.
All: Amen.

He sprinkles it with holy water.

2. CONSECRATION OF A PATEN AND A CHALICE

(From the new Roman Pontifical of 1962)

{The consecration of a paten and of a chalice may be delegated to a priest, who follows the same rite given here for a bishop, omitting, however, the directions that do not pertain to a priest.}

The consecration of a paten and chalice may take place on any day and at any convenient place.

The following are prepared: holy chrism and whatever materials are necessary for cleansing and wiping the chalice and paten as well as the bishop's hands. The chalice and paten should be placed on a table covered with a white-linen cloth or on the altar.

If several chalices and patens are to be consecrated the bishop performs the anointings successively on each of them, but he says the orations only once and in the plural form.

The bishop, standing and wearing the rochet, white stole, and gold-embroidered mitre, says:

Celebrant: Our help is in the name of the Lord.

All: Who made heaven and earth.

C: Let us pray, my dear brethren, that by the help of God's grace this paten (these patens) may be consecrated and hallowed for the purpose of breaking over it (them) the body of our Lord Jesus Christ, who suffered death on the cross for the salvation of us all.

Then, removing the mitre, he says:
C: The Lord be with you.
All: May He also be with you.

Let us pray.
Almighty everlasting God, who instituted the laws of sacrifice, and ordered among other things that the sprinkled wheaten flour should be carried to the altar on plates of gold and silver; be pleased to bless, hallow,   and consecrate this paten (these patens), destined for the administration of the Eucharist of Jesus Christ, your Son, who for our salvation and that of all
mankind chose to immolate Himself on the gibbet of the cross to you, God the Father, with whom He lives and reigns, forever and ever.
All: Amen.

Having put on the mitre, he dips the thumb of his right hand into the holy chrism, anoints the paten from rim to rim in the form of a cross, and then rubs the holy chrism all over the upper side of the paten, while saying the following formula:

Lord God, may you deign to consecrate and to hallow this paten by this anointing and our blessing, in Christ Jesus our Lord, who lives and reigns with you forever and ever.
All: Amen.

Then (still standing and wearing the mitre) he proceeds to the blessing of the chalice, saying:

Let us pray, my dear brethren, that our Lord and God, by His heavenly grace and inspiration, may hallow this chalice (these chalices), about to be consecrated for use in His ministry, and that He may add the fulness of His divine favor to the consecration performed by us; through Christ our Lord.
All: Amen.

Then, removing the mitre, he says:
C: The Lord be with you.
All: May He also be with you.

Let us pray.
O Lord our God, be pleased to bless this chalice (these chalices), made by your devout people for your holy service. Bestow that same blessing which you bestowed on the hallowed chalice of your servant, Melchisedech. And what we cannot make worthy of your altars by our craft and metals, do you nonetheless make worthy by your blessing; through Christ our Lord.
All: Amen.

Having put on the mitre, he dips the thumb of his right hand into the holy chrism and anoints each chalice on the inside from rim to rim In the form of a cross, while saying the following formula:
Lord God, may it please you to consecrate and to hallow this chalice by this anointing and our blessing, in Christ Jesus our Lord, who lives and reigns with you forever and ever.
All: Amen.

Then, removing the mitre, he says the following over the chalice and paten (chalices and patens):

C: The Lord be with you.
All: May He also be with you.

Let us pray.
Almighty everlasting God, we beg you to impart to our hands the
virtue of your blessing, so that by our blessing this vessel and
paten (these vessels and patens) may be hallowed and become, by
the grace of the Holy Spirit, a new sepulchre for the body and
blood of our Lord Jesus Christ; through Christ our Lord.
All: Amen.

When the consecration is over a priest cleans the chalice and paten
with crumbs of bread and purifies them thoroughly. These
cleansing materials are put into the sacrarium.

3. BLESSING OF A TABERNACLE, PYX, CIBORIUM

For reserving the holy Eucharist

{The blessings of the sacred appurtenances or furnishings (sacra
supellex) required in sacred worship--vessels, utensils, vestments,
linens, and the like--used to be reserved to cardinals, bishops,
pastors, priests especially delegated thereto, and religious
superiors. Now according to the new "Instruction" of September
26, 1964, any priest may confer them. In view of past
interpretation of the Congregation of Sacred Rites, this would
apply only to blessings in which no special anointing is required.}

P: Our help is in the name of the Lord.
All: Who made heaven and earth.
P: The Lord be with you.
All: May He also be with you.

Let us pray.
Almighty everlasting God, we humbly entreat your sovereignty to

consecrate with your blessing ✠ this tabernacle (or ciborium or pyx) made to contain the body of your Son, our Lord Jesus Christ; through Christ our Lord.
All: Amen.

It is sprinkled with holy water.

4. BLESSING OF A MONSTRANCE OR OSTENSORIUM

For exposition of the Blessed Sacrament

P: Our help is in the name of the Lord.
All: Who made heaven and earth.
P: The Lord be with you.
All: May He also be with you.

Let us pray.
Almighty everlasting God, be pleased to bless and to hallow this vessel made to expose, for the faithful's adoration, the body of your Son, our Lord Jesus Christ. May all who in this life piously adore your only-begotten Word possess Him in the life to come as their everlasting recompense; through Christ our Lord.
All: Amen.

It is sprinkled with holy water.

5. BLESSING OF A RELIQUARY

P: Our help is in the name of the Lord
All: Who made heaven and earth.
P: The Lord be with you.
All: May He also be with you.

Let us pray.
Lord, bless ✠ this reliquary made to contain the holy remains of your saints; and grant that by the prayers of your saints all who devoutly venerate their relics may obtain pardon for sin and

protection from every adversity; through Christ our Lord.
All: Amen.

It is sprinkled with holy water.

6. BLESSING OF OIL-STOCKS

P: Our help is in the name of the Lord.
All: Who made heaven and earth.
P: The Lord be with you.
All: May He also be with you.

Let us pray.
Most gracious Lord and Father, hear our prayers, and bless and
hallow these vessels prepared for the sacred ministry of your
Church; through Christ our Lord.
All: Amen.

Let us pray.
Almighty everlasting God, by whom all unclean things are made
clean, and in whom all things made clean retain their lustre, we
humbly implore your sovereign power that these vessels and
ornaments offered to you by your servants may be freed from
contamination of every unclean spirit, and that by your blessing
they remain hallowed for the use and ministry of the holy altar and
of your Church; through Christ our Lord.
All: Amen.

They are sprinkled with holy water.

7. BLESSING OF SACRED VESSELS

Or ornaments in general

This blessing and the following ones, nos. 8, 9, 10, 11, 12, and 13,
are revised in accordance with the new Roman Missal of 1962. The
blessing of a purificator is a new one, i.e. not heretofore

contained in the liturgical books. And a corporal and a pall are each blessed separately, instead of together as happened formerly.

P: Our help is in the name of the Lord.
All: Who made heaven and earth.
P: The Lord be with you.
All: May He also be with you.

Let us pray. Almighty everlasting God, by whom all unclean things are made clean, and in whom all things made clean retain their lustre, we humbly implore your sovereign power that these vessels and ornaments offered to you by your servants may be freed from contamination of every unclean spirit, and that by your blessing they remain hallowed for the use and service of the holy altar and of your Church; through Christ our Lord.
All: Amen.

They are sprinkled with holy water.

8. BLESSING OF ALTAR-LINENS

P: Our help is in the name of the Lord.
All: Who made heaven and earth.
P: The Lord be with you.
All: May He also be with you.

Let us pray.
Lord God almighty, who for forty days instructed Moses, your servant, how to make linens and sacred appointments, which even Mary wove and made for the service of the Old Covenant; be pleased to bless   these linens (this linen) made to cover and envelop the altar of your glorious Son, our Lord Jesus Christ, who lives and reigns with you forever and ever.
All: Amen.

They are (it is) sprinkled with holy water.

9. BLESSING OF A CORPORAL

P: Our help is in the name of the Lord.
All: Who made heaven and earth.
P: The Lord be with you.
All: May He also be with you.

Let us pray.
Most gracious Lord, whose power is indescribable, and whose mysteries are celebrated with wondrous ceremonies; grant, we pray, that by your kindness this linen may be hallowed by your blessing, and serve for the consecration of the body and blood of your Son, our Lord and God Jesus Christ, who lives and reigns with you forever and

All: Amen.

It is sprinkled with holy water.

10. BLESSING OF A PALL

P: Our help is in the name of the Lord.
All: Who made heaven and earth.
P: The Lord be with you.
All: May He also be with you.

Let us pray.
Almighty everlasting God, be pleased to bless   this pall, which is to be used in covering the body and blood of our Lord Jesus Christ, your Son, who lives and reigns forever and ever.
All: Amen.

It is sprinkled with holy water.

11. BLESSING OF A PURIFICATOR

P: Our help is in the name of the Lord.

All: Who made heaven and earth.
P: The Lord be with you.
All: May He also be with you.

Let us pray.
Hearken to our prayers, O Lord, and be pleased to bless this linen prepared for use in purifying the sacred chalice; through Christ our Lord.
All: Amen.

It is sprinkled with holy water

12. BLESSING OF PRIESTLY VESTMENTS

in general

P: Our help is in the name of the Lord,
All: Who made heaven and earth.
P: The Lord be with you.
All: May He also be with you.

Let us pray.
Almighty everlasting God, who decreed through Moses, your servant, that the vesture of high-priest, priest, and levite, used in fulfilling their ministry in your sight, should be worn to dignify and beautify the worship rendered to your holy name; mercifully heed our prayers, and be pleased, through our lowly ministry, to bless ~ these priestly vestments (this priestly vestment), bedewing them (it) with your grace, so that they (it) become hallowed and suitable for divine worship and the sacred mysteries. Let every bishop, priest, or deacon clothed in these sacred vestments (this sacred vestment) be strengthened and defended from all assault or temptation of wicked spirits; let them perform and celebrate your mysteries reverently and well; and let them always carry out their ministry in a devout and pleasing manner; through Christ our Lord.
All: Amen.

They are (it is) sprinkled with holy water.

13. BLESSING OF ANY PRIESTLY VESTMENT

P: Our help is in the name of the Lord.
All: Who made heaven and earth.
P: The Lord be with you.
All: May He also be with you.

Let us pray.
Almighty everlasting God, giver of all good things and bountiful
bestower of all graces, we humbly beg you to endow us with the
power of your blessing. May it also please you to bless,   by the
work of the Holy Spirit, this amice (or alb, or cincture, or stole, or
maniple, or tunic, or dalmatic, or chasuble, or cope, or humeral
veil) made ready for divine worship. Kindly let the
grace of your holy mysteries descend on all who are to use it, so
that they may appear holy, pure, and blameless in your presence,
and may be aided by your mercy; through Christ our Lord.
All: Amen.

It is sprinkled with holy water.

14. SOLEMN BLESSING OF A CROSS

If a cross is to be exposed for public veneration, it should be
solemnly blessed.

P: Our help is in the name of the Lord.
All: Who made heaven and earth.
P: The Lord be with you.
All: May He also be with you.

Let us pray.
Holy Lord, almighty Father, everlasting God, be pleased to bless
this cross, that it may be a saving help to mankind. Let it be the
support of faith, an encouragement to good works, the redemption
of souls; and let it be consolation, protection, and a shield against

the cruel darts of the enemy; through Christ our Lord.
All: Amen.

Let us pray.
Lord Jesus Christ, bless this cross by which you snatched the
world from Satan's grasp, and on which you overcame by your
suffering the tempter to sin, who rejoiced in the first man's fall in
eating of the forbidden tree. Here it is sprinkled with holy water.
May this cross be hallowed in the name of the Father, and of the
Son, and of the Holy Spirit; and may all who kneel and pray before
this cross in honor of our Lord find health in body and soul;
through Christ our Lord.
All: Amen.

After this the priest, kneeling before the cross, devoutly
venerates and kisses it, and others may do likewise.

15. MORE SOLEMN BLESSING OF A CROSS

At hand are a thurible and holy water. The priest, vested in surplice
red stole and cope, says:

P: Our help is in the name of the Lord.
All: Who made heaven and earth.
P: The Lord be with you.
All: May He also be with you.

Let us pray.
Lord Jesus Christ, bless this cross by which you snatched the
world from Satan's grasp, and overcame by your suffering the
tempter to sin, who rejoiced in the first man's fall in eating of the
forbidden tree. We ask this of you who live and reign with God the
Father and the Holy Spirit forever and ever.
All: Amen.

Let us pray.
Holy Lord, almighty Father, everlasting God, be pleased, we beg
you, to bless this cross, so that it may be a saving help to
mankind. Let it be the support of faith, an encouragement to good

works, the redemption of souls; and let it be consolation, protection, and a shield against thecruel darts of the enemy; through Christ our Lord.
All: Amen.

Then with hands outstretched before his breast he says the following preface in a moderately loud voice:

P: Forever and ever.
All: Amen.
P: The Lord be with you.
All: May He also be with you.
P: Lift up your hearts.
All: We have lifted them up to the Lord.
P: Let us give thanks to the Lord our God.
All: It is fitting and right to do so.

It is indeed fitting and right, worthy and salutary that we should always and everywhere give thanks to you, O holy Lord, almighty Father, everlasting God; for among your visible creatures even fruitful trees never cease to praise and bless your holy and awesome name. In figure of your only-begotten Wisdom you beautified in the beginning the Garden of Eden with the tree of life, and by its fruit, as by a holy sign, you admonished our first parents to beware of death and to seek everlasting life. Condemned as we were to a just death by the touch of the forbidden tree, you mercifully recalled us from death to life by the selfsame co-eternal Wisdom, Jesus Christ, our Lord and God. Therefore, we your suppliants pray that you may hallow with a blessing   from on high this singular sign, wrought and raised up for the faithful's devotion in remembrance of that first holy standard on which you conquered by the precious blood
of your Son. May all who kneel before it, imploring your sovereignty, experience true compunction and obtain forgiveness of their transgressions; and by the merits of the victorious suffering and death of your only-begotten Son may they seek only what pleases you, and speedily obtain what they request. Grant, we pray, O most loving Father in whom we live, and move, and have our being, that as often as we gaze upon and call to mind the

triumphant sign of your divine humility, which crushed the pride
of our foe, we may be filled with hope and be strengthened against
the wiles of that same foe, and receive greater grace to live humbly
and devoutly in your sight. And on that dreadful judgment day,
when you will appear in majesty, when the elements shall quake
and the powers of heaven be moved, and this glorified sign of our
redemption shall appear in the heavens, may we pass from death to
life, and deserve to see the everlasting joys of a blessed
resurrection. What follows is said in a subdued tone, loud enough,
however, to be heard by the bystanders: Through our Lord Jesus
Christ, your Son, who lives and reigns with you, in the unity of the
Holy Spirit, God, forever and ever.
All: Amen.

Let us pray.
God, who by the gibbet of the holy cross, a onetime instrument of
punishment for criminals, restored life to the redeemed, grant that
your faithful people may find in it a strong support, who see in it
their standard of battle. Let the cross be for them a foundation of
faith, a pillar of hope, a safeguard in adversity, an aid in prosperity;
let it be victory amid enemies, a guard in cities, a shield in the
country, a prop in their homes. By it may the Good Shepherd keep
His flock unharmed, for on it did the Lamb who has conquered
win our salvation; through Christ our Lord.
All: Amen.

Then incense in a boat is brought before the priest, who blesses it
saying:

Let us pray.
Lord God almighty, before whom the host of angels stands in awe,
and renders you a spiritual service glowing with love, be pleased to
look with favor on this creature, incense, to bless   and to hallow
it. May all weakness, all infirmity, and all assaults of the enemy,
sensing its fragrance, flee and be kept far from your creature, man,
that he, whom you redeemed by the precious blood of your Son,
may never again suffer from the sting of the ancient serpent;
through Christ our Lord.
All: Amen.

After this the priest puts incense into the thurible, and then sprinkles the cross with holy water and incenses it.

If the cross is made of wood he adds the prayer indicated by 1; if of metal or stone, the prayer indicated by 2:

(1): May this wood be sanctified, in the name of the Father, and of the Son, and of the Holy   Spirit. And may the blessing of this wood, on which were hung the sacred members of our Savior, remain ever in it, so that all who kneel in prayer before this cross in God's honor may have health in body and soul; through Christ our Lord.
All: Amen.

Then the priest, kneeling before the cross, devoutly venerates it and kisses it, and others who wish may do likewise.

(2): God of glory, God of hosts, the mighty Emmanuel, God, Father of truth, Father of wisdom, Father of holiness. Father, you enlighten us and keep watch over us. You rule the world and reign over all kingdoms. You are the giver of all grace and the dispenser of all gifts. All nations, peoples, tribes, and tongues serve you. All legions of angels minister before you. You bestow on your servants the power to believe and to praise your name, enabling them to offer due worship to you. You desire first of all faith in those who offer sacrifice to you, even before the gift is sacrificed. We appeal, then, to your tender-hearted mercy, asking that you hallow   and consecrate   this cross made by your servants in a spirit of total faith and devotion, to serve as a reminder of your victory and our redemption, a victorious and glorious sign of Christ's love. Behold this unconquerable sign of the cross by which diabolical power was destroyed and human liberty restored, which once was a symbol of shame, but now by your grace has been turned into a symbol of honor; which once punished the guilty with death, but now absolves criminals from their debt. And how can it please you, except that by it you were pleased to redeem us? And now no gift can any longer give you due honor except that which onetime had the sacred body nailed to it; nor can any offering

please you more than that which onetime was made holy by your arms outstretched on it. Therefore, accept this cross with those hands that once embraced the first cross, and by the holiness of that cross make holy   this one. And as the world's guilt was expiated by that cross, so may your servants merit deliverance from sin by this one, as they honor it in praise of you. Under the protection of the true cross may they advance step by step as victors. Here on the cross may the splendor of your only-begotten Son, our Lord, sparkle in the gold of your glance; may the renown of His death on the wood shine out; may our redemption from death, the purification of our life, be reflected in the effulgent crystal of the cross. Let the cross be a safeguard and assurance to its followers; let it unite them in faith with the people of all nations, bringing them together in peace and in hope, advancing them in victories, increasing their good fortunes, helping them for all time to advance toward everlasting life, thus assuring their happiness in this life, and leading them by its mighty power to the glory of the heavenly kingdom. May you grant this by the appeasing blood of your Son, by Him who is the giver of all gifts, who gave Himself for the redemption of many, who offered Himself as a holocaust for sin, who in being exalted on the wood of the cross humbled the principalities and powers, who with you, in the undivided unity of the Holy Spirit, sits on the heavenly throne forevermore.
All: Amen.

Then the priest, kneeling before the cross, devoutly venerates and kisses it, and others who wish may do likewise.

16. SOLEMN BLESSING OF AN IMAGE

Of our Lord Jesus Christ,the blessed Virgin Mary, or any saint

If such images are exposed for public veneration they should be solemnly blessed.

P: Our help is in the name of the Lord.
All: Who made heaven and earth.

P. The Lord be with you.
All: May He also be with you.

Let us pray.
Almighty everlasting God, who do not forbid us to carve or paint
likenesses of your saints, in order that whenever we look at them
with our bodily eyes we may call to mind their holy lives, and
resolve to follow in their footsteps; may it please you to bless and
to hallow this statue (or picture), which has been made in memory
and honor of your only-begotten Son, our Lord Jesus
Christ (or the blessed Virgin Mary, Mother of our Lord Jesus
Christ), (or blessed N., your apostle, or martyr, or pontiff, or
confessor, or virgin). And grant that all who in its presence pay
devout homage to your only-begotten Son (or the blessed Virgin,
or the glorious apostle, or martyr, or pontiff, or confessor, or
virgin) may by His (or his or her) merits (and intercession) obtain
your grace in this life and everlasting glory in the life to come;
through Christ our Lord.
All: Amen.

The image is sprinkled with holy water.

17. BLESSING OF A CLERICAL CASSOCK

A candidate for holy orders, who has obtained permission to wear
the clerical cassock, may wish to have this garment blessed. The
clerical aspirant, holding the cassock folded over his outstretched
arms, kneels before the priest.

P: Our help is in the name of the Lord.
All: Who made heaven and earth.
P: The Lord be with you.
All: May He also be with you.

Let us pray.
Lord Jesus Christ, who condescended to clothe yourself in our
mortal nature, we beg you in your boundless goodness to bless
this cassock which the holy fathers have sanctioned as the garb for

clerics, in token of the innocence and humility which should be theirs. Laying aside the vanity of secular garb, may these servants (this servant) of yours, who are (is) to wear the cassock, likewise put on you, and be recognized as men (a man) dedicated to your service. We ask this of you who are God, living and reigning forever and ever.
All: Amen.

The cassock is sprinkled with holy water.

18. BLESSING OF A CINCTURE

To be worn in honor of our Lord Jesus Christ

P: Our help is in the name of the Lord.
All: Who made heaven and earth.
P: The Lord be with you.
All: May He also be with you.

Let us pray.
God, who willed, in redeeming your servant, that your Son should be bound by impious hands, we beg you to bless this cincture; and grant that your servant, who is to wear it as a reminder of bodily mortification, may always venerate the bonds of our Lord Jesus Christ, and may acknowledge that he (she) is bound to your service; through Christ our Lord.
All: Amen.

It is sprinkled with holy water.

19. BLESSING OF A CINCTURE

To be worn in honor of the blessed Virgin Mary or a canonized saint

P: Our help is in the name of the Lord.
All: Who made heaven and earth.

P: The Lord be with you.
All: May He also be with you.

Let us pray.
Lord Jesus Christ, we beg you to bless   this cincture; and grant
that he (she) who is to wear it may, by the help and protection of
the blessed Virgin Mary, your mother, (or of St. N.), be shielded
from every danger and obtain health of body and soul. We ask this
of you who live andreign forever and ever.
All: Amen.

It is sprinkled with holy water.

20. BLESSING OF A HABIT

To be worn in honor of the blessed Virgin Mary

P: Our help is in the name of the Lord.
All: Who made heaven and earth.
P: The Lord be with you.
All: May He also be with you.

Let us pray.
Lord, bless   this habit which is to be worn in honor of the blessed
Virgin Mary, and under her patronage; and grant that he (she) who
is to wear it may obtain health in body and protection in soul;
through Christ our Lord
All: Amen.

It is sprinkled with holy water.

21. BLESSING OF A HABIT

To be worn in honor of the blessed Virgin Mary or a canonized
saint

P: Our help is in the name of the Lord.

All: Who made heaven and earth.
P: The Lord be with you.
All: May He also be with you.

Let us pray.
Lord Jesus Christ, who in becoming man for our salvation deigned
to assume our vesture of flesh, bless   this habit with a holy
benediction, for your servant is to wear it in thanksgiving to you
and in veneration of the blessed Virgin Mary (or of St. N.). Pour
out on him (her), we pray, your holy blessing, so that when he
(she) first puts on this garb, which is like that of a religious, he
(she) may obtain, through the prayers of the blessed Virgin Mary
(or of St. N.), your grace to protect him (her) from every evil of
mind or body. We ask this of you who live and reign forever and
ever.
All: Amen.

It is sprinkled with holy water.

22. BLESSING OF A CINCTURE

To be worn in honor of St. Joseph, spouse of our Lady

(Approved by the Congregation of Sacred Rites, Sept. 19, 1859)

The priest, vested in surplice and white stole, says:

P: Our help is in the name of the Lord.
All: Who made heaven and earth.
P: The Lord be with you.
All: May He also be with you.

Let us pray.
Lord Jesus Christ, who inculcated the counsel and love of
virginity, and gave the precept of chastity, we appeal to your
kindness, asking that you bless and hallow this cincture as a token
of purity. Let all who gird themselves with it as a safeguard of
chastity be enabled, by the prayers of St. Joseph, spouse of your

holy Mother, to practice that continence which is so pleasing to you, and to live in obedience to your commandments. May they also obtain pardon of their sins, health in mind and body, and finally attain everlasting life. We ask this of you who live and reign with God the Father, in the unity of the Holy Spirit, God, forever and ever.

All: Amen.

Let us pray.

Almighty everlasting God, grant, we pray, that those who revere the inviolate virginity of the most pure Virgin Mary and of Joseph, her spouse, may by their prayers be pure in mind and body; through Christ our Lord.

All: Amen.

Let us pray. Almighty everlasting God. who committed the boy Jesus and the most pure Mary, ever a Virgin, to the care of the chaste man Joseph, we humbly entreat you that those who are girded with this cincture in honor of St. Joseph and under his patronage may, by your help and his prayers, persevere in holy chastity for all time; through Christ our Lord.

All: Amen.

Let us pray.

God, the lover and restorer of innocence, we pray that your faithful who are to wear this cincture may, by the prayers of St. Joseph, spouse of your holy Mother, have their loins girded and hold burning lamps in their hands, and thus be likened to men who wait for their Lord when He shall return for a wedding, that when He comes and knocks they may open to Him, and be found worthy of being taken into everlasting joys; through you who live and reign forever and ever.

All: Amen.

Then the priest puts incense into the censer, sprinkles the cincture with holy water, saying:

Sprinkle me with hyssop, Lord, and I shall be clean of sin. Wash me, and I shall be whiter than snow.

After this he incenses the cincture, and then continues:

P: Save your servants.

All: Who trust in you, my God.

P: Lord, send them aid from your holy place.

All: And watch over them from Sion.

P: Lord, heed my prayer.

All: And let my cry be heard by you.

P: The Lord be with you.

All: May He also be with you.

Let us pray.
O God of mercy, God of goodness, who are pleased with all good things, and without whom no good work is begun, no good work is finished; kindly hear our prayers, and defend your faithful, who are to wear this blessed cincture in honor of St. Joseph and under his protection, from the pit-falls of this world and all its lusts. Help them to persist in their holy resolution and to obtain pardon of their sins, and thus merit to be numbered among your elect; through Christ our Lord.
All: Amen.

23. BLESSING OF LILIES

On the feast of St. Anthony of Padua

(Approved by the Congregation of Sacred Rites, Feb. 26, 1901)

The priest vests in surplice and white stole, and says:

P: Our help is in the name of the Lord.
All: Who made heaven and earth.
P: The Lord be with you.
All: May He also be with you.

Let us pray.
God, the Creator and preserver of the human race, the lover of holy purity, the giver of supernatural grace, and the dispenser of everlasting salvation; bless these lilies which we, your humble servants, present to you today as an act of thanksgiving and in honor of St. Anthony, your confessor, and with a request for your blessing. Pour out on them, by the saving sign of the holy cross, your dew from on high. You in your great kindness have given them to man, and endowed them with a sweet fragrance to lighten the burden of the sick. Therefore, let them be filled with such power that, whether they are used by the sick, or kept in homes or other places, or devoutly carried on one's person, they may serve to drive out evil spirits, safeguard holy chastity, and turn away illness--all this through the prayers of St. Anthony--and finally impart to your servants grace and peace; through Christ our Lord.
All: Amen.

Then he sprinkles the lilies with holy water, saying:

Sprinkle me with hyssop, Lord, and I shall be clean of sin. Wash me, and I shall be whiter than snow.

P: Pray for us, St. Anthony.
All: That we may be worthy of Christ's promise.

Let us pray.
We beg you, O Lord, that your people may be helped by the constant and devout intercession of Blessed Anthony, your illustrious confessor. May he assist us to be worthy of your grace in this life, and to attain everlasting joys in the life to come; through Christ our Lord.
All: Amen.

After this the lilies are distributed to the people.

24. BLESSING OF A PROCESSIONAL BANNER

Of any society

P: Our help is in the name of the Lord.
All: Who made heaven and earth.
P: The Lord be with you.
All: May He also be with you.

Let us pray.
Lord Jesus Christ, whose Church is like a well ordered battle-array,
bless this banner; and grant that all who fight under this standard
for your sake, O Lord God, may by the prayers of St. N. overcome
their visible and invisible enemies in this life, and after this victory
come as conquerors to the kingdom of heaven. We ask this through
you, Jesus Christ, who live and reign with God the Father and the
Holy Spirit forever and ever.
All: Amen.

It is sprinkled with holy water.

25. BLESSING OF CANDLES

P: Our help is in the name of the Lord.
All: Who made heaven and earth.
P: The Lord be with you.
All: May He also be with you.

Let us pray.
Lord Jesus Christ, Son of the living God, bless these candles at our
lowly request. Endow them, Lord, by the power of the holy cross,
with a blessing from on high, you who gave them to mankind in
order to dispel darkness. Let the blessing that they receive from the
sign of the holy cross be so effectual that, wherever they are
lighted or placed, the princes of darkness may depart in trembling

from all these places, and flee in fear, along with all their legions, and never more dare to disturb or molest those who serve you, the almighty God, who live and reign forever and ever.
All: Amen.

They are sprinkled with holy water.

26. BLESSING OF A CHURCH ORGAN

P: Our help is in the name of the Lord.
All: Who made heaven and earth.

Psalm 150

P: Praise the Lord in His sanctuary, * praise Him in the firmament of His strength.

All: Praise Him for His mighty deeds, * praise Him for His sovereign majesty.

P: Praise Him with the blast of the trumpet, * praise Him with lyre and harp,

All: Praise Him with timbrel and dance, * praise Him with strings and pipe.

P: Praise Him with sounding cymbals, praise Him with clanging cymbals. * Let everything that has breath praise the Lord!

All: Glory be to the Father.

P: As it was in the beginning.

P: Praise Him with timbrel and dance.

All: Praise Him with strings and pipes.

P: The Lord be with you.

All: May He also be with you.

Let us pray.
God, who by Moses, your servant, ordered the sound of trumpets to accompany the sacrifices offered to your name, and willed that the children of Israel sing praise to your name with trumpets and timbrels; we beg you to bless this organ which we dedicate to your service. And grant that your faithful who are gladdened with holy songs here on earth may attain everlasting gladness in heaven; through Christ our Lord.
All: Amen.

It is sprinkled with holy water.

27. BLESSING OF A CHURCH BELL

Designated for a church that is merely blessed or for an oratory*

(Approved by the Congregation of Sacred Rites, Jan. 22, 1908)

* Reserved to the Ordinary or to a priest delegated by him. There is a consecration of bells destined for a consecrated church in the Roman Pontifical.

P: Our help is in the name of the Lord.
All: Who made heaven and earth.

Psalm 50

Psalm 53

P: God, by your name save me, * and by your might defend my cause.

All: God, hear my prayer; * hearken to the words of my mouth.

P: For haughty men have risen up against me, and fierce men seek my life; * they set not God before their eyes.

All: See, God is my helper; * the Lord sustains my life.

P: Turn back the evil upon my foes; * in your faithfulness destroy them.

All: Freely will I offer you sacrifice; * I will praise your name, Lord, for its goodness,

P: Because from all distress you have rescued me, * and my eyes look down upon my enemies.

All: Glory be to the Father.

P: As it was in the beginning.

Psalm 56

P: Have pity on me, O God; have pity on me, * for in you I take refuge.

All: In the shadow of your wings I take refuge, * till harm pass by.

P: I call to God the Most High, * to God, my benefactor.

All: May He send from heaven and save me; may He make those a reproach who trample upon me; * may God send His kindness and His faithfulness.

P: I lie prostrate in the midst of lions * which devour men;

All: Their teeth are spears and arrows, * their tongue is a sharp sword.

P: Be exalted above the heavens, O God; * above all the earth be your glory!

All: They have prepared a net for my feet; * they have bowed me down;

P: They have dug a pit before me; * may they fall into it.

All: My heart is steadfast, O God; my heart is steadfast; * I will sing and chant praise.

P: Awake, my soul; awake, lyre and harp! * I will wake the dawn.

All: I will give thanks to you among the peoples, Lord, * I will chant your praise among the nations.

P: For your kindness towers to the heavens, * and your faithfulness to the skies.

All: Be exalted above the heavens, O God; * above all the earth be your glory!

P: Glory be to the Father.

All: As it was in the beginning.

Psalm 66

Psalm 69

Psalm 85

Psalm 129

P: Lord, have mercy. Christ, have mercy. Lord, have mercy. Our Father (the rest inaudibly until:)

P: And lead us not into temptation.

All: But deliver us from evil.

P: Blessed be the name of the Lord.

All: Both now and forevermore.

P: Lord, heed my prayer.

All: And let my cry be heard by you.

P: The Lord be with you.

All: May He also be with you.

Let us pray.
God, who decreed through blessed Moses, your servant and lawgiver, that silver trumpets should be made and be sounded at the time of sacrifice, in order to remind the people by their clear tones to prepare for your worship and to assemble for its celebration. Grant, we pray, that this bell, destined for your holy Church, may be hallowed by the Holy Spirit through our lowly ministry, so that when it is tolled and rung the faithful may be invited to the house of God and to the everlasting recompense. Let the people's faith and piety wax stronger whenever they hear its melodious peals. At its sound let all evil spirits be driven afar; let thunder and lightning, hail and storm be banished; let the power of your hand put down the evil powers of the air, causing them to tremble at the sound of this bell, and to flee at the sight of the holy cross engraved thereon. May our Lord Himself grant this, who overcame death on the gibbet of the cross, and who now reigns in the glory of God the Father, in the unity of the Father and the Holy Spirit, forever and ever.
All: Amen.

The priest puts incense into the thurible, and sprinkles the bell with holy water while walking around it. While he does so the choir sings the Asperges (see p. 398). Then he incenses it, again walking around it, as the choir sings the following antiphon (for the music see the music supplement):

Antiphon: Lord, let my prayer come like incense before you.

Then the celebrant continues:

Let us pray.
O Christ, the almighty ruler, as you once calmed the storm at sea when awakened in the boat from the sleep of your human nature, so now come with your benign help to the needs of your people, and pour out on this bell the dew of the Holy Spirit. Whenever it rings may the enemy of the good take flight, the Christian people hear the call to faith, the empire of Satan be terrified, your people be strengthened as they are called together in the Lord, and may the Holy Spirit be with them as He delighted to be with David when he played his harp. And as onetime thunder in the air frightened away a throng of enemies, while Samuel slew an unweaned lamb as a holocaust to the eternal King, so when the peal of this bell resounds in the clouds may a legion of angels stand watch over the assembly of your Church, the first-fruits of the faithful, and afford your ever-abiding protection to them in body and spirit. We ask this through you, Jesus Christ, who live and reign with God the Father, in the unity of the Holy Spirit, God, forever and ever.
All: Amen.

P: To the honor of St. N.
All: Amen.

Lastly the priest signs the blessed bell with the sign of the cross, and departs with his assistants.

If this blessing of a bell has to do with consecrated churches, due care must be taken that it is bestowed by a bishop or by a priest having the apostolic indult, and the rite used is that given in the Roman Pontifical.

28. RITE FOR ERECTING STATIONS OF THE CROSS

{This rite was formerly reserved to the Order of Friars Minor, but for some time bishops have been empowered to delegate it to their own priests. Now, by the "Motu Proprio" of Paul VI, dated November 30, 1963 (see "Ephemerides Liturgicae" 78 [1964] 2), the privilege has been extended, and bishops may give priests the faculty to erect the stations of the cross, with all indulgences. And more recently, by virtue of the "Instruction" of September 26, 1964, it is no longer reserved to the Friars Minor but only to bishops.}

The priest who has this faculty vests in surplice and purple stole. He should be assisted by at least one cleric, who at the times designated hands him the aspersory and the thurible. First the priest goes up to the altar predella and addresses the people briefly on the excellence and value of the devotion of the Way of the Cross. After this he kneels on the lowest step of the altar and intones the "Veni Creator," which is continued by the choir. When the hymn is finished he says:

P: Send forth your Spirit and all things shall be recreated.
All: And you shall renew the face of the earth.

Let us pray.
God, who instructed the hearts of the faithful by the light of the Holy Spirit, guide us by your Spirit to desire only what is good and so always to find joy in His comfort.

Lord, we beg you to protect this people from every adversity, by the intercession of blessed Mary, ever a Virgin; and as they bow down fervently before you shield them by your benevolence from all wiles of the enemy.

We beg you, Lord, let a breath of your grace prompt our undertakings and guide them along their course, so that our least prayer and work may begin in you and end in you; through Christ our Lord.
All: Amen.

Then if the paintings or images of the stations are right at hand (and not already hung in their place) the priest blesses them as follows:

P: Our help is in the name of the Lord.
All: Who made heaven and earth.
P: The Lord be with you.
All: May He also be with you.

Let us pray.
Almighty everlasting God, who do not forbid us to carve or paint likenesses of your saints, in order that whenever we look at them with our bodily eyes we may call to mind their holy lives, and resolve to follow in their footsteps; may it please you to bless and to hallow these images, which have been made in memory and honor of your only begotten Son, our Lord Jesus Christ. And grant that all who in their presence pay devout homage to your only begotten Son may by His merits and primacy obtain your grace in this life and everlasting glory in the life to come; through Christ our Lord.
All: Amen.

The priest sprinkles them with holy water and incenses them. In a private oratory the incensation may be omitted.

Next the priest blesses the fourteen crosses which must be made of wood.

P: Our help is in the name of the Lord.
All: Who made heaven and earth.
P: The Lord be with you.
All: May He also be with you.

Let us pray.
Holy Lord, almighty Father, everlasting God, we beg that it may please you to bless   these crosses, so that they may be saving helps to mankind. Let them be the support of faith, an encouragement to good works, the redemption of souls; and let them be consolation, protection, and shields against the cruel darts of the enemy; through Christ our Lord.
All: Amen.

Let us pray.
Lord Jesus Christ, bless   these crosses, for by your holy cross you
snatched the world from Satan's grasp, and overcame by your
suffering the tempter to sin, who rejoiced in the first man's fall in
eating of the forbidden tree.

Then the priest sprinkles them with holy water, saying:

May these crosses be hallowed, in the name of the Father, and of
the Son, and of the Holy   Spirit; so that all who kneel in prayer
before these crosses in our Lord's honor may have health in body
and soul; through Christ our Lord.
All: Amen.

If there is a procession the following hymns are sung (for the
music of these two hymns see the music supplement):

Hymn: Vexilla Regis

> Abroad the regal banners fly,
> Now shines the cross's mystery;
> Upon it Life did death endure,
> And yet by death did life procure.
>
> Who, wounded with a direful spear,
> Did, purposely to wash us clear
> From stain of sin, pour out a flood
> Of precious water mixed with blood.
>
> That which the prophet-king of old
> Has in mysterious verse foretold,
> Is now accomplished, while we see
> God ruling nations from a tree.
>
> O lovely and refulgent tree,
> Adorned with purpled majesty;
> Culled from a worthy stock to bear

Those limbs which sanctified were.

Blest tree, whose happy branches bore
The wealth that did the world restore;
The beam that did that body weigh
Which raised up hell's expected prey.

Hail, cross, of hopes the most sublime!
Now in this mournful passion time, *
Improve religious souls in grace.
The sins of criminals efface.

Blest Trinity, salvation's spring,
May every soul your praises sing;
To those you grant a conquest by
The holy cross, rewards apply. Amen.

* Outside of passiontime this line reads: "Now in your glorious reign in time." In paschaltime it reads: "Which bears the joys of paschaltime."

Hymn: Stabat Mater

At the cross her station keeping,
Stood the mournful Mother weeping,
Close to Jesus to the last.

Through her heart, His sorrows sharing,
All His bitter anguish bearing,
Now at length the sword had passed.

Oh, how sad and sore distressed
Was that Mother highly blest
Of the sole-begotten One.

Christ above in torment hangs;
She beneath beholds the pangs
Of her dying glorious Son.

Is there one who would not weep,
Whelmed in miseries so deep
Christ's dear Mother to behold?

Can the human heart refrain
From partaking in her pain,
In that Mother's pain untold?

Bruised, derided, cursed, defiled,
She beheld her tender child
All with bloody scourges rent.

For the sins of His own nation,
Saw Him hang in desolation,
Till his spirit forth He sent.

O you Mother, fount of love!
Touch my spirit from above,
Make my heart with yours accord.

Make me feel as you have felt,
Make my soul to glow and melt
With the love of Christ my Lord. Amen.

P: We adore you, Christ, and we bless you.
All: For by your holy cross you have redeemed the world.

Let us pray.
God, who by the illustrious suffering of your Son taught us to
arrive at everlasting glory by the way of the cross, grant that we,
who devoutly unite ourselves with Him on Calvary, may reign
triumphantly with Him in glory. We ask this of Him who lives and
reigns with you forever and ever.
All: Amen.

The priest goes to the place of the first station, where he kisses the
cross and then hangs it in place, either himself or with the help of a
layman who is properly clothed for this service. He then reads the
meditation and prayers proper to this station; and the same is done

at the other stations. After this the Te Deum is sung along with its versicles and oration.

Lastly the priest blesses the people with a crucifix.

The fastening of the stations to the walls may be done privately by anyone and without ceremony, either before or after the blessing by the priest.

Following is an example of the formal testimonial that the stations of the cross were erected in a given place:

By virtue of the faculty granted me, I, N. N. erected the Way of the Cross with its annexed indulgences in the place named above in the delegation, in accord with the rules prescribed by the Congregation of Sacred Indulgences on May 10, 1742. In testimony of which I have affixed my signature on this day, etc.

(Then Sign)

8

BLESSINGS OF THINGS DESIGNATED FOR ORDINARY USE

1. BLESSING OF BREAD AND PASTRIES

P: Our help is in the name of the Lord.
All: Who made heaven and earth.
P: The Lord be with you.
All: May He also be with you.

Let us pray.
Lord Jesus Christ, bread of angels, living bread for everlasting life, bless this bread as you once blessed the five loaves in the wilderness; so that all who eat it reverently may thereby obtain the health they desire for body and soul. We ask this of you who live and reign forever and ever.
All: Amen.

It is sprinkled with holy water.

There is another blessing of bread among the special blessings for Eastertime; in which section there are also other blessings of food.

2. BLESSING OF GRAPES

P: Our help is in the name of the Lord.
All: Who made heaven and earth.
P: The Lord be with you.
All: May He also be with you.

Let us pray.
Lord, bless this new fruit of the vineyard, which in your benevolence you have ripened by heavenly dew, an abundance of rainfall, gentle breezes, and fair weather; and have given us to use with gratitude in the name of our Lord Jesus Christ, who lives and reigns with you, in the unity of the Holy Spirit, God, forever and ever.
All: Amen.

They are sprinkled with holy water.

3. BLESSING OF WINE FOR THE SICK

P: Our help is in the name of the Lord.
All: Who made heaven and earth.
P: The Lord be with you.
All: May He also be with you.

Let us pray.
Lord, Jesus Christ, Son of the living God, who in Cana of Galilee changed water into wine, be pleased to bless and to hallow this creature, wine, which you have given as refreshment for your servants. And grant that whenever it is taken as drink or poured into wounds it will be accompanied by an outpouring of grace

from on high.

Let us pray.
Almighty eternal God, everlasting salvation to those who believe in you; graciously hear us on behalf of your sick servant, for whom we beg your merciful aid, so that having recovered from his (her) illness he (she) may give thanks to you in your Church; through Christ our Lord
All: Amen.

It is sprinkled with holy water.

4. BLESSING OF ANY KIND OF MEDICINE

P: Our help is in the name of the Lord.
All: Who made heaven and earth.
P: The Lord be with you.
All: May He also be with you.

Let us pray.
God, who in a wonderful way created man and still more wondrously renewed him; who were pleased to aid with many healing remedies the various infirmities that beset the human condition; mercifully pour out your holy   blessing on this medicine, so that he (she) who takes it may have health in mind and body; through Christ our Lord.
All: Amen.

It is sprinkled with holy water.

5. BLESSING OF BEER

P: Our help is in the name of the Lord.
All: Who made heaven and earth.
P: The Lord be with you.
All: May He also be with you.

Let us pray.

Lord, bless this creature, beer, which by your kindness and power has been produced from kernels of grain, and let it be a healthful drink for mankind. Grant that whoever drinks it with thanksgiving to your holy name may find it a help in body and in soul; through Christ our Lord.

All: Amen.

It is sprinkled with holy water.

6. BLESSING OF CHEESE OR BUTTER

P: Our help is in the name of the Lord.
All: Who made heaven and earth.
P: The Lord be with you.
All: May He also be with you.

Let us pray.

Lord God almighty, if it please you, bless and sanctify this creature, cheese (or butter), which by your power has been made from the fat of animals. Grant that those of your faithful who eat it may be sated with a blessing from on high, with your grace and all good things; through Christ our Lord.

All: Amen.

It is sprinkled with holy water.

7. BLESSING OF LARD

P: Our help is in the name of the Lord.
All: Who made heaven and earth.
P: The Lord be with you.
All: May He also be with you.

Let us pray.

Lord, bless this creature, lard, and let it be a healthful food for mankind. Grant that everyone who eats it with thanksgiving to

your holy name may find it a help in body and in soul; through
Christ our Lord.
All: Amen.

It is sprinkled with holy water.

8. BLESSING OF OIL

P: Our help is in the name of the Lord.
All: Who made heaven and earth.

God's creature, oil, I cast out the demon from you by God the
Father almighty, who made heaven and earth and sea, and all that
they contain. Let the adversary's power, the devil's legions, and all
Satan's attacks and machinations be dispelled and driven afar from
this creature, oil. Let it bring health in body and mind to all who
use it, in the name of God the Father almighty, and of our Lord
Jesus Christ, His Son, and of the Holy Spirit, the Advocate, as well
as in the love of the same Jesus Christ our Lord, who is coming to
judge both the living and the dead and the world by fire.
All: Amen.

P: Lord, heed my prayer.
All: And let my cry be heard by you.
P: The Lord be with you.
All: May He also be with you.

Let us pray.
Lord God almighty, before whom the hosts of angels stand in awe,
and whose heavenly service we acknowledge; may it please you to
regard favorably and to bless   and hallow   this creature, oil, which
by your power has been pressed from the juice of olives. You have
ordained it for anointing the sick, so that, when they are made well,
they may give thanks to you, the living and true God. Grant, we
pray, that those who will use this oil, which we are blessing   in
your name, may be delivered from all suffering, all infirmity, and
all wiles of the enemy. Let it be a means of
averting any kind of adversity from man, made in your image and

redeemed by the precious blood of your Son, so that he may never again suffer the sting of the ancient serpent; through Christ our Lord.
All: Amen.

It is sprinkled with holy water.

9. BLESSING OF SALT OR OATS FOR ANIMALS

P: Our help is in the name of the Lord.
All: Who made heaven and earth.
P: The Lord be with you.
All: May He also be with you.

Let us pray.
Lord God, Creator and preserver of all things, in whose hand is the life and breath of every creature; we beg you to listen to the prayers of your faithful, and to pour out on this creature, salt (or oats), your blessing   and the unseen working of your might. May the animals, which you have kindly given for the service of man, be spared every kind of sickness when they eat this salt (or oats), and under your protection escape every affliction of hateful evil spirits; through Christ our Lord.
All: Amen.

It is sprinkled with holy water.

10. BLESSING OF SEED

P: Our help is in the name of the Lord.
All: Who made heaven and earth.
P: The Lord be with you.
All: May He also be with you.

Let us pray.
Lord, we earnestly beg you to bless   these seeds, to protect and preserve them with gentle breezes, to make them fertile with

heavenly dew, and to bring them, in your benevolence, to the
fullest harvest for our bodily and spiritual welfare; through Christ
our Lord.
All: Amen.

They are sprinkled with holy water.

11. BLESSING OF ANY VICTUAL

P: Our help is in the name of the Lord.
All: Who made heaven and earth.
P: The Lord be with you.
All: May He also be with you.

Let us pray.
Lord, bless   this creature, N., and let it be a healthful food for
mankind. Grant that everyone who eats it with thanksgiving to
your holy name may find it a help in body and in soul; through
Christ our Lord.
All: Amen.

It is sprinkled with holy water.

12. BLESSING OF FIRE

P: Our help is in the name of the Lord.
All: Who made heaven and earth.
P: The Lord be with you.
All: May He also be with you.

Let us pray.
Lord God, almighty Father, maker of all light, and the light that
never fails; hallow   this new fire, and grant that after the darkness
of this world we may come with pure hearts to you, our perpetual
light; through Christ our Lord.
All: Amen.

It is sprinkled with holy water.

13. BLESSING OF LINENS FOR THE SICK

P: Our help is in the name of the Lord.
All: Who made heaven and earth.
P: The Lord be with you.
All: May He also be with you.

Let us pray.
Lord Jesus Christ, who, at a touch of the hem of your garment, healed the woman suffering from hemorrhage; who throughout your life on earth healed many other sick; who by your Apostle Paul cast out infirmities and evil spirits from the sick when they touched his handkerchief and leather apron; grant, we beseech you, that all who will be clothed or be covered with these various linens for the sick which we bless in your name, may obtain health of mind and body. We ask this of you who live and reign forever and ever.
All: Amen.

They are sprinkled with holy water.

14. BLESSING OF A STRETCHER, AMBULANCE, WHEELCHAIR

P: Our help is in the name of the Lord.
All: Who made heaven and earth.
P: The Lord be with you.
All: May He also be with you.

Let us pray.
Lord Jesus Christ, Son of the living God, who during your earthly sojourn went about doing good, alleviating the people's suffering and infirmities, and restoring bodily and spiritual vigor to the paralytic lying on his pallet; look with favor, we pray, on the faith and compassion of your servants who, animated with true charity

by your example as well as by your command, have constructed this stretcher (or ambulance or wheelchair) to bear the wounded and the sick to the place of healing. By the blessing we impart to it in the power of your name, O gentle Jesus, let it become for the sick that will be carried on it a comfort on the way, a safeguard in perils, a relief from suffering. Grant that in the company of your angels they may be borne in comfort to the place of healing, and there recover their former good health. Thus made aware of how they have been favored by your mercy and by the prayers of Mary, your blessed Mother, may they return to their homes praising and glorifying you, the true God, who live and reign with the Father and the Holy Spirit forever and ever.
All: Amen.

They are sprinkled with holy water.

15. BLESSING OF AN AUTOMOBILE OR OTHER VEHICLE

P: Our help is in the name of the Lord.
All: Who made heaven and earth.
P: The Lord be with you.
All: May He also be with you.

Let us pray.
Lord God, be well disposed to our prayers, and bless this vehicle with your holy hand. Appoint your holy angels as an escort over it, who will always shield its passengers and keep them safe from accidents. And as once by your deacon, Philip, you bestowed faith and grace upon the Ethiopian seated in his carriage and reading Holy Writ, so also now show the way of salvation to your servants, in order that, strengthened by your grace and ever intent upon good works, they may attain, after all the successes and failures of this life, the certain happiness of everlasting life; through Christ our Lord.
All: Amen.

It is sprinkled with holy water.

16. BLESSING OF AN AIRPLANE

(Approved by the Congregation of Sacred Rites, March 24, 1920)

P: Our help is in the name of the Lord.
All: Who made heaven and earth.
P: The Lord be with you.
All: May He also be with you.

Let us pray.
God, who made all things for your glory, yet destined every lower being in this world for man's service, we beg you to bless this airplane (these airplanes). Let it (them) serve to carry far and wide the fame and glory of your name, and in expediting more speedily the affairs of mankind without loss and accident. And let it (them) foster in the souls of all the faithful who travel in it (them) a longing for the things above; through Christ our Lord.
All: Amen.

Let us pray.
God, who by the mystery of the incarnation mercifully consecrated the dwelling-place of the blessed Virgin Mary, and wondrously transferred it to the heart of your Church; we beg you to pour out your blessing on this airplane (these airplanes), so that all who fly in it (them) may, under the protection of the Blessed Virgin, happily reach their destination and then safely return home; through Christ our Lord.
All: Amen.

Let us pray.
God, the salvation of those who trust in you, kindly appoint a good angel from on high as an escort for your servants who make an airplane voyage and who call on you for help. Let him shield the passengers throughout the flight and conduct them safely to their destination; through Christ our Lord.
All: Amen.

It is sprinkled with holy water

17. BLESSING OF A RAILWAY AND ITS CARS

P: Our help is in the name of the Lord.
All: Who made heaven and earth.
P: The Lord be with you.
All: May He also be with you.

Let us pray.
Almighty everlasting God, who made all creatures for your glory and for man's use, be pleased, we pray, to bless this railway and its equipment, and to watch over it at all times with your kindly solicitude; so that your servants, as they speed along its course, may likewise advance in your law and your commandments, and thus happily arrive in your heavenly kingdom; through Christ our Lord.
All: Amen.

Let us pray.
Lord God, be well disposed to our prayers, and bless   these cars with your holy hand. Appoint your holy angels as an escort over them, who will always shield their passengers and keep them safe from accidents. And as once by your deacon, Philip, you bestowed faith and grace upon the Ethiopian seated in his carriage and reading Holy Writ, so also now show the way of salvation to your servants, in order that, strengthened by your grace and ever intent upon good works, they may attain, after all the successes and failures of this life, the certain happiness of everlasting life; through Christ our Lord.
All: Amen.

The tracks and cars are sprinkled with holy water.

18. A MORE SOLEMN BLESSING OF A RAILWAY AND ITS CARS

From the nearest church or another place designated for the

purpose the clergy go in solemn procession to the railroad station, singing or reciting the following (for the music see the music supplement):

Antiphon: May the almighty and merciful Lord lead you in the way of peace and prosperity. May the Angel Raphael be your companion on the journey and bring you back to your homes inpeace, health, and happiness.

Then the Canticle of Zachary is said; and after the canticle the above antiphon is repeated. Then the priest continues:

Lord, have mercy. Christ, have mercy. Lord, have mercy. Our Father (the rest inaudibly until:)

P: And lead us not into temptation.

All: But deliver us from evil.

P: Save your servants.

All: Who trust in you, my God.

P: Lord, send them aid from your holy place.

All: And watch over them from Sion.

P: Let them find in you, Lord, a fortified tower.

All: In the face of the enemy.

P: Let the enemy have no power over them.

All: And the son of iniquity be powerless to harm them.

P: May the Lord be praised at all times.

All: May God, our helper, grant us a happy journey.

P: Lord, show us your ways.

All: And lead us along your paths.

P: Oh, that our life be bent.

All: On keeping your precepts.

P: For the crooked ways will be made straight.

All: And the rough places plain.

P: God has given His angels charge over you.

All: To guard you in all your undertakings.

P: Lord, heed my prayer.

All: And let my cry be heard by you.

P: The Lord be with you.

All: May He also be with you.

Let us pray.

Almighty everlasting God, who made all creatures for your glory
and for man's use, be pleased, we pray, to bless this railway and its
equipment, and to watch over it at all times with your kindly
solicitude; so that your servants, as they speed along its course,
may likewise advance in your law and your commandments, and
thus happily arrive in your heavenly kingdom; through Christ our
Lord.
All: Amen.

Let us pray.

Lord God, be well disposed to our prayers, and bless   these cars
with your holy hand. Appoint your holy angels as an escort over

them, who will always shield their passengers and keep them safe from accidents. And as once by your deacon, Philip, you bestowed faith and grace upon the Ethiopian seated in his carriage and reading Holy Writ, so also now show the way of salvation to your servants, in order that, strengthened by your grace and ever intent upon good works, they may attain, after all the successes and failures of this life, the certain happiness of everlasting life; through Christ our Lord.
All: Amen.

Then he sprinkles the tracks and cars with holy water.

After the blessing (and the previous one too) the Te Deum is said along with its versicles and oration.

19. BLESSING OF A SHIP OR BOAT

P: Our help is in the name of the Lord.
All: Who made heaven and earth.
P: The Lord be with you.
All: May He also be with you.

Let us pray.

Lord, be well disposed to our prayers, and by your holy hand bless this ship (boat) and its passengers, as you were pleased to let your blessing hover over Noah's ark in the Deluge. Reach out your hand to them, Lord, as you did to blessed Peter as he walked upon the sea. Send your holy angel from on high to watch over it and all on board, to ward off any threat of disaster, and to guide its course through calm waters to the desired port. Then after a time, when they have successfully transacted their business, may you in your loving providence bring them back with glad hearts to their own country and home. We ask this of you who live and reign forever and ever.
All: Amen.

It is sprinkled with holy water.

20. SOLEMN BLESSING OF A FISHING-BOAT

(Approved by the Congregation of Sacred Rites, April 10. 1912)

P: Our help is in the name of the Lord.
All: Who made heaven and earth.
P: The Lord be with you.
All: May He also be with you.

Then the priest intones the antiphon, which is continued by the chanters; and the first verse of psalm 8 is directly attached to the antiphon (music):

Antiphon: O Lord, * our Lord, how glorious is your name over all the earth; * you have exalted your majesty above the heavens.

Psalm 8

After the psalm the antiphon is repeated thus:

All: Ant.: O Lord, our Lord, * how glorious is your name over all the earth.

P: The Lord be with you.
All: May He also be with you.

Let us pray.
Lord, be well disposed to our prayers, and by your holy hand bless this fishing-boat and the fishermen, as you were pleased to let your blessing hover over Noah's ark in the Deluge. Reach out your hand to them, Lord, as you did to blessed Peter as he walked upon the sea. Send your holy angel from on high to watch over it and all on board, to ward off any threat of disaster, and to guide its course through calm waters to the desired port. Then after a time, when they have had good success in their labors, may you in your loving providence bring them back with glad hearts to their own shores

and homes. We ask this of you who live and reign forever and ever.

All: Amen.

P: A lesson from the holy Gospel according to St. John.

All: Glory be to you, O Lord.

John 21:1-24

On a later occasion Jesus showed himself again to the disciples, this time by the Lake of Tiberias. He did so under the following circumstances: Simon Peter, Thomas called the Twin, Nathanael of Cana in Galilee, the sons of Zebedee, and two others of His disciples, happened to be together. Simon Peter said to them: "I am going fishing." "We will go along with you," they replied. So they set out and got into the boat, and during that entire night they caught nothing. But just as day was breaking, Jesus stood on the beach. The disciples did not know, however, that it was Jesus. "Well, lads," Jesus said to them, "you have no fish there, have you?" "No," they replied. "Cast your net to the right of the boat," He said to them, "and you will find something." So they cast it, and now they were not strong enough to haul it up into the boat because of the great number of fish in it. Then the disciple whom Jesus loved said to Peter: "It is the Master!" No sooner did Simon Peter learn that it was the Master than he girt his upper garment about him--for he was wearing little--and plunged into the lake. Meanwhile the other disciples came on in the boat--for they were not far from the shore, only about two hundred yards--dragging along the net full of fish.

When they had come ashore, they noticed hot embers on the ground, with fish lying on the fire and bread. Jesus said to them: "Bring some of the fish you caught just now." So Simon Peter boarded the boat and hauled the net upon the beach. It was full of fish, one hundred and fifty-three in all, and in spite of the great number the net did not break. "Come, now," Jesus said to them, "and have breakfast." Not one of His disciples could find it in his heart to ask Him, "Who are you?" They knew it was the Master. Then Jesus approached, took the bread in His hands, and gave them of it. He did the same with the fish. This was now the third time that Jesus showed Himself to the disciples after He had risen from the dead.

After they had breakfasted, Jesus said to Simon Peter: "Simon, son of John, do you love me more than these others do?" "Yes, my Master," he replied; "you know that I really love you." "Then," Jesus said to him, "feed my lambs." He asked him a second time: "Simon, son of John, do you love me?" "Yes, Master," he replied, "you know that I really love you." "Then," He said to him, "be a shepherd to my sheep." For the third time He put the question to him: "Simon, son of John, do you really love me?" It grieved Peter that He had asked him the third time: "Do you really love me?" and he replied: "Master, you know everything; you know that I really love you!" "Then," Jesus said to him, "feed my sheep. I tell you the plain truth: when you were young, you used to put on your own belt and go where you wished; but when you grow old, you will stretch out your arms for someone else to gird you and carry you where you have no wish to go." He said this to signify the kind of death by which He was to glorify God. And having said this, He said to him: "Follow me."

Turning round, Peter saw the disciple whom Jesus loved following them, the same who at the supper had been resting against his bosom and had asked: "Master, who is it that is going to betray you?" So, at sight of him, Peter said to Jesus: "And what about him, Master?" Jesus replied: "If I want him to stay till I return, what difference does this make to you? Your duty is to follow me." Accordingly, the report became current among the brethren that that disciple was not going to die. But Jesus had not said to him that he was not to die, but simply: "If I want him to stay till I return, what difference does this make to you?"

This is the disciple who is both the witness of these facts and the recorder of these facts; and we know that his testimony is true.

All: Praise be to you, O Christ.

P: The Lord be with you.
All: May He also be with you.

Let us pray.
God, who divided the waters from the dry land and created every
living thing they contain; who willed that man should have
dominion over the fishes of the sea; who walked on the crest of the
waves and stilled the winds and the sea; who miraculously filled
the nets of the apostles with fishes; grant, we pray, that your
servants may have you as their captain, and so be delivered from
all perils, haul into their boats a good catch of fish, and come
finally to the port of everlasting blessedness laden with the merits
of good works; through Christ our Lord.
All: Amen.

Let us pray.
We beg you, Lord and Savior, be pleased to bless the labors of
your servants, as you once blessed your apostles when you said:
"Cast your net to the right of the boat, and you will find
something." Thus gladdened by your bountiful blessing, may we
praise you, our Redeemer, now and forevermore.
All: Amen.

Have regard, O Lord, for the prayers of the blessed Virgin Mary,
St. Peter and the other apostles, and St. N. (the patron of the boat),
and do not disdain the work of our hands. Rather, give us your
holy blessing, keep us from all sin, avert all dangers, and be
prodigal with your gifts; through Christ our Lord.

All: Amen.

The priest sprinkles the boat with holy water, saying:

May the peace and blessing of almighty God, Father, Son, and
Holy Spirit, come upon this boat and on all who are to sail in it,
and remain forever.
All: Amen.

21. BLESSING OF TOOLS FOR SCALING MOUNTAINS

(Approved by Pope Pius XI on October 14, 1931)

P: Our help is in the name of the Lord.
All: Who made heaven and earth.
P: The Lord be with you.
All: May He also be with you.

Let us pray.
Lord, we beg you to bless these ropes, staves, mattocks, and these other tools, so that all who will use them in scaling the mountains' heights and precipices, in ice and snow and raging storms, may be preserved from all accidents and catastrophe, safely reach the summits, and return unharmed to their homes; through Christ our Lord.
All: Amen.

Let us pray.
Protect these servants of yours, O Lord, by the prayers of St. Bernard, whom you have made patron of mountain dwellers and travelers; and grant that along with scaling these heights they may also reach that mountain which is Christ; through the same Christ our Lord.
All: Amen.

They are sprinkled with holy water.

22. BLESSING OF A SEISMOGRAPH

(Approved by the Congregation of Sacred Rites, Feb. 13, 1924)

P: Our help is in the name of the Lord.
All: Who made heaven and earth.
P: The Lord be with you.
All: May He also be with you.

Let us pray.
Almighty everlasting God, whose very gaze causes the earth to tremble, pour out your blessing on this seismograph; and grant that the signs of the earth's tremors may be precisely recorded by it, and then rightly interpreted by man, both for the benefit of your people and for the greater glory of your name; through Christ our Lord.
All: Amen.

O Virgin Mary, in view of your own sorrows take pity on us and pray for us.

St. Emidius, pray for us, and in the name of Jesus Christ of Nazareth, protect us and also this seismograph from the terror of earthquakes.

It is sprinkled with holy water.

23. BLESSING OF A TELEGRAPH

From the nearest church or from another place designated for this purpose the clergy go to the telegraph station, chanting or reciting the following (for the music see the music supplement):

Canticle of Zachary

On arriving at the station the priest intones the antiphon, which is continued by the choir and followed by psalm 103.

Antiphon: Blessed are you, O Lord, * who make the clouds your chariot, who travel on the wings of the wind; * who make the winds your messengers, and flaming fire your ministers.

Psalm 103

P: Bless the Lord, my soul! * Lord, my God, you are great indeed!

All: You are clothed with majesty and glory, * robed in light as with a cloak.

P: You have spread out the heavens like a tent-cloth; * you have constructed your palace upon the waters.

All: You make the clouds your chariot; * you travel on the wings of the wind.

P: You make the winds your messengers, * and flaming fire your ministers.

All: You fixed the earth upon its foundation, * not to be moved forever;

P: With the ocean, as with a garment, you covered it; * above the mountains the waters stood.

All: At your rebuke they fled, * at the sound of your thunder they took to flight;

P: As the mountains rose, they went down the valleys * to the place you had fixed for them.

All: You set a limit they may not pass, * nor shall they cover the earth again.

P: You send forth springs into the watercourses * that wind among the mountains,

All: And give drink to every beast of the field, * till the wild asses quench their thirst.

P: Beside them the birds of heaven dwell; * from among the branches they send forth their song.

All: You water the mountains from your palace; * the earth is replete with the fruit of your works.

P: You raise grass for the cattle, * and vegetation for men's use,

All: Producing bread from the earth, * and wine to gladden men's hearts,

P: So that their faces gleam with oil, * and bread fortifies the hearts of men.

All: Well watered are the trees of the Lord, * the cedars of Lebanon, which He planted;

P: In them the birds build their nests; * fir trees are the home of the stork.

All: The high mountains are for wild goats; * the cliffs are a refuge for rock-badgers.

P: You made the moon to mark the seasons; the sun knows the hour of its setting.

All: You bring darkness, and it is night; * then all the beasts of the forest roam about;

P: Young lions roar for the prey * and seek their food from God.

All: When the sun rises, they withdraw * and couch in their dens.

P: Man goes forth to his work * and to his tillage till the evening.

All: How manifold are your works, O Lord! * In wisdom you have wrought them all--the earth is full of your creatures;

P: The sea also, great and wide, in which are schools without number * of living things both small and great,

All: And where ships move about * with Leviathan, which you formed to play there.

P: They all look to you * to give them food in due time.

All: When you give it to them, they gather it; * when you open your hand, they are filled with good things.

P: If you hide your face, they are dismayed; if you take away their breath, they perish * and return to their dust.

All: When you send forth your spirit, they are created, * and you renew the face of the earth.

P: May the glory of the Lord endure forever; * may the Lord be glad in His works!

All: He who looks upon the earth, and it trembles; * who touches the mountains and they smoke!

P: I will sing to the Lord all my life; * I will sing praise to my God while I live.

All: Pleasing to Him be my theme; * I will be glad in the Lord.

P: May sinners cease from the earth, and may the wicked be no more. * Bless the Lord, my soul!

All: Glory be to the Father.

P: As it was in the beginning.

All: Ant.: Blessed are you, O Lord, who make the clouds your chariot, who travel on the wings of the wind; * who make the winds your messengers, and flaming fire your ministers.

P: Our help is in the name of the Lord.
All: Who made heaven and earth.
P: The Lord be with you.
All: May He also be with you.

Let us pray.
We entreat you, Lord God, grant us, your servants, the enjoyment

of lasting health of body and mind; and by the glorious intercession of blessed Mary, ever a Virgin, free us from present sorrow and give us everlasting joy; through Christ our Lord.
All: Amen.

Let us pray.
God, who ride on the wings of the wind, and who alone work wonders; just as you have empowered this metal to carry messages to-and-fro more quickly than a lightning flash; so also grant that we, inspired by these new inventions and aided by your bounteous grace, may in a similar way come more swiftly and easily to you; through Christ our Lord.
All: Amen.

The priest sprinkles the telegraph with holy water.

24. BLESSING OF AN ELECTRIC DYNAMO

From the nearest church or from another place designated for the purpose the clergy go in solemn manner to the electric plant, chanting or reciting the following (for the music see the music supplement):

Canticle of Zachary

On arriving at the plant the priest intones the antiphon, which is continued by the choir and followed by psalm 96:

Antiphon: Light dawns for the just, * and gladness for the upright of heart.

Psalm 96

P: The Lord is king; let the earth rejoice; * let the many isles be glad.

All: Clouds and darkness are round about Him, * justice and

judgment are the foundation of His throne.

P: Fire goes before Him * and consumes His foes round about.

All: His lightnings illumine the world; * the earth sees and trembles.

P: The mountains melt like wax before the Lord, * before the Lord of all the earth.

All: The heavens proclaim His justice, * and all peoples see His glory.

P: All who worship graven things are put to shame, who glory in the things of nought; * all gods are prostrate before him.

All: Sion hears and is glad, and the cities of Juda rejoice * because of your judgments, O Lord.

P: Because you, O Lord, are the Most High over all the earth, * exalted far above all gods.

All: The Lord loves those that hate evil; He guards the lives of His faithful ones; * He delivers them from the hand of the wicked.

P: Light dawns for the just; * and gladness for the upright of heart.

All: Be glad in the Lord, you just, * and give thanks to His holy name.

P: Glory be to the Father.

All: As it was in the beginning.

All: Ant.: Light dawns for the just, * and gladness for the pright of heart.

P: Our help is in the name of the Lord.
All: Who made heaven and earth.

P: Lord, heed my prayer.
All: And let my cry be heard by you.
P: The Lord be with you.
All: May He also be with you.

Let us pray.
We entreat you, Lord God, grant us, your servants, the enjoyment
of lasting health of body and mind; and by the glorious
intercession of blessed Mary, ever a Virgin, free us from present
sorrow and give us everlasting joy; through Christ our Lord.

All: Amen.

Let us pray.
Lord God almighty, Creator of all light, bless   this generator built
to create light anew; and grant that after the darkness of this world
we may come to you who are never ending light; through
Christ our Lord.
All: Amen.

He sprinkles the dynamo with holy water.

25. BLESSING OF A FIRE-ENGINE

(Approved by the Congregation of Sacred Rites, April 10, 1912)

From the nearest church or another place designated for the
purpose the clergy go to the fire-station, chanting or reciting the
following antiphon and psalm. The priest intones the antiphon,
which is then continued by the choir (music):

Antiphon: The fire's fury was tamed, and its overpowering heat
quenched, * as your beloved youths, Lord, were preserved
unharmed.

Psalm 65

P: Shout joyfully to God, all you on earth, sing praise to the glory of His name; * proclaim His glorious praise.

All: Say to God, "How tremendous are your deeds! * for your great strength your enemies fawn upon you.

P: Let all on earth worship and sing praise to you, * sing praise to your name!"

All: Come and see the works of God, * His tremendous deeds among men.

P: He has changed the sea into dry land; through the river they passed on foot; * therefore let us rejoice in Him.

All: He rules by His might forever; His eyes watch the nations; * rebels may not exalt themselves.

P: Bless our God, you peoples, * loudly sound His praise;

All: He has given life to our souls, * and has not let our feet slip.

P: For you have tested us, God! * You have tried us as silver is tried by fire;

All: You have brought us into a snare; * you have laid a heavy burden on our backs.

P: You let men ride over our heads; we went through fire and water, * but you have led us out to refreshment.

All: I will bring holocausts to your house; * to you I will fulfill the vows

P: Which my lips uttered and my words promised * in my distress.

All: Holocausts of fatlings I will offer you, with burnt offerings of rams; * I will sacrifice oxen and goats.

P: Hear now, all you who fear God, while I declare * what He has done for me!

All: When I appealed to Him in words, * praise was on the tip of my tongue.

P: Were I to cherish wickedness in my heart, * the Lord would not hear;

All: But God has heard; * He has hearkened to the sound of my prayer.

P: Blessed be God who refused me not * my prayer or His kindness!

All: Glory be to the Father.

P: As it was in the beginning.

All: Ant.: The fire's fury was tamed, and its overpowering heat quenched, * as your beloved youths, Lord, were preserved unharmed.

P: Lord, have mercy. Christ, have mercy. Lord, have mercy. Our Father (the rest inaudibly until:)

P: And lead us not into temptation.

All: But deliver us from evil.

P: Save your servants.

All: Who trust in you, my God.

P: Lord, send them aid from your holy place.

All: And watch over them from Sion.

P: Let the enemy have no power over them.

All: And the son of iniquity be powerless to harm them.

P: Fire and heat, bless the Lord.

All: Praise and exalt Him above all forever.

P: You sons of men, bless the Lord.

All: Praise and exalt Him above all forever.

P: Who delivers us from the devouring flames.

All: And leads us out of the encircling fires.

P: Let us praise the Lord, for He is good.

All: And His mercy endures forever.

P: Our help is in the name of the Lord.
All: Who made heaven and earth.
P: Lord, heed my prayer.
All: And let my cry be heard by you.
P: The Lord be with you.
All: May He also be with you.

Let us pray.
God, who by your angel assuaged the flames of fire for the sake of the three youths cast into the furnace in Babylon; we implore you to extinguish by your hand the evil lusts that burn in our hearts, and to deliver us from all fires, both in this world and in the world to come through Christ our Lord.
All: Amen.

Let us pray.
God, in whose hands we are, dependent on you in our every thought, word, and deed; stand by your servants with your most generous aid, so that whenever we are threatened by dreaded fire we may have the protection of these technical devices; through Christ our Lord.

All: Amen.

Let us pray.
God, the just and loving ruler of mankind, to whom as its Creator
your creature, fire, is so readily subject that on the one hand it
blazes out to torment the impious, and on the other it burns lightly
to serve the needs of the devout; kindly hear our prayers, and pour
out your blessing on this fire-engine. Whenever this efficient tool
is used with lively faith and fervent prayers against the ravages of
fire, may the stream of water gushing forth from it extinguish the
roaring flames, completely wiping out their destructive force, so
that no injury befalls the faithful who trust in you, and no damage
is done to their possessions. Thus may it come about that all who
experience your protection against the fright and dangers of fire
will turn away from sin with all their heart, and, mindful of your
benefits, sincerely acknowledge that such visitations are a
consequence of their sinful ways, and cease only when you deign
to show your mercy; through Christ our Lord.
All: Amen.

It is sprinkled with holy water.

26. BLESSING OF MOLTEN METAL FOR A BELL

P: Our help is in the name of the Lord.
All: Who made heaven and earth.
P: The Lord be with you.
All: May He also be with you.

Let us pray.
Lord God almighty, who honored even inanimate creatures in
designating them for your worship, we beg you to pour out your
blessing on this metal; and as it now issues forth a molten stream,
let your hand guide it and your grace protect it, so that it will be
cast into a good and artistic bell (or bells) for summoning the
faithful to church, there to praise and to glorify your name; through
Christ our Lord.
All: Amen.

The metal is sprinkled with holy water. And after the casting is successfully completed the priest adds:

Psalm 116

P: Praise the Lord, all you nations, * glorify Him, all you peoples.

All: For steadfast is His kindness toward us, * and the fidelity of the Lord endures forever.

P: Glory be to the Father.

All: As it was in the beginning.

Let us pray.
We beg you, Lord, let a breath of your grace prompt our undertakings and guide them along their course, so that our least prayer and work may ever begin in you and end in you; through Christ our Lord.

All: Amen.

27. BLESSING OF A BELL

Not designated for a church or oratory

P: Our help is in the name of the Lord.
All: Who made heaven and earth.

Then the seven penitential psalms are said.

After the psalms the priest continues:

Lord, have mercy. Christ, have mercy. Lord, have mercy. Our Father (the rest inaudibly until:)

P: And lead us not into temptation.

All: But deliver us from evil.

P: Blessed be the name of the Lord.

All: Both now and forevermore.

P: Lord, heed my prayer.
All: And let my cry be heard by you.
P: The Lord be with you.
All: May He also be with you.

Let us pray.
Almighty everlasting God, who arranged the purpose of all creatures with indescribable wisdom; be pleased, we pray, to pour out the dew of your blessing   on this bell, destined to ring out the order of the day's activities and have them proceed in orderly fashion, thus forestalling any disturbance from the spiteful demon; through Christ our Lord.
All: Amen.

The celebrant puts incense into the thurible and blesses it. Then he walks around the bell, sprinkling it with holy water, during which the choir sings (music):

Purify me with hyssop, Lord, and I shall be clean of sin. Wash me, and I shall be whiter than snow.

Then he again walks around the bell, incensing it, while the choir sings the following antiphon (music see the music):

Lord, let my prayer come like incense before you.

Lastly the priest signs the bell with the sign of the cross, and departs with his assistants.

28. BLESSING OF MOBILE FILM UNITS FOR ROAD

SAFETY

{On August 9, 1961, Good Pope John blessed forty mobile film units, designed by the Italian government to inform the people, both pedestrians and motorists, about safety rules in the streets and on the highways. Anyone who knows Italy will appreciate how opportune this business was. In a little talk explaining this new liturgical blessing, Pope John admonished the people to bear in mind the commandment, "Thou shalt not kill."}

P: Our help is in the name of the Lord.
All: Who made heaven and earth.
P: The Lord be with you.
All: May He also be with you.

Let us pray.
Almighty everlasting God, who willed that the works of man be ordered both to the glory of your name and the welfare of mankind, pour out the grace of your blessing on these machines, destined to disseminate the rules for road safety. May your servants, both pedestrians and drivers, learn by means of them to be prudent and vigilant and possessed by a fear of you, and so always be sure to have regard for their own safety and the safety of others. Lord, let no harm befall them, whether it be from the difficulty of the journey, or from weariness, or from rash speeding. May they show no lack of consideration, no lack of alertness. And as you onetime assigned the Archangel Raphael as a companion to your son, Tobias, on his travels, so may you now assign the angels as guardians of your faithful, helping them to walk before you in holiness while on earth, and to reach the goal of everlasting salvation; through Christ our Lord.
All: Amen.

They are sprinkled with holy water.

29. BLESSING OF ANYTHING

This form may be used by any priest for the blessing of anything that does not have its own special blessing in the Roman Ritual.

P: Our help is in the name of the Lord.
All: Who made heaven and earth.
P: The Lord be with you.
All: May He also be with you.

Let us pray.
God, whose word suffices to make all things holy, pour out your blessing   on this object (these objects); and grant that anyone who uses it (them) with grateful heart and in keeping with your law and will, may receive from you, its (their) Maker, health in body and protection of soul by calling on your holy name; through Christ our Lord.
All: Amen.

It (they) is (are) sprinkled with holy water.

9

GENERAL RULES
CONCERNING PROCESSIONS

1. The sacred public processions and solemn rites of petition used in the Catholic Church were instituted in very early times by the holy fathers. Their purpose is to arouse the faithful's devotion, to commemorate God's benefits to man and to thank Him for them, and to call upon Him for further assistance; hence they ought to be celebrated in a truly religious manner. For they are the bearers of sublime and godly mysteries, and all who devoutly take part in them receive from God the salutary fruits of Christian piety. It is the pastors' duty to explain them to the faithful at the proper time.

2. Priests especially, but others in holy orders as well, should see to it that during these processions such decorum and reverence prevail as befits these devout exercises, both on the part of themselves and the rest who participate.

3. All members of the clergy who are to take part will be properly clothed, in surplices or in other sacred vestments (no hats should be worn unless rain threatens). They will walk two by two, bearing themselves with gravity, reserve, and piety. Talking, laughing, and

gazing about should be conspicuously absent; rather they should be so intent on prayer that they will
invite the people to join in fervent petitions.

4. All who march in the procession should be praying. The men should be separate from the women, and the laity separate from the clergy.

5. A cross is carried at the head of the procession, and where it is the custom also a banner with sacred images, but not one that has a military character or a triangular form.

6. Let pastors be sedulous in abolishing the abuse of eating and drinking, as well as carrying along food and drink during any of the sacred processions or on the occasions when the fields are blessed or when a pilgrimage is made to a church lying outside the city. And the faithful should repeatedly be admonished, especially on the Sunday prior to the Rogation days, how unseemly this abuse is.

7. The processions should take place before the solemn celebration of Mass, unless occasionally the Ordinary or the clergy decide otherwise for a good reason.

8. Certain processions are of regular occurrence, that is, specified for particular days of the year, as those of Candlemas, Palm Sunday, the Greater Litany on the feast of St. Mark the Evangelist, the Lesser Litanies on the three Rogation days before Ascension, and Corpus Christi, or on other days according to the usage of local churches.

9. But some processions are of all extraordinary nature--those which are ordered for other public causes at special times.

CHAPTER II: CANDLEMAS PROCESSION

1. Following the blessing and distribution of candles, as prescribed

in the Roman Missal, the procession takes place. First the celebrant puts incense into the thurible; and then the deacon turns to the people and sings (the music for this and all other parts is given in the music supplement):

Deacon: Let us go forth in peace.
All: In Christ's name. Amen.

2. The order of the procession is: first the thurifer carrying the thurible with burning incense; the subdeacon vested in tunic and carrying the processional cross, and on either side of him the acolytes with lighted candles; the clergy in order of their rank; the celebrant accompanied by the deacon at his left. All carry lighted candles. During the procession the following antiphons are sung:

Antiphon I

Sion, adorn your nuptial bower For the mystic marriage with Christ the King. Greet in loving embrace, the Virgin Mary, heaven's portal, Who bears in her arms the King of glory, Christ, the new Light of the world. The Virgin's footsteps halt as she presents her Son, Begotten before the morning-star. Simeon takes the Child into his cradled arms, And proclaims to the people that He is the Lord, Lord over life and death, Savior of the world.

Antiphon II

Luke 2:26-29

It had been revealed to Simeon by the Holy Spirit that he was not to see death before seeing the Lord's Anointed. And when the parents had brought the Child into the temple he took Him into his arms and spoke this hymn to God: "Now you may release your bondsman in peace, O Master!"

As the procession reenters the church the following responsory is sung:

Responsory

Luke 2:22-24

They offered for Him to the Lord a pair of turtle-doves or two young pigeons, * according to the regulation in the Law of the Lord. V. When the prescribed days had elapsed, it was time for Mary to be purified according to the Law of Moses. So they took Jesus to Jerusalem in order to present Him to the Lord. * According to the regulation in the Law of the Lord. V. Glory be to the Father, and to the Son, and to the Holy Spirit. * According to the regulation in the Law of the Lord.

3. At the end of the procession the celebrant and the ministers remove the purple vestments and vest in white for Mass. Lighted candles are held during the chanting of the Gospel, and again from the beginning of the Canon until the end of the communion of the priest.

PROCESSION ON PALM SUNDAY

1. On Palm Sunday, after the blessing and distribution of the palms or olive branches, the procession takes place. First the celebrant puts incense into the thurible; and then the deacon turns to the people and sings (music):

Deacon: Let us go forth in peace.
All: In Christ's name. Amen.

2. The order of the procession is: first the thurifer carrying the thurible with the burning incense; the subdeacon vested in tunic and carrying the processional cross, and on either side of him the acolytes with lighted candles; the clergy in order of their rank; the celebrant accompanied by the deacon at his left.
All carry palms. During the procession the following antiphons are sung, either some or all of them:

Antiphon 1: The multitude, carrying flowers and palms, goes out to meet the Redeemer, paying Him homage worthy of a triumphant conqueror. The people proclaim the Son of God, praising Christ with voices echoing to the skies: "Hosanna in high heaven."

Antiphon 2: Let us prove our faith with the angels and children, singing to the conqueror of death: "Hosanna in high heaven."

Antiphon 3: The great multitude that had gathered for the festival cried out to the Lord: "Blessed is He who comes in the name of the Lord. Hosanna in high heaven."

Antiphon 4: The great crowds came down the way rejoicing, and they praised God for all the miracles they had seen, crying aloud: "Blessed is the King who comes in the name of the Lord. Peace on earth and glory in high heaven."

In the course of the procession the following hymn is sung, with the choir and people alternating as indicated below:

Choir: All glory, laud, and honor to you, Redeemer, King, to whom the lips of children made glad hosannas ring.

People: All glory, laud, and honor to you, Redeemer, King, to whom the lips of children made glad hosannas ring.

Choir: You are the King of Israel, you David's royal Son, who in the Lord's name comes, the King and blessed One.

People: All glory, laud, and honor to you, Redeemer, King, to whom the lips of children made glad hosannas ring.

Choir: The company of angels are praising you on high; and mortal men and all things created make reply.

People: All glory, laud, and honor to you, Redeemer, King, to whom the lips of children made glad hosannas ring.

Choir: The people of the Hebrews with palms before you went; our praise and prayers and anthems before you we present.

People: All glory, laud, and honor to you, Redeemer, King, to whom the lips of children made glad hosannas ring.

Choir: To you before your passion they sang their hymns of praise; to you, now high exalted, our melody we raise.

People: All glory, laud, and honor to you, Redeemer, King, to whom the lips of children made glad hosannas ring.

Choir: You did accept their praises; accept the prayers we bring, who take delight in good things, O gracious, clement King.

People: All glory, laud, and honor to you, Redeemer, King, to whom the lips of children made glad hosannas ring.

Antiphon and Psalm 147

All: Ant.: Let all voices join in praising your name and saying: * "Blessed is He who comes in the name of the Lord. Hosanna in high heaven."

Psalm 147

The choir or priest sings or recites the parts marked P, and the people the parts marked All. After the psalm the antiphon given above is repeated by all.

Antiphon 6: Let us strew our graceful palms in the way of our Lord. Let us go to meet Him with hymns and songs, praising Him and saying: "Blessed be the Lord."

Antiphon 7: Hail, our King, David's Son, the world's Redeemer, the house of Israel's Savior, whose coming the prophets foretold. The Father sent you into the world to be its saving victim, whom all holy men longed for from the beginning. Therefore, let us sing: "Hosanna to the Son of David. Blessed is He who comes in the name of the Lord. Hosanna in high heaven."

It would also be fitting for the people to sing the hymn "Christ Conquers," or any other hymn in honor of Christ the King.

When the procession has reentered the church, the choir begins the last antiphon, just as the priest is entering the door:

Antiphon 8: As our Lord entered the Holy City the Hebrew children announced beforehand the resurrection of Life; and waving their palms they cried out: "Hosanna in high heaven." When the people heard that Jesus was coming to Jerusalem, they went forth to meet Him; and waving their palms they cried out: "Hosanna in high heaven."

When the celebrant comes to the altar he makes the proper reverence, and ascends the altar with his ministers. Standing between them with his hands folded (a cleric holds the book), and facing the people, he sings the concluding prayer in the ferial tone:

P: The Lord be with you.
All: May He also be with you.

Let us pray.
Lord Jesus Christ, King and Redeemer, in whose honor we have sung our solemn praises, holding these palm branches in our hands; be pleased to send the grace of your blessing on every place where these branches are to be taken. Grant, too, that all wickedness and deceit of evil spirits may be overthrown; and reach out your hand to shield those whom you have redeemed. We ask this of you who live and reign with God the Father, in the unity of the Holy Spirit, God, forever and ever.
All: Amen.

PROCESSION ON THE FEAST OF ST. MARK THE EVANGELIST AND ON THE
THREE ROGATION DAYS BEFORE ASCENSION*

* The local Ordinary may transfer the celebration of the Rogation days to three consecutive days that are more convenient.

1. The clergy and people assemble in church at the appointed hour of the morning, where they kneel and devote a few moments to humble and contrite prayer. The celebrant and his ministers are vested in amice, alb, and cincture. The celebrant wears also a stole and cope; or at least a surplice and purple stole. This same color is always used in the other processions, except on Corpus Christi, on solemn feast days, or for the procession of thanksgiving, on which days the color proper to the occurring solemnity is used. The rest of the priests and clerics wear a surplice. All stand as the following antiphon is sung (music):

All: Ant. Rise up, O Lord, and help us, * and deliver us for your name's sake.

P: We have heard, O God, with our own ears * the things which our fathers told us.

All: Glory be to the Father, and to the Son, * and to the Holy Spirit.

P: As it was in the beginning, is now, and ever shall be, * world without end. Amen.

All: Ant.: Rise up, O Lord, and help us, * and deliver us for your name's sake.

2. Then all kneel again, and two clerics who are kneeling at the altar begin the chant of the Litany of the Saints.

3. As soon as the invocation Holy Mary has been sung, all rise, and continuing the litany march out in the proper order. The cross is carried at the head of the procession; then come the faithful followed by the clergy, and last of all the priest, vested as described above. He is accompanied by his ministers who are clothed in sacred vestments, as circumstances dictate.

4. If the procession takes a long time the litany can be repeated, or else after the last Kyrie of the litany (excluding the orations), some

of the penitential or gradual psalms can be added. However, hymns or sacred songs of a joyous character should not be sung during the Rogation processions or any procession which has a penitential purpose.

5. If one or several churches are visited along the way, then, having entered the church, the litany or the psalms are interrupted, and the antiphon of the patron of that church is sung, along with the versicle and oration. On leaving the church the chanting of the litany or psalms is resumed, and the procession continues in the same order as before until it has reentered the church from which it started. Here the service ends with the final prayers and orations prescribed for the conclusion of the Litany of the Saints.

6. Should it happen that the feast of St. Mark the Evangelist is transferred to another day, the procession is held nevertheless, unless the feast falls on Easter Sunday or Monday, in which case the procession is transferred to Easter Tuesday.

CORPUS CHRISTI PROCESSION

1. The church as well as the streets through which the procession will pass should be fittingly decorated with tapestry, drapery, and sacred images; not, however, with profane or meaningless images or any unworthy ornamentation.

2. The priest first celebrates Mass, during which he consecrates two hosts. After he has consumed one at his communion he exposes the other in the monstrance to be used in the procession. The part of the monstrance which holds the host should be enclosed with glass so that the host is visible to the worshippers. When Mass is over and the procession has begun (in the same order as mentioned above in the Rogation procession), the priest, vested in white cope, kneels and incenses the Blessed Sacrament with a threefold incensation.

3. Then one of the clerics places a humeral veil over the priest's shoulders. Having covered both hands with the ends of the veil, the

priest reverently receives the monstrance from the deacon. Holding the Blessed Sacrament before his face he turns toward the people and joins the procession, walking beneath the canopy accompanied by his ministers Two acolytes or clerics carrying thuribles with burning incense walk in front of him.

4. All march with bared heads, holding lighted candles, and devoutly singing the following hymns, or as many as time allows.

Hymn I: Pange lingua

Hymn II: Sacris sollemniis

> At this our solemn feast,
> Let holy joys abound,
> And from the inmost breast
> Let songs of praise resound;
> Let ancient rites depart,
> And all be new around,
> In ev'ry act and voice and heart.
>
> Remember we that eve,
> When, the Last Supper spread,
> Christ, as we all believe,
> The lamb, with leavenless bread,
> Among His brethren shared,
> And thus the Law obeyed,
> Of old unto their sires declared.
>
> The lamb as type consumed,
> The legal feast complete,
> The Lord unto the twelve
> His body gave to eat;
> The whole to all, no less
> The whole to each, did mete
> With His own hands, as we confess.
>
> He gave them, weak and frail,
> His flesh, their food to be;

On them, downcast and sad,
His blood bestowed He;
And thus to them He spake,
"Receive this cup from me,
And all of you of this partake."

So He this Sacrifice
To institute did will,
And charged His priests alone
That office to fulfill;
In them He did confide,
To whom it pertains still
To take and to the rest divide.

Thus angels' bread is made
The bread of man today;
The living bread from heaven
With figures does away.
A wondrous gift indeed!
The poor and lowly may
Upon their Lord and Master feed.

O Triune Deity,
To you we meekly pray,
So may you visit us,
As we our homage pay;
And in your footsteps bright
Conduct us on our way
To where you dwell in cloudless light. Amen.

Hymn III: Verbum supernum

The heav'nly Word proceeding forth,
Yet leaving not the Father's side,
And going to His work on earth
Had reached at length life's eventide.

By false disciple to be given

To foemen for His blood athirst,
Himself, the living bread from heaven,
He gave to His disciples first.

To them He gave in twofold kind
His very flesh, His very blood;
In love's own fulness thus designed
Of the whole man to be the food.

By birth our fellowman was He;
Our meat, while sitting at the board;
He died, our ransomer to be;
He ever reigns, our great reward.

O saving Victim, opening wide
The gate of heaven to man below,
Our foes press on from every side,
Your aid supply, your strength bestow.

To your great name be endless praise,
Immortal Godhead, One in Three;
O grant us endless length of days
In our true native land to see. Amen.

Hymn IV: Salutis humanae

Redeemer, come to take man's part,
Jesu, the joy of every heart;
Great Maker of the world's wide frame,
And purest love's delight and flame.

What nameless mercy you o'ercame,
To bear our load of sin and shame?
For guiltless, you your life did give,
That sinful erring man might live.

The realms of woe are forced to see
Its captives from their chains set free;

And you, amid your ransomed train,
At God's right hand do victor reign.

Let mercy sweet with you prevail,
To cure the wounds we now bewail;
Oh, bless us with your holy sight,
And fill us with eternal light.

Our guide, our way to heavenly rest,
Be you the aim of every breast;
Be you the soother of our tears,
Our sweet reward above the spheres. Amen.

Hymn V: Aeterne Rex

Eternal Monarch, King most High,
Whose blood has brought redemption nigh,
By whom the death of death was wrought
And conquering grace's battle fought.

Ascending to your starry height,
Were lifted in a cloud of light,
By heaven to power unending called,
And by no human hand installed.

That so, in nature's triple frame,
Each heavenly and each earthly name,
And things in hell's abyss abhorred,
May bend the knee and own Him Lord.

Yes, angels tremble when they see
How changed is our humanity;
That flesh has purged what flesh had stained,
And God, the flesh of God, has reigned.

Be you our joy, O mighty Lord,
As you will be our great reward;
Earth's joys to you are nothing worth,

You joy and crown of heaven and earth.

To you we therefore humbly pray
That you would purge our sins away,
And draw our hearts by cords of grace
To your celestial dwelling-place.

So when the judgment day shall come,
And all must rise to meet their doom,
You will remit the debts we owe,
And our lost crowns again bestow.

All glory, Lord, to you we pay,
Ascending o'er the stars today;
All glory, as is ever meet,
To Father, and to Paraclete. Amen.

In addition to the hymns given above the following may be sung or recited: Te Deum; Canticle of Zachary; the Magnificat.

5. At the end of the procession when the Blessed Sacrament has been brought back to the church and placed on the altar, all kneel in reverent adoration and sing the last stanzas of the Tantum ergo, followed by the versicles and oration.

6. Having made a genuflection the priest blesses the people with the monstrance, making a single sign of the cross and not saying anything. After this the Blessed Sacrament is reposed in the tabernacle.

7. The manner of blessing described above is observed in every procession with the Blessed Sacrament.

PROCESSION FOR IMPLORING RAIN

The same procedure is followed as that given above in the Rogation procession, until the invocation in the litany That you grant eternal rest to all the faithful departed, etc. After this invocation the following is sung twice:

V. That you grant to your faithful the much needed rainfalls.
R. We beg you to hear us.

At the end of the litany the following is added:

P: Our Father (the rest inaudibly until :)

P: And lead us not into temptation.

All: But deliver us from evil.

Psalm 146

At the end of the psalm the following prayers are said:

P: Lord, cover the heavens with clouds.

All: And prepare rain for the earth.

P: That grass may spring up in the hills.

All: And vegetation for men's use.

P: Sprinkle the hills from the clouds up above.

All: And the earth will be saturated from the work of your hands.

P: Lord, heed my prayer.
All: And let my cry be heard by you.
P: The Lord be with you.
All: May He also be with you.

Let us pray.
God, in whom we live and move and have our being, grant us rain in plenty, so that as we amply experience your gifts of the present time we may all the more confidently desire those of eternity.

Grant, we beg you, almighty God, that we who put our trust in you in this affliction may ever be shielded from all adversities.

Lord, give us, we pray, a plentiful rainfall, and graciously pour out on the parched earth moisture from the heavenly vaults; through Christ our Lord.
All: Amen.

P: The Lord be with you.

All: May He also be with you.

P: Let us bless the Lord.

All: Thanks be to God.

P: May the almighty and merciful Lord be pleased to hear us.

All: Amen.

P: May the souls of the faithful departed through the mercy of God rest in peace.

All: Amen.

PROCESSION FOR IMPLORING FAIR WEATHER

The same procedure is followed as that given above in the Rogation procession, until the invocation in the litany that you grant eternal rest to all the faithful departed, etc. After this invocation the following is sung twice:

V. That you grant to your faithful fair weather.

R. We beg you to hear us.

At the end of the litany the following is added:

P: Our Father (the rest inaudibly until:)

P: And lead us not into temptation.

All: But deliver us from evil.

Psalm 66

At the end of the psalm the following prayers are said:

P: Lord, you sent a wind over the earth.

All: And the rain from the heavens was withheld.

P. When I bring clouds over the earth.

All: My bow will appear, and I will remember my covenant.

P: Lord, let your countenance shine upon your servants

All: And bless those who trust in you.

P: Lord, heed my prayer.
All: And let my cry be heard by you.
P: The Lord be with you.
All: May He also be with you.

Let us pray.
God, who are offended by our sins but appeased by our penances, may it please you to hear the entreaties of your people and to turn away the stripes that our transgressions rightly deserve.

Graciously hear us, O Lord, as we cry out to you, and grant fair weather to us, your suppliants; and although we are justly afflicted for our sins, may we nonetheless know your mercy and so appreciate your clemency.

Almighty God, we appeal to your kindness, asking that you hold back the inundation of rainfall, and be pleased to show us the cheerfulness of your countenance; through Christ our Lord.
All: Amen.

PROCESSION FOR AVERTING TEMPEST

The church bells are rung, and all who can assemble in church. Then the Litany of the Saints is said, in which the following invocation is said twice:

From lightning and tempest, Lord, deliver us.

At the end of the litany the following is added:

P: Our Father (the rest inaudibly until:)

P: And lead us not into temptation.

All: But deliver us from evil.

Psalm 147

P: Glorify the Lord, O Jerusalem; * praise your God, O Sion.

All: For He has strengthened the bars of your gates; * He has blessed your children within you.

P: He has granted peace in your borders; * with the best of wheat He fills you.

All: He sends forth His command to the earth; * swiftly runs His word!

P: He spreads snow like wool; * He strews frost like ashes.

All: He scatters His hail like crumbs; * the waters freeze before

His cold.

P: He sends His word and melts them; * He lets His breeze blow and the waters run.

All: He has proclaimed His word to Jacob, * His statutes and His ordinances to Israel.

P: He has not done thus for any other nation; * He has not made known His ordinances to them.

All: Glory be to the Father.

P: As it was in the beginning.

P: Our help is in the name of the Lord.

All: Who made heaven and earth.

P: Lord, show us your mercy.

All: And grant us your salvation.

P: Help us, O God, our Savior.

All: And deliver us, O Lord, for your name's sake.

P: Let the enemy have no power over us.

All: And the son of iniquity be powerless to harm us.

P: May your mercy, Lord, remain with us always.

All: For we put our whole trust in you.

P: Save your faithful people, Lord.

All: Bless all who belong to you.

P: You withhold no good thing from those who walk in sincerity.

All: Lord of hosts, happy the men who trust in you.

P: Lord, heed my prayer.
All: And let my cry be heard by you.
P: The Lord be with you.
All: May He also be with you.

Let us pray.
God, who are offended by our sins but appeased by our penances, may it please you to hear the entreaties of your people and to turn away the stripes that our transgressions rightly deserve.

We beg you, Lord, to repel the wicked spirits from your family, and to ward off the destructive tempestuous winds

Almighty everlasting God, spare us in our anxiety and take pity on us in our abasement, so that after the lightning in the skies and the force of the storm have calmed, even the very threat of tempest may be an occasion for us to offer you praise.

Lord Jesus, who uttered a word of command to the raging tempest of wind and sea and there came a great calm; hear the prayers of your family, and grant that by this sign of the holy   cross all ferocity of the elements may abate.

Almighty and merciful God, who heal us by your chastisement and save us by your forgiveness; grant that we, your suppliants, may be heartened and consoled by the tranquil weather we desire, and so may ever profit from your gracious favors; through Christ our Lord.
All: Amen.

He sprinkles the surroundings with holy water.

PROCESSION IN TIME OF FAMINE

The same order is followed as on the feast of St. Mark until the last part of the Litany of the Saints, in which the following invocation is sung twice:

That you give and preserve the fruits of the earth.

R. We beg you to hear us.

After the litany the priest says:

P: Our Father (the rest inaudibly until:)

P: And lead us not into temptation.

All: But deliver us from evil.

Psalm 22

After the psalm the priest continues:

P: Deal not with us, Lord, as our sins deserve.

All: Nor take vengeance on us for our transgressions.

P: The eyes of all look to you, O Lord.

All: To give them food in due time.

P: Remember your people.

All: Who have been yours from the beginning.

P: The Lord will be gracious.

All: And our land will bring forth fruit.

P: Lord, heed my prayer.
All: And let my cry be heard by you.

P: The Lord be with you.
All: May He also be with you.

Let us pray.
Show us, O Lord, your inexpressible mercy, blot out our transgressions, and graciously deliver us from the condemnation they deserve.

We beg you, Lord, to hear our sincere pleas, and graciously to avert this famine which afflicts us; so that mortal hearts may acknowledge that such scourges come from your wrath and cease only when you are moved to pity.

Lord, kindly help your people, now suffering this famine in punishment for their sins, to turn back as loyal subjects to you. For you promised that those who seek first your kingdom shall have all other things besides. We ask this of you who live and reign with God the Father, in the unity of the Holy Spirit, God, forever and ever.
All: Amen.

PROCESSION IN TIME OF EPIDEMIC AND PLAGUE

The same order is followed as on the feast of St. Mark until the last part of the Litany of the Saints, in which the following invocation is sung twice:

From plague, famine, and war. R. Lord, deliver us.

And after the invocation "That you grant eternal rest to all the faithful departed," etc. the following invocation is said twice:

That you deliver us from the scourge of pestilence.

R. We beg you to hear us.

After the litany the priest says:

P: Our Father (the rest inaudibly until:)

P: And lead us not into temptation.

All: But deliver us from evil.

Psalm 6

P: Deal not with us, Lord, as our sins deserve.

All: Nor take vengeance on us for our transgressions.

P: Help us, O God, our Savior.

All: And deliver us, O Lord, for your name's sake.

P: Lord, do not keep in mind our former sins.

All: Let us soon know your compassion, for we are exceedingly poor.

P: St. Sebastian, pray for us.

All: That we may be worthy of Christ's promise.

P: Lord, heed my prayer.
All: And let my cry be heard by you.
P: The Lord be with you.
All: May He also be with you.

Let us pray.
Hear us, O God, our Savior, and by the prayers of glorious Mary, Mother of God, and ever a Virgin, of St. Sebastian, your martyr, and of all the saints, deliver your people from your wrath, and in your bounty let them feel certain of your mercy.

Lord, mercifully heed our supplications, and heal our infirmities of body and soul; so that knowing your forgiveness we may ever rejoice in your blessing.

We beg you, Lord, to hear our sincere pleas, and graciously to avert this plague which afflicts us; so that mortal hearts may acknowledge that such scourges come from your wrath and cease only when you are moved to pity; through Christ our Lord.
All: Amen.

PROCESSION IN TIME OF WAR

Having observed the same order as given for the feast of St. Mark, the following is added at the end of the litany:

P: Our Father (the rest inaudibly until:)

P: And lead us not into temptation.

All: But deliver us from evil.

Psalm 45

After the psalm the priest continues:

P: Rise up, O Lord, and help us.

All: And deliver us for your name's sake.

P: Lord, save your people.

All: Who trust in you, my God.

P: Let peace reign in your dominion.

All: And prosperity in your fortress.

P: Let us find in you, Lord, a fortified tower.

All: In the face of the enemy.

P: He breaks the bow and cuts spears in two.

All: And hurls armor into the fire.

P: Lord, send us aid from your holy place.

All: And watch over us from Sion.

P: Lord, heed my prayer.
All: And let my cry be heard by you.
P: The Lord be with you.
All: May He also be with you.

Let us pray.
God, who put down wars and overthrow by your mighty defense those who assail your trustful followers, stand by your servants as they appeal to your mercy; and once the savagery of our enemies has been suppressed, may we praise you in a spirit of constant gratitude.

God, from whom come holy desires, right counsels, and good works, give to your servants that peace which the world cannot give; so that our hearts may be dedicated to the observance of your law, freed from fear of our enemies, and tranquil in the knowledge of your protection.

We beg you, O Lord, to confound the haughtiness of our foe, and to crush with your mighty arm their insolence; through Christ our Lord.

All: Amen.

2. If, however, the war is being waged against the enemies of his Church, then the following petition is said twice in the proper place in the litany:

That you humble the enemies of holy Church. R. We beg you to hear us.

And after the litany the following is added:

P: Our Father (the rest inaudibly until:)

P: And lead us not into temptation.

All: But deliver us from evil.

Psalm 78

P: O God, the nations have come into your inheritance; they have defiled your holy temple, * they have laid Jerusalem in ruins.

All: They have given the corpses of your servants as food to the birds of heaven, * the flesh of your faithful ones to the beasts of the earth.

P: They have poured out their blood like water round about Jerusalem, * and there is no one to bury them.

All: We have become the reproach of our neighbors, * the scorn and derision of those around us.

P: O Lord, how long? Will you be angry forever? * Will your jealousy burn like fire?

All: Pour out your wrath upon the nations that do not acknowledge you, * upon the kingdoms that do not call on your name;

P: For they have devoured Jacob * and laid waste his dwelling.

All: Do not hold the iniquities of the past against us; may your compassion quickly come to us, * for we are brought very low.

P: Help us, O God our savior, because of the glory of your name; * deliver us and pardon our sins for your name's sake.

All: Why should the nations say, * "Where is their God?"

P: Let it be known among the nations in our sight * that you avenge the shedding of your servants' blood.

All: Let the prisoners' sighing come before you; * with your great power free those doomed to death.

P: And repay our neighbors seven-fold into their bosoms * the disgrace they have inflicted on you, O Lord.

All: Then we, your people and the sheep of your pasture, will give thanks to you forever; * through all generations we will declare your praise.

P: Glory be to the Father.

All: As it was in the beginning.

After the psalm the priest continues:

P: Save your servants.

All: Who trust in you, my God.

P: Let us find in you, Lord, a fortified tower.

All: In the face of the enemy.

P: Let the enemy have no power over us.

All: And the son of iniquity be powerless to harm us.

P: Lord, confound the haughtiness of those opposed to your name.

All: And crush with your mighty arm their insolence.

P: Let them be like dust before the wind.

All: And may the Lord's messenger pursue them.

P: Pour out your wrath on the nations that deny you.

All: And on kingdoms that refuse to call on your name.

P: Lord, send us aid from your holy place.

All: And watch over us from Sion.

P: Lord, heed my prayer.
All: And let my cry be heard by you.
P: The Lord be with you.
All: May He also be with you.

Let us pray.
God of mercy, we pray that your Church, made one body in the Holy Spirit, may in nowise be perturbed by the assaults of her foes.

God, who are offended by our sins but appeased by our penances, may it please you to hear the entreaties of your people and to turn away the stripes of your wrath that Our transgressions rightly deserve.

Almighty everlasting God, in whose hand are all authority and all rights of empire, come to the aid of your Christian people; so that our enemies, trusting in their savagery, may be crushed by your mighty arm; through Christ our Lord.
All: Amen.

P: May the Lord graciously hear us.

All: Amen.

PROCESSION IN TIME OF ANY TRIBULATION

the same order is observed as on the feast of St. Mark; at the end of the litany the following is added:

P: Our Father (the rest inaudibly until:)

P: And lead us not into temptation.

All: But deliver us from evil.

Then psalm 19 is said; or in place of it psalm 90. After the psalm the priest continues:

P: God is our refuge and our strength.

All: A helper in all tribulations.

P: Lord, save your servants.

All: Who trust in you, my God.

P: O holy God! O holy strong One! O holy immortal

All: Have mercy on us.

P: Help us, O God, our Savior.

All: And deliver us, O Lord, for the glory of your name.

P: Lord, heed my prayer.
All: And let my cry be heard by you.
P: The Lord be with you.
All: May He also be with you.

Let us pray.
Almighty God, do not disdain your people who cry to you in their affliction, but for the glory of your name be pleased to help us who are so sorely troubled. Show us, O Lord, your inexpressible mercy, blot out our transgressions, and graciously deliver us from the condemnation they deserve.

We entreat you, Lord God, grant us, your servants, the enjoyment of lasting health of body and mind; and by the glorious intercession of blessed Mary, ever a Virgin, free us from present sorrow and give us everlasting joy.

Graciously hear us, O Lord, in our tribulation, and turn away the stripes of your wrath which we justly deserve. God, our refuge and our strength and source of all goodness, heed the holy prayers of your Church, and grant that we fully obtain whatever we ask for in faith; through Christ our Lord.
All: Amen.

PROCESSION OF THANKSGIVING

1. At the beginning of the procession the Te Deum is sung.

2. After the hymn the following psalms may be said:

Psalm 65

Psalm 80

P: Sing joyfully to God our strength; * acclaim the God of Jacob.

All: Take up a melody, and sound the timbrel, * the pleasant harp and the lyre.

P: Blow the trumpet at the new moon, * at the full-moon, on our solemn feast;

All: For it is a statute in Israel, * an ordinance of the God of Jacob,

P: Who made it a decree for Joseph * when he came forth from the land of Egypt.

All: An unfamiliar speech I hear: "I relieved his shoulder of the burden; * his hands were freed from the basket.

P: In distress you called, and I rescued you; unseen, I answered you in thunder; * I tested you at the waters of Meriba.

All: Hear, my people, and I will admonish you; * O Israel, will you not hear me?

P: There shall be no strange god among you * nor shall you worship any alien god.

All: I, the Lord, am your God who led you forth from the land of Egypt; * open wide your mouth, and I will fill it.

P: But my people heard not my voice, * and Israel obeyed me not;

All: So I gave them up to the hardness of their hearts; * let them walk according to their own counsels.

P: If only my people would hear me, * and Israel walk in my ways,

All: Quickly would I humble their enemies; * I would turn my hand against their foes.

P: Those who hated the Lord would seek to flatter him, * but their fate would endure forever,

All: While Israel I would feed with the best of wheat, * and with honey from the rock I would fill them."

P: Glory be to the Father.

All: As it was in the beginning.

Psalm 95

Psalm 99

P: Sing joyfully to the Lord, all you lands; * serve the Lord with gladness;

All: Come before Him * with joyful song.

P: Know that the Lord is God; He made us, His we are; * His people, the flock He tends.

All: Enter His gates with thanksgiving, His courts with praise; * give thanks to Him; bless His name.

P: For He is good: the Lord, whose kindness endures forever, * and His faithfulness to all generations.

All: Glory be to the Father.

P: As it was in the beginning.

Psalm 102

P: Bless the Lord, O my soul; * and all my being, bless His holy name.

All: Bless the Lord, O my soul, * and forget not all His benefits;

P: He pardons all your iniquities, * He heals all your ills.

All: He redeems your life from destruction, * He crowns you with goodness and compassion,

P: He fills your lifetime with good; * your youth is renewed like the eagle's.

All: The Lord performs just deeds * and secures the rights of all the oppressed.

P: He has made known His ways to Moses, * and His deeds to the children of Israel.

All: Merciful and gracious is the Lord, * slow to anger and abounding in kindness.

P: He will not always chide, * nor does He keep His wrath forever.

All: He does not deal with us according to our sins, * nor does He requite us according to our crimes.

P: For as the heavens are high above the earth, * so surpassing is His kindness toward those who fear Him.

All: As far as the east is from the west, * so far has He put our transgressions from us.

P: As a father has compassion on his children, * so the Lord has compassion on those who fear Him,

All: For He knows how we are formed; * He remembers that we are dust.

P: Man's days are like those of grass; * like a flower of the field he blooms;

All: The wind sweeps over him and He is gone, * and his place knows him no more.

P: But the kindness of the Lord is from eternity to eternity toward those who fear Him, * and His justice toward children's children.

All: Among those who keep His covenant * and remember to fulfill His precepts.

P: The Lord has established His throne in heaven, * and His kingdom rules over all.

All: Bless the Lord, all you His angels, you mighty in strength, who do His bidding, * obeying His spoken word.

P: Bless the Lord, all you His hosts, * His ministers, who do His will.

All: Bless the Lord, all His works, everywhere in His domain. *
Bless the Lord, O my soul!

All: Bless the Lord, all His works, everywhere in His domain. *
Bless the Lord, O my soul!

P: Glory be to the Father.

All: As it was in the beginning.

Psalm 116

P: Praise the Lord, all you nations; * glorify Him, all you peoples!

All: For steadfast is His kindness toward us, * and the fidelity of
the Lord endures forever.

P: Glory be to the Father.

All: As it was in the beginning.

Psalm 148

Psalm 149

P: Sing to the Lord a new song * of praise in the assembly of the
faithful.

All: Let Israel be glad in their maker, * let the children of Sion
rejoice in their king.

P: Let them praise His name in the festive dance, * let them sing
praise to Him with timbrel and harp.

All: For the Lord loves His people, * and He adorns the lowly with victory.

P: Let the faithful exult in glory; * let them sing for joy upon their couches.

All: Let the high praises of God be in their throats * and let two-edged swords be in their hands:

P: To execute vengeance on the nations, * punishments on the peoples;

All: To bind their kings with chains, * their nobles with fetters of iron;

P: To execute on them the written sentence. * This is the glory of all His faithful.

All: Glory be to the Father.

P: As it was in the beginning.

Psalm 150

Canticle of the Three Youths

Daniel 3:57-88 and 56

P: Bless the Lord, all you works of the Lord, * praise and exalt Him above all forever.

All: Angels of the Lord, bless the Lord, * you heavens, bless the Lord.

P: All you waters above the heavens, bless the Lord; * all you hosts of the Lord, bless the Lord.

All: Sun and moon, bless the Lord; * stars of heaven, bless the Lord.

P: Every shower and dew, bless the Lord; * all you winds. bless the Lord.

All: Fire and heat, bless the Lord; * cold and chill, bless the Lord.

P: Dew and rain, bless the Lord; * frost and cold, bless the Lord.

All: Ice and snow, bless the Lord; * nights and days, bless the Lord.

P: Light and darkness, bless the Lord; * lightnings and clouds, bless the Lord.

All: Let the earth bless the Lord, * praise and exalt Him above all forever.

P: Mountains and hills, bless the Lord; * everything growing from the earth, bless the Lord.

All: You springs, bless the Lord; * seas and rivers, bless the Lord.

P: You dolphins and all water creatures, bless the Lord; * all you birds of the air, bless the Lord.

All: All you beasts, wild and tame, bless the Lord; * praise and exalt Him above all forever.

P: You sons of men, bless the Lord; * O Israel, bless the Lord.

All: Priests of the Lord, bless the Lord; * servants of the Lord, bless the Lord.

P: Spirits and souls of the just, bless the Lord; * holy men of humble heart, bless the Lord.

All: Ananias, Azarias, Misael, bless the Lord; * praise and exalt

Him above all forever.

P: Let us bless the Father and the Son and the Holy Spirit, * let us praise and exalt God above all forever.

All: Blessed are you, Lord, in the firmament of heaven, * praiseworthy and glorious forever!

After the above canticle the Canticle of Zachary may be said.

3. The foregoing psalms and canticles may be sung in whole or in part, depending on the duration of the procession. Having come into the stational church the following versicles and prayers are said in front of the altar:

P: Blessed are you, Lord God of our fathers.

All: And praiseworthy and glorious forever.

P: Let us bless the Father and the Son and the Holy Spirit.

All: Let us praise and exalt Him above all forever.

P: Blessed are you, Lord, in the firmament of heaven.

All: Praiseworthy and glorious and exalted above all forever.

P: Bless the Lord, O my soul.

All: And never forget His many benefactions.

P: Lord, heed my prayer.
All: And let my cry be heard by you.
P: The Lord be with you.
All: May he also be with you.

Let us pray.

For the three orations that follow here see the end of the Te Deum.

PROCESSION FOR TRANSFERRING SACRED RELICS

The church and the streets in the path of the procession ought to be decorated as fittingly as possible. The priests and other ministers should be clothed in sacred vestments, either white or red, depending on the saints whose relics are being transferred. All who accompany the sacred relics are to carry lighted candles. During the procession the Litany of the Saints is sung, in which will be inserted the names of the saints to whom honor is being paid. In addition to the litany the following hymns and psalms may be sung: the "Te Deum"; psalm 148; psalm 149; and psalm 150; or any other psalms and hymns from the Proper or Common of the saints concerned.

10

EXORCISM

INTRODUCTION

That there is a world of demons is a teaching of revealed religion which is perfectly clear to all who know Sacred Scripture and respect and accept its word as inspired of God. It is part of the whole Christian-Judaeo heritage. There are some who hold that even if revelation were not so absolute, an inference of the existence of evil spirits can be drawn from the magnitude of evil in the world. They say that human malice and depravity even at its worst is not sufficient to account for it, and it must be concluded that the devil is a real person and that his sway is tremendous. As Francois Mauriac writes in his life of St. Margaret of Cortona: "Evil is Someone, Someone who is multiple and whose name is legion.... It is one thing to be in the realm of the demons, as we all are when we have lost the state of grace, and quite another to be held and surrounded, literally possessed by him."

One gets the impression that the teaching about the devil's existence is not a particularly popular one in our time. C. S. Lewis in his "Screwtape Letters" says something to the effect that if the little inexperienced novice devils, about to start out on their work of seducing men, can convince men that the devil does not exist, and then half the battle is already won.

The first book of the Holy Bible recounts the seduction of Adam and Eve by the Prince of Darkness; but it is to the last book that we must go for his origin. "Then war broke out in heaven. Michael and his angels had to fight the dragon; the dragon fought, and so did his angels. But they were defeated, and a place was no longer found for them in heaven. That huge dragon, the ancient serpent, was hurled down, he who is called the devil and Satan, he who leads the whole world astray. He was hurled down to death, and his angels were hurled down with him."

Christ our Lord overcame Satan on the cross, and ever since the latter's empire is shaken. Man is delivered from the power of darkness and transferred to the kingdom of the Son. Yet the devil is not completely vanquished or trodden underfoot once for all, and the warfare against him is carried out by Christ and His Church until the end of time. Therefore, St. Paul is prompted to admonish us: "Put on all the armor that God has forged, that you may be able to make a stand against the devil's cunning tricks. Our wrestling is not against weak human nature, but against the Principalities and the Powers, against those that rule the world of darkness, the wicked spirits that belong to an order higher than ours.... With all this take up the shield of faith, with which you will be enabled to put out all the flaming arrows of the wicked enemy."

Against these unclean spirits the Church uses as her weapons prayers, blessings, holy water, and other sacramentals to combat the ordinary power that the former wield over men. But apart from this ordinary and general power that Providence allows Satan there is also a special and terrible satanic influence called possession-- the domination by the demon over man's bodily organs and his lower spiritual faculties. In later Christian times the term obsession is used instead of possession, the former connoting a lesser kind of demonic disturbance. That Christ reckoned with this satanic power in the same way that the Church has throughout her centuries is evident from the New Testament; see for example Mt 9.32-34, Lk 8.2, Mk 9.13 ff.

To be possessed can mean that Satan has gained mastery over the will so devastatingly that sinfulness passes beyond ordinary depravity in the world, and its cause must be sought in a power above the order of nature. To be possessed can mean that Satan has beclouded the intellect, so that the light of faith cannot illuminate it. To be possessed can mean that Satan has befuddled a person's reason; in fact, simple and superstitious folk have wrongly made lunacy synonymous with diabolical infestation. In some instances of possession recounted in the New Testament, molestation by the devil is manifested in various disturbances of the human body itself, where he has gained control over a man's sight, hearing, speech, or the physical organism in general.

Christ handed down to the Church the power He once exercised over demons. The early Christians were deeply influenced by what they had learned of their Master's dealing with evil spirits, and there was on their part frequent use of the charismatic gifts of healing the sick and driving out devils. But the prayers and forms used for exorcism in the first centuries have not come down to us, outside the ones used in baptism. Exorcism became part of the baptismal rite somewhere around 200 A.D. Thus the ancient liturgical records which date from the third century those dealing with baptism, give us the early Christians' belief about Satan and his intervention in the affairs of man. In the devil's hatred for God he turned on man, who is made in God's image. In consequence of original sin men are no longer temples of the Holy Spirit but rather the habitations of the demon. Not too much distinction is made between the possessed and the unbaptized. Isidore of Seville puts both on the same level, and says that exorcism is the ceremony of banishing the wicked influence of the devil from catechumens and possessed alike.

However, always bear in mind that exorcisms were NOT limited to Christianity, now even the Jewish faith. Exorcism had appeared in earlier religions, even the basic Egyptian Religion of Thalamic Magick. The fellow known as Horus, who predated Jesus by 1,500 years was even known to have been born to a human virgin mother, was baptized and even performed exorcisms. Now this should NOT dismay you from your faith, as the basic principal has always been light versus dark, or good versus evil. And any form of great light can always defeat the darkness. However it is those who go into a battle with this darkness, with an overbearing smugness that they will win, are the ones who stand to lose. It is one thing to be confident, however one should always be on guard, even if Christ himself is standing beside you.

It is difficult to fix precisely the time of origin of a special rite for exorcism. The evidence would indicate that in the early Church acts of exorcism consisted mainly in the sign of the cross, invoking the name of Jesus, and renunciations of Satan and adjurations and threats uttered against him. But later on, especially in the Latin Church, the rites of exorcism become more and more numerous, until in the highly imaginative Middle Ages there is actually a profusion of them. To this period we must attribute beliefs and practices which are superstitious to an extreme. Devils are believed to exist in the guise of certain material bodies. Demonic possession is confounded with epilepsy and other mental or psychic disorders. Rituals of this time prescribe that the subject remain in the presence of the exorcist throughout the period of exorcism, that he observe a strict fast and limit his diet to blessed water, salt, and vegetables, that he wear new clothes, that he abstain from the marital act. No less complicated are the injunctions for the exorcist. And by the time we come to the fourteenth century magical practices have been introduced into the ceremonies.

No doubt the present rite for exorcism will undergo improvement and revision along with the general revision of the liturgical books recommended by Vatican Council II. But compared to former times the rite as given in the Roman Ritual today is characterized by great sobriety. Some minds might still discern traces of a certain naiveté, yet at any rate it has been purged of the unfortunate accretions of a period ruled much more by human credulity than by the unadulterated doctrine of the Church. No longer, for example, does the official text afford any grounds for the erroneous notion that diabolical possession is necessarily a divine retribution visited upon a grievous sinner. God allows this terrible evil in His wisdom without the afflicted person being necessarily at fault. It is one thing to have fallen into the slavery of sin or to be afflicted with a bodily or mental infirmity, and quite another to have the devil enter into a man and take possession of him.

The general rules for exorcism that follow are a clear indication that we have come a long way from the superstitious notions that prevailed in the era of the Middle Ages. Noteworthy among these rules are the ones that direct that the parties concerned should have recourse to the holy sacraments, and that the sacred words of Holy Writ should be employed rather than any forms devised by the exorcist or someone else. The instructions given below indicate that the Church has carefully guarded the extraordinary power over Satan committed to her by Christ, and that Catholic exorcism is poles removed from any form of dabbling in the spirit world which springs from human chicanery or malice.

EXORCISM

GENERAL RULES CONCERNING EXORCISM

1. A priest--one who is expressly and particularly authorized by the Ordinary--when he intends to perform an exorcism over persons tormented by the devil, must be properly distinguished for his piety, prudence, and integrity of life. He should fulfill this devout undertaking in all constancy and humility, being utterly immune to any striving for human aggrandizement, and relying, not on his own, but on the divine power. Moreover, he ought to be of mature years, and revered not alone for his office but for his moral qualities.

2. In order to exercise his ministry rightly, he should resort to a great deal more study of the matter (which has to be passed over here for the sake of brevity), by examining approved authors and cases from experience; on the other hand, let him carefully observe the few more important points enumerated here.

3. Especially, he should not believe too readily that a person is possessed by an evil spirit; but he ought to ascertain the signs by which a person possessed can be distinguished from one who is suffering from some illness, especially one of a psychological nature. Signs of possession may be the following: ability to speak with some facility in a strange tongue or to understand it when spoken by another; the faculty of divulging future and hidden events; display of powers which are beyond the subject's age and natural condition; and various other indications which, when taken together as a whole, build up the evidence.

4. In order to understand these matters better, let him inquire of the person possessed, following one or the other act of exorcism, what the latter experienced in his body or soul while the exorcism was being performed, and to learn also what particular words in the form had a more intimidating effect upon the devil, so that hereafter these words may be employed with greater stress and frequency.

5. He will be on his guard against the arts and subterfuges which the evil spirits are wont to use in deceiving the exorcist. For oft times they give deceptive answers and make it difficult to understand them, so that the exorcist might tire and give up, or so it might appear that the afflicted one is in no wise possessed by the devil.

6. Once in a while, after they are already recognized, they conceal themselves and leave the body practically free from every molestation, so that the victim believes himself completely delivered. Yet the exorcist may not desist until he sees the signs of deliverance.

7. At times, moreover, the evil spirits place whatever obstacles

they can in the way, so that the patient may not submit to exorcism, or they try to convince him that his affliction is a natural one. Meanwhile, during the exorcism, they cause him to fall asleep, and dangle some illusion before him, while they seclude themselves, so that the afflicted one appears to be freed.

8. Some reveal a crime which has been committed and the perpetrators thereof, as well as the means of putting an end to it. Yet the afflicted person must beware of having recourse on this account to sorcerers or necromancers or to any parties except the ministers of the Church, or of making use of any superstitious or forbidden practice.

9. Sometimes the devil will leave the possessed person in peace and even allow him to receive the holy Eucharist, to make it appear that he has departed. In fact, the arts and frauds of the evil one for deceiving a man are innumerable. For this reason the exorcist must be on his guard not to fall into this trap.

10. Therefore, he will be mindful of the words of our Lord, to the effect that there is a certain type of evil spirit who cannot be driven out except by prayer and fasting. Therefore let him avail himself of these two means above all for imploring the divine assistance in expelling demons, after the example of the holy fathers; and not only himself, but let him induce others, as far as possible, to do the same.

11. If it can be done conveniently the possessed person should be led to church or to some other sacred and worthy place, where the exorcism will be held, away from the crowd. But, if the person is ill, or for any valid reason, the exorcism may take place in a private home.

12. The subject, if in good mental and physical health, should be exhorted to implore God's help, to fast, and to fortify himself by frequent reception of penance and Holy Communion, at the discretion of the priest. And in the course of the exorcism he should be fully recollected, with his intention fixed on God, whom he should entreat with firm faith and in all humility. And if he is all

the more grievously tormented, he ought to bear this patiently, never doubting the divine assistance.

13. He ought to have a crucifix at hand or somewhere in sight. If relics of the saints are available, they are to be applied in a reverent way to the breast or the head of the person possessed (the relics must be properly and securely encased and covered). One will see to it that these sacred objects are not treated improperly or that no injury is done them by the evil spirit. However, one should not hold the holy Eucharist over the head of the person or in any way apply it to his body, owing to the danger of desecration.

14. The exorcist must not digress into senseless prattle nor ask superfluous questions or such as are prompted by curiosity, particularly if they pertain to future and hidden matters, all of which have nothing to do with his office. Instead, he will bid the unclean spirit keep silence and answer only when asked. Neither ought he to give any credence to the devil if the latter maintains that he is the spirit of some saint or of a deceased party, or even claims to be a good angel.

15. But necessary questions are, for example: the number and name of the spirits inhabiting the patient, the time when they entered into him, the cause thereof, and the like. As for all jesting, laughing, and nonsense on the part of the evil spirit--the exorcist should prevent it or contemn it, and he will exhort the bystanders (whose number must be very limited) to pay no attention to such goings on; neither are they to put any question to the subject. Rather they should intercede for him to God in all humility and urgency.

16. Let the priest pronounce the exorcism in a commanding and authoritative voice, and at the same time with great confidence, humility, and fervor; and when he sees that the spirit is sorely vexed, then he oppresses and threatens all the more. If he notices that the person afflicted is experiencing a disturbance in some part of his body or an acute pain or a swelling appears in some part, he traces the sign of the cross over that place and sprinkles it with holy water, which he must have at hand for this purpose.

17. He will pay attention as to what words in particular cause the evil spirits to tremble, repeating them the more frequently. And when he comes to a threatening expression, he recurs to it again and again, always increasing the punishment. If he perceives that he is making progress, let him persist for two, three, four hours, and longer if he can, until victory is attained.

18. The exorcist should guard against giving or recommending any medicine to the patient, but should leave this care to physicians.

19. While performing the exorcism over a woman, he ought always to have assisting him several women of good repute, who will hold on to the person when she is harassed by the evil spirit. These assistants ought if possible to be close relatives of the subject and for the sake of decency the exorcist will avoid saying or doing anything which might prove an occasion of evil thoughts to himself or to the others.

20. During the exorcism he shall preferably employ words from Holy Writ, rather than forms of his own or of someone else. He shall, moreover, command the devil to tell whether he is detained in that body by necromancy, by evil signs or amulets; and if the one possessed has taken the latter by mouth, he should be made to vomit them; if he has them concealed on his person, he should expose them; and when discovered they must be burned. Moreover, the person should be exhorted to reveal all his temptations to the exorcist.

21. Finally, after the possessed one has been freed, let him be admonished to guard himself carefully against falling into sin, so as to afford no opportunity to the evil spirit of returning, lest the last state of that man become worse than the former.

RITE FOR EXORCISM

1. The priest delegated by the Ordinary to perform this office should first go to confession or at least elicit an act of contrition, and, if convenient, offer the holy Sacrifice of the Mass, and implore God's help in other fervent prayers. He vests in surplice and purple stole. Having before him the person possessed (who should be bound if there is any danger), he traces the sign of the cross over him, over himself, and the bystanders, and then sprinkles all of them with holy water. After this he kneels and says the Litany of the Saints, exclusive of the prayers which follow it. All present are to make the responses. At the end of the litany he adds the following:

Antiphon: Do not keep in mind, O Lord, our offenses or those of our parents, nor take vengeance on our sins. Our Father (the rest inaudibly until:)

P: And lead us not into temptation.

All: But deliver us from evil.

Psalm 53

After the psalm the priest continues:

P: Save your servant.

All: Who trusts in you, my God.

P: Let him (her) find in you, Lord, a fortified tower.

All: In the face of the enemy.

P: Let the enemy have no power over him (her).

All: And the son of iniquity be powerless to harm him (her).

Lord, send him (her) aid from your holy place.

All: And watch over him (her) from Sion.

P: Lord, heed my prayer.
All: And let my cry be heard by you.
P: The Lord be with you.
All: May He also be with you.

Let us pray.
God, whose nature is ever merciful and forgiving, accept our prayer that this servant of yours, bound by the fetters of sin, may be pardoned by your loving kindness.

Holy Lord, almighty Father, everlasting God and Father of our Lord Jesus Christ, who once and for all consigned that fallen and apostate tyrant to the flames of hell, who sent your only-begotten Son into the world to crush that roaring lion; hasten to our call for help and snatch from ruination and from the clutches of the noonday devil this human being made in your image and likeness. Strike terror, Lord, into the beast now laying waste your vineyard. Fill your servants with courage to fight manfully against that reprobate dragon, lest he despise those who put their trust in you, and say with Pharaoh of old: "I know not God, nor will I set Israel free." Let your mighty hand cast him out of your servant, N., so he may no longer hold captive this person whom it pleased you to make in your image, and to redeem through your Son; who lives and reigns with you, in the unity of the Holy Spirit, God, forever and ever.
All: Amen.

2. Then he commands the demon as follows:

I command you, unclean spirit, whoever you are, along with all your minions now attacking this servant of God, by the mysteries of the incarnation, passion, resurrection, and ascension of our Lord Jesus Christ, by the descent of the Holy Spirit, by the coming of our Lord for judgment, that you tell me by some sign your name, and the day and hour of your departure. I command you, moveover, to obey me to the letter, I who am a minister of God despite my unworthiness; nor shall you be emboldened to harm in any way this creature of God, or the bystanders, or any of their possessions.

3. Next he reads over the possessed person these selections from the Gospel, or at least one of them.

A Lesson from the holy Gospel according to St. John

John 1.1-14

As he says these opening words he signs himself and the possessed on the brow, lips, and breast.

A Lesson from the holy Gospel according to St. Mark

Mark 16.15-18

At that time Jesus said to His disciples: "Go into the whole world and preach the Gospel to all creation. He that believes and is baptized will be saved; he that does not believe will be condemned. And in the way of proofs of their claims, the following will accompany those who believe: in my name they will drive out demons; they will speak in new tongues; they will take up serpents in their hands, and if they drink something deadly, it will not hurt them; they will lay their hands on the sick, and these will recover."

A Lesson from the holy Gospel according to St. Luke

Luke 10.17-20

At that time the seventy-two returned in high spirits. "Master," they said, "even the demons are subject to us because we use your name!" "Yes," He said to them, "I was watching Satan fall like lightning that flashes from heaven. But mind: it is I that have given you the power to tread upon serpents and scorpions, and break the dominion of the enemy everywhere; nothing at all can injure you. Just the same, do not rejoice in the fact that the spirits are subject to you, but rejoice in the fact that your names are engraved in heaven."

A Lesson from the holy Gospel according to St. Luke

Luke 11.14-22

At that time Jesus was driving out a demon, and this particular demon was dumb. The demon was driven out, the dumb man spoke, and the crowds were enraptured. But some among the people remarked: "He is a tool of Beelzebul, and that is how he drives out demons!" Another group, intending to test Him, demanded of Him a proof of His claims, to be shown in the sky. He knew their inmost thoughts. "Any kingdom torn by civil strife," He said to them, "is laid in ruins; and house tumbles upon house. So, too, if Satan is in revolt against himself, how can his kingdom last, since you say that I drive out demons as a tool of Beelzebul. And furthermore: if I drive out demons as a tool of Beelzebul, whose tools are your pupils when they do the driving out? Therefore, judged by them, you must stand condemned. But, if, on the contrary, I drive out demons by the finger of God, then, evidently the kingdom of God has by this time made its way to you. As long as a mighty lord in full armor guards his premises, he is in peaceful possession of his property; but should one mightier than he attack and overcome him, he will strip him of his armor, on which he had relied, and distribute the spoils taken from him."

P: Lord, heed my prayer.
All: And let my cry be heard by you.
P: The Lord be with you.
All: May He also be with you.

Let us pray.
Almighty Lord, Word of God the Father, Jesus Christ, God and Lord of all creation; who gave to your holy apostles the power to

tramp underfoot serpents and scorpions; who along with the other
mandates to work miracles was pleased to grant them the authority
to say: "Depart, you devils!" and by whose might Satan was made
to fall from heaven like lightning; I humbly call on your holy name
in fear and trembling, asking that you grant me, your unworthy
servant, pardon for all my sins, steadfast faith, and the power--
supported by your mighty arm--to confront with confidence and
resolution this cruel demon. I ask this through you, Jesus Christ,
our Lord and God, who are coming to judge both the living and the
dead and the world by fire.
All: Amen.

4. Next he makes the sign of the cross over himself and the one
possessed, places the end of the stole on the latter's neck, and,
putting his right hand on the latter's head, he says the following in
accents filled with confidence and faith:

P: See the cross of the Lord; begone, you hostile powers!

All: The stem of David, the lion of Juda's tribe has conquered.

P: Lord, heed my prayer.
All: And let my cry be heard by you.
P: The Lord be with you.
All: May He also be with you.

Let us pray.
God and Father of our Lord Jesus Christ, I appeal to your holy
name, humbly begging your kindness, that you graciously grant me
help against this and every unclean spirit now tormenting this
creature of yours; through Christ our Lord.
All: Amen.

Exorcism

I cast you out, unclean spirit, along with every satanic power of the
enemy, every spectre from hell, and all your fell companions; in
the name of our Lord Jesus   Christ Begone and stay far from this

creature of God.   For it is He who commands you, He who flung you headlong from the heights of heaven into the depths of hell. It is He who commands you, He who once stilled the sea and the wind and the storm. Hearken, therefore, and tremble in fear, Satan, you enemy of the faith, you foe of the human race, you begetter of death, you robber of life, you corrupter of justice, you root of all evil and vice? seducer of men, betrayer of the nations, instigator of envy, font of avarice, fomentor of discord, author of pain and sorrow. Why, then, do you stand and resist, knowing as you must that Christ the Lord brings your plans to nothing? Fear Him, who in Isaac was offered in sacrifice, in Joseph sold into bondage, slain as the paschal lamb, crucified as man, yet triumphed over the powers of hell. (The three signs of the cross which follow are traced on the brow of the possessed person). Begone, then, in the name of the Father, and of the Son,   and of the Holy Spirit. Give place to the Holy Spirit by this sign of the holy cross of our Lord Jesus Christ, who lives and reigns with the Father and the Holy Spirit, God, forever and ever.
All: Amen.

P: Lord, heed my prayer.
All: And let my cry be heard by you.
P: The Lord be with you.
All: May He also be with you.

Let us pray.
God, Creator and defender of the human race, who made man in your own image, look down in pity on this your servant, N., now in the toils of the unclean spirit, now caught up in the fearsome threats of man's ancient enemy, sworn foe of our race, who befuddles and stupefies the human mind, throws it into terror, overwhelms it with fear and panic. Repel, O Lord, the devil's power, break asunder his snares and traps, put the unholy tempter to flight. By the sign   (on the brow) of your name, let your servant be protected in mind and body. (The three crosses which follow are traced on the breast of the possessed person). Keep watch over the inmost recesses of his (her)   heart; rule over his (her) emotions; strengthen his (her)   will. Let vanish from his (her) soul the temptings of the mighty adversary. Graciously grant, O Lord, as

we call on your holy name, that the evil spirit, who hitherto terrorized over us, may himself retreat in terror and defeat, so that this servant of yours may sincerely and steadfastly render you the service which is your due; through Christ our Lord.
All: Amen.

I adjure you, ancient serpent, by the judge of the living and the dead, by your Creator, by the Creator of the whole universe, by Him who has the power to consign you to hell, to depart forthwith in fear, along with your savage minions, from this servant of God, N., who seeks refuge in the fold of the Church. I adjure you again, (on the brow) not by my weakness but by the might of the Holy Spirit, to depart from this servant of God, N., whom almighty God has made in His image. Yield, therefore, yield not to my own person but to the minister of Christ. For it is the power of Christ that compels you, who brought you low by His cross. Tremble before that mighty arm that broke asunder the dark prison walls and led souls forth to light. May the trembling that afflicts this human frame, (on the breast) the fear that afflicts this image (on the brow) of God, descend on you. Make no resistance nor delay in departing from this man, for it has pleased Christ to dwell in man. Do not think of despising my command because you know me to be a great sinner. It is God Himself who commands you; the majestic Christ who commands you. God the Father commands you; God the Son commands you; God the Holy Spirit commands you. The mystery of the cross commands you. The faith of the holy apostles Peter and Paul and of all the saints commands you. The blood of the martyrs commands you. The continence of the confessors commands you. The devout prayers of all holy men and women command you. The saving mysteries of our Christian faith command you.

Depart, then, transgressor. Depart, seducer, full of lies and cunning, foe of virtue, persecutor of the innocent. Give place, abominable creature, give way, you monster, give way to Christ, in whom you found none of your works. For He has already stripped you of your powers and laid waste your kingdom, bound you prisoner and plundered your weapons. He has cast you forth into the outer darkness, where everlasting ruin awaits you and your abettors. To what purpose do you insolently resist? To what purpose do you brazenly refuse? For you are guilty before almighty God, whose laws you have transgressed. You are guilty before His Son, our Lord Jesus Christ, whom you presumed to tempt, whom you dared to nail to the cross. You are guilty before the whole human race, to whom you proffered by your enticements the poisoned cup of death.

Therefore, I adjure you, profligate dragon, in the name of the spotless Lamb, who has trodden down the asp and the basilisk, and overcome the lion and the dragon, to depart from this man (woman) (on the brow), to depart from the Church of God (signing the bystanders). Tremble and flee, as we call on the name of the Lord, before whom the denizens of hell cower, to whom the heavenly Virtues and Powers and Dominations are subject, whom the Cherubim and Seraphim praise with unending cries as they sing: Holy, holy, holy, Lord God of Sabaoth. The Word made flesh commands you; the Virgin's Son commands you; Jesus of Nazareth commands you, who once, when you despised His disciples, forced you to flee in shameful defeat from a man; and when He had cast you out you did not even dare, except by His leave, to enter into a herd of swine. And now as I adjure you in His name, begone from this man (woman) who is His creature. It is futile to resist His will. It is hard for you to kick against the goad. The longer you delay, the heavier your punishment shall be; for it is not men you are contemning, but rather Him who rules the living and the dead, who is coming to judge both the living and the dead and the world by fire.
All: Amen.

P: Lord, heed my prayer.
All: And let my cry be heard by you.
P: The Lord be with you.
All: May He also be with you.

Let us pray.
God of heaven and earth, God of the angels and archangels, God of

284

the prophets and apostles, God of the martyrs and virgins, God who have power to bestow life after death and rest after toil; for there is no other God than you, nor can there be another true God beside you, the Creator of heaven and earth, who are truly a King, whose kingdom is without end; I humbly entreat your glorious majesty to deliver this servant of yours from the unclean spirits; through Christ our Lord.

All: Amen.

Therefore, I adjure you every unclean spirit, every spectre from hell, every satanic power, in the name of Jesus Christ of Nazareth, who was led into the desert after His baptism by John to vanquish you in your citadel, to cease your assaults against the creature whom He has formed from the slime of the earth for His own honor and glory; to quail before wretched man, seeing in him the image of almighty God, rather than his state of human frailty. Yield then to God,   who by His servant, Moses, cast you and your malice, in the person of Pharaoh and his army, into the depths of the sea. Yield to God,   who, by the singing of holy canticles on the part of David, His faithful servant, banished you from the heart of King Saul. Yield to God, who condemned you in the person of Judas Iscariot, the traitor. For He now flails you with His divine scourges,   He in whose sight you and your legions once cried out: "What have we to do with you, Jesus, Son of the Most High God? Have you come to torture us before the time?" Now He is driving you back into the everlasting fire, He who at the end of time will say to the wicked: "Depart from me, you accursed, into the everlasting fire which has been prepared for the devil and his angels." For you, O evil one, and for your followers there will be worms that never die. An unquenchable fire stands ready for you and for your minions, you prince of accursed murderers, father of lechery, instigator of sacrileges, model of vileness, promoter of heresies, inventor of every obscenity.

Depart, then,   impious one, depart,   accursed one, depart with all your deceits, for God has willed that man should be His temple. Why do you still linger here? Give honor to God the Father

almighty, before whom every knee must bow. Give place to the Lord Jesus   Christ, who shed His most precious blood for man. Give place to the Holy   Spirit, who by His blessed apostle Peter openly struck you down in the person of Simon Magus; who cursed your lies in Annas and Saphira; who smote you in King Herod because he had not given honor to God; who by His apostle Paul afflicted you with the night of blindness in the magician Elyma, and by the mouth of the same apostle bade you to go out of Pythonissa, the soothsayer. Begone,   now! Begone, seducer! Your place is in solitude; your abode is in the nest of serpents; get down and crawl with them. This matter brooks no delay; for see, the Lord, the ruler comes quickly, kindling fire before Him, and it will run on ahead of Him and encompass His enemies in flames. You might delude man, but God you cannot mock. It is He who casts you out, from whose sight nothing is hidden. It is He who repels you, to whose might all things are subject. It is He who expels you, He who has prepared everlasting hellfire for you and your angels, from whose mouth shall come a sharp sword, who is coming to judge both the living and the dead and the world by fire.
All: Amen.

5. All the above may be repeated as long as necessary, until the one possessed has been fully freed.

6. It will also help to say devoutly and often over the afflicted person the Our Father, Hail Mary, and the Creed, as well as any of the prayers given below.

7. The Canticle of our Lady, with the doxology; the Canticle of Zachary, with the doxology.

Athanasian Creed

P: Whoever wills to be saved * must before all else hold fast to the Catholic faith.

All: Unless one keeps this faith whole and untarnished, * without doubt he will perish forever.

P: Now this is the Catholic faith: * that we worship one God in Trinity, and Trinity in unity;

All: Neither confusing the Persons one with the other, * nor making a distinction in their nature.

P: For the Father is a distinct Person; and so is the Son, * and so is the Holy Spirit.

All: Yet the Father, Son, and Holy Spirit possess one Godhead, * co-equal glory, co-eternal majesty.

P: As the Father is, so is the Son, * so also is the Holy Spirit.

All: The Father is uncreated, the Son is uncreated, * the Holy Spirit is uncreated.

P: The Father is infinite, the Son is infinite, * the Holy Spirit is infinite.

All: The Father is eternal, the Son is eternal, * the Holy Spirit is eternal.

P: Yet they are not three eternals, * but one eternal God.

All: Even as they are not three uncreated, or three infinites, * but one uncreated and one infinite God.

P: So likewise the Father is almighty, the Son is almighty, * the Holy Spirit is almighty.

All: Yet they are not three almighties, * but they are the one Almighty.

P: Thus the Father is God, the Son is God, * the Holy Spirit is God.

All: Yet they are not three gods, * but one God.

P: Thus the Father is Lord, the Son is Lord, * the Holy Spirit is Lord.

All: Yet there are not three lords, * but one Lord.

P: For just as Christian truth compels us to profess that each Person is individually God and Lord, * so does the Catholic religion forbid us to hold that there are three gods or lords.

All: The Father was not made by any power; * He was neither created nor begotten.

P: The Son is from the Father alone, * neither created nor made, but begotten.

All: The Holy Spirit is from the Father and the Son, * neither made nor created nor begotten, but He proceeds.

P: So there is one Father, not three; one Son, not three; * one Holy Spirit, not three.

All: And in this Trinity one Person is not earlier or later, nor is one greater or less; * but all three Persons are co-eternal and co-equal.

P: In every way, then, as already affirmed, * unity in Trinity and Trinity in unity is to be worshipped.

All: Whoever, then, wills to be saved * must assent to this doctrine of the Blessed Trinity.

P: But it is necessary for everlasting salvation * that one also firmly believe in the incarnation of our Lord Jesus Christ.

All: True faith, then, requires us to believe and profess * that our Lord Jesus Christ, the Son of God, is both God and man.

P: He is God, begotten of the substance of the Father from eternity; * He is man, born in time of the substance of His Mother.

All: He is perfect God, and perfect man * subsisting in a rational soul and a human body.

P: He is equal to the Father in His divine nature, * but less than the Father in His human nature as such.

All: And though He is God and man, * yet He is the one Christ, not two;

P: One, however, not by any change of divinity into flesh, * but by the act of God assuming a human nature. All: He is one only, not by a mixture of substance, * but by the oneness of His Person.

P: For, somewhat as the rational soul and the body compose one man, * so Christ is one Person who is both God and man;

All: Who suffered for our salvation, who descended into hell, * who rose again the third day from the dead;

P: Who ascended into heaven, and sits at the right hand of God the Father almighty, * from there He shall come to judge both the living and the dead.

All: At His coming all men shall rise again in their bodies, * and shall give an account of their works.

P: And those who have done good shall enter into everlasting life, * but those who have done evil into ever lasting fire.

All: All this is Catholic faith, * and unless one believes it truly and firmly one cannot be saved.

P: Glory be to the Father

All: As it was in the beginning.

{Here follow a large number of psalms which may be used at the exorcist's discretion but are not a necessary part of the rite. Some of them occur in other parts of the Ritual and are so indicated; the others may be taken from the Psalter. Psalm 90; psalm 67; psalm 69; psalm 53; psalm 117; psalm 34; psalm 30; psalm 21, psalm 3; psalm 10; psalm 12.}

Prayer Following Deliverance

Almighty God, we beg you to keep the evil spirit from further molesting this servant of yours, and to keep him far away, never to return. At your command, O Lord, may the goodness and peace of our Lord Jesus Christ, our Redeemer, take possession of this man (woman). May we no longer fear any evil since the Lord is with us; who lives and reigns with you, in the unity of the Holy Spirit, God, forever and ever.

All: Amen.

11

EXORCISM OF SATAN AND THE FALLEN ANGELS

{Whereas the preceding rite of exorcism is designated for a particular person, the present one is for general use--to combat the power of the evil spirits over a community or locality.}

The following exorcism can be used by bishops, as well as by priests who have this authorization from their Ordinary.

In the name of the Father, and of the Son, and of the Holy Spirit. Amen.

Prayer to St. Michael the Archangel

St. Michael the Archangel, illustrious leader of the heavenly army, defend us in the battle against principalities and powers, against the rulers of the world of darkness and the spirit of wickedness in high places. Come to the rescue of mankind, whom God has made in His own image and likeness, and purchased from Satan's tyranny at so great a price. Holy Church venerates you as her patron and guardian. The Lord has entrusted to you the task of leading the souls of the redeemed to heavenly blessedness. Entreat the Lord of peace to cast Satan down under our feet, so as to keep him from further holding man captive and doing harm to the Church. Carry our prayers up to God's throne, that the mercy of the Lord may quickly come and lay hold of the beast, the serpent of old, Satan and his demons, casting him in chains into the abyss, so that he can no longer seduce the nations.

In the name of Jesus Christ, our Lord and God, by the intercession of Mary, spotless Virgin and Mother of God, of St. Michael the Archangel, of the blessed apostles Peter and Paul, and of all the saints, and by the authority residing in our holy ministry, we steadfastly proceed to combat the onslaught of the wily enemy.

Psalm 67

P: God arises; His enemies are scattered, * and those who hate Him flee before Him.

All: As smoke is driven away, so are they driven; * as wax melts before the fire, so the wicked perish before God.

P: See the cross of the Lord; begone, you hostile powers!

All: The stem of David, the lion of Juda's tribe has conquered.

P: May your mercy, Lord, remain with us always.

All: For we put our whole trust in you.

We cast you out, every unclean spirit, every satanic power, every onslaught of the infernal adversary, every legion, every diabolical group and sect, in the name and by the power of our Lord Jesus Christ. We command you, begone and fly far from the Church of God, from the souls made by God in His image and redeemed by the precious blood of the divine Lamb. No longer dare, cunning serpent, to deceive the human race, to persecute God's Church, to strike God's elect and to sift them as wheat. For the Most High God commands you, He to whom you once proudly presumed yourself equal; He who wills all men to be saved and come to the knowledge of truth. God the Father commands you. God the Son commands you. God the Holy Spirit commands you. Christ, the eternal Word of God made flesh, commands you, who humbled Himself, becoming obedient even unto death, to save our race from the perdition wrought by your envy; who founded His Church upon a firm rock, declaring that the gates of hell should never prevail against her, and that He would remain with her all days, even to the end of the world. The sacred mystery of the cross commands you, along with the power of all mysteries of Christian faith. The exalted Virgin Mary, Mother of God, commands you, who in her lowliness crushed your proud head from the first moment of her Immaculate Conception. The faith of the holy apostles Peter and Paul and the other apostles commands you. The blood of martyrs and the devout prayers of all holy men and women command you.

Therefore, accursed dragon and every diabolical legion, we adjure you by the living God, by the true God, by the holy God, by God, who so loved the world that He gave His only-begotten Son, that whoever believes in Him might not perish but have everlasting

life; to cease deluding human creatures and filling them with the poison of everlasting damnation; to desist from harming the Church and hampering her freedom. Begone, Satan, father and master of lies, enemy of man's welfare. Give place to Christ, in whom you found none of your works. Give way to the one, holy, catholic, and apostolic Church, which Christ Himself purchased with His blood. Bow down before God's mighty hand, tremble and flee as we call on the holy and awesome name of
Jesus, before whom the denizens of hell cower, to whom the heavenly Virtues and Powers andDominations are subject, whom the Cherubim and Seraphim praise with unending cries as they sing: Holy, holy, holy, Lord God of Sabaoth.

P: Lord, heed my prayer.
All: And let my cry be heard by you.
P: The Lord be with you.
All: May He also be with you.

Let us pray.
God of heaven and earth, God of the angels and archangels, God of the patriarchs and prophets, God of the apostles and martyrs, God of the confessors and virgin God who have power to bestow life after death and rest after toil; for there is no other God than you, nor can there be another true God beside you, the Creator of all things visible and invisible, whose kingdom is without end; we humbly entreat your glorious majesty to deliver us by your might from every influence of the accursed spirits, from their every evil snare and deception, and to keep us from all harm; through Christ our Lord.
All: Amen.

P: From the snares of the devil.

All: Lord, deliver us.

P: That you help your Church to serve you in security and freedom.

All: We beg you to hear us.

P: That you humble the enemies of holy Church.

All: We beg you to hear us.

The surroundings are sprinkled with holy water.

12
LITANIES

LITANY OF THE HOLY NAME OF JESUS

Lord, have mercy.

Christ, have mercy.

Lord, have mercy.

Jesus, hear us.

Jesus, graciously hear us.

God, the Father in heaven, have mercy on us.* (After each invocation: "Have mercy on us.")

God, the Son, Redeemer of the world,

God, the Holy Spirit,

Holy Trinity, one God,

Jesus, Son of the living God,

Jesus, splendor of the Father,

Jesus, brightness of eternal light,

Jesus, king of glory,

Jesus, sun of justice,

Jesus, Son of the Virgin Mary,

Jesus, most amiable,

Jesus, most admirable,

Jesus, God of power,

Jesus, father of the world to come,

Jesus, angel of great counsel,

Jesus, most powerful,

Jesus, most patient,

Jesus, most obedient,

Jesus, meek and humble of heart,

Jesus, lover of chastity,

Jesus, lover of us,

Jesus, God of peace,

Jesus, author of life,

Jesus, model of virtue,

Jesus, zealous for souls,

Jesus, our God,

Jesus, our refuge,

Jesus, father of the poor,

Jesus, treasure of the faithful,

Jesus, good shepherd,

Jesus, true light,

Jesus, eternal wisdom,

Jesus, infinite goodness

Jesus, our way and our life,

Jesus, joy of angels,

Jesus, king of patriarchs,

Jesus, master of the apostles,

Jesus, teacher of the evangelists,

Jesus, strength of martyrs,

Jesus, light of confessors,

Jesus, purity of virgins,

Jesus, crown of all saints,

Be merciful, spare us, O Jesus.

Be merciful, graciously hear us, O Jesus.

From all evil, Jesus, deliver us.* (After each invocation: "Jesus, deliver us.")

From all sin,

From your wrath,

From the snares of the devil,

From all lewdness,

From eternal death,

From the neglect of your inspirations,

By the mystery of your holy incarnation,

By your birth,

By your infancy,

By your truly divine life,

By your labors,

By your agony and passion,

By your cross and dereliction,

By your sufferings,

By your death and burial,

By your resurrection,

By your ascension,

By your joys,

By your glory,

Lamb of God, who take away the sins of the world, spare us, O Jesus.

Lamb of God, who take away the sins of the world, graciously hear us, O Jesus.

Lamb of God, who take away the sins of the world, have mercy on us, O Jesus.

P: Jesus, hear us.

All: Jesus, graciously hear us.

Let us pray.
Lord Jesus Christ, who said: "Ask, and you shall receive; seek, and you shall find; knock, and it shall be opened to you"; we beg you to heed our prayers, and grant us the gift of your divine charity, that we may ever love you with all our heart, word, and deed, and never cease to praise you.

Help us, O Lord, always to love and revere your holy name, for you never cease to guide those whom you have firmly established in your love; who live and reign forever and ever.
All: Amen.

LITANY OF THE SACRED HEART OF JESUS

Lord, have mercy.

Christ, have mercy.

Lord, have mercy.

Christ, hear us.

Christ, graciously hear us.

God, the Father in heaven, have mercy on us.* (After each invocation: "Have mercy on us.")

God, the Son, Redeemer of the world,

God, the Holy Spirit,

Holy Trinity, one God,

Heart of Jesus, Son of the eternal Father,

Heart of Jesus, formed by the Holy Spirit in the womb of the Virgin Mother,

Heart of Jesus, substantially united to the Word of God,

Heart of Jesus, infinite in majesty,

Heart of Jesus, sacred temple of God,

Heart of Jesus, tabernacle of the Most High,

Heart of Jesus, house of God and gate of heaven,

Heart of Jesus, aflame with love for men,

Heart of Jesus, abode of justice and love,

Heart of Jesus, full of goodness and love,

Heart of Jesus, endless source of all virtues,

Heart of Jesus, worthy of all praise,

Heart of Jesus, King and center of all hearts,

Heart of Jesus, in whom are all the treasures of wisdom and knowledge,

Heart of Jesus, in whom dwells the fulness of divinity,

Heart of Jesus, in whom the Father was well pleased,

Heart of Jesus, of whose fulness we have all received,

Heart of Jesus, desire of the everlasting hills,

Heart of Jesus, patient and merciful,

Heart of Jesus, enriching all who call upon you,

Heart of Jesus, fountain of life and holiness,

Heart of Jesus, atonement for our sins,

Heart of Jesus, loaded down with opprobrium,

Heart of Jesus, bruised for our offences,

Heart of Jesus, obedient unto death,

Heart of Jesus, pierced with a lance,

Heart of Jesus, source of all consolation,

Heart of Jesus, our life and resurrection,

Heart of Jesus, our peace and reconciliation,

Heart of Jesus, victim for sin,

Heart of Jesus, salvation of those who trust in you,

Heart of Jesus, hope of those who die in you,

Heart of Jesus, delight of all the saints,

Lamb of God, who take away the sins of the world, spare us, O Lord.

Lamb of God, who take away the sins of the world, graciously hear us, O Lord.

Lamb of God, who take away the sins of the world, have mercy on us.

P: Jesus, meek and humble of heart.

All: Let our hearts resemble yours.

Let us pray.
Almighty everlasting God, look upon the heart of your dearly beloved Son, and upon the praise and satisfaction He offers you in the name of sinners and for those who seek your mercy. Be appeased, and grant us pardon in the name of Jesus Christ, your Son, who lives and reigns with you forever and ever.

All: Amen.

LITANY OF THE PRECIOUS BLOOD

{This litany was approved by Pope John XXIII, and on his recommendation included in the Roman Ritual on February 24, 1960.}

Lord, have mercy.

Christ, have mercy.

Lord, have mercy.

Christ, hear us.

Christ, graciously hear us.

God, the Father in heaven, have mercy on us.*(After each invocation: "Have mercy on us.")

God, the Son, Redeemer of the world,

God, the Holy Spirit,

Holy Trinity, one God,

Blood of Christ, the only-begotten Son of the eternal Father, save us.** (After each invocation: "Save us.")

Blood of Christ, Word of God made flesh,

Blood of Christ, of the New and everlasting Covenant,

Blood of Christ, trickling to the earth in the agony in the garden,

Blood of Christ, pouring from your body in the scourging,

Blood of Christ, flowing from your head in the crowning with thorns,

Blood of Christ, shed on the cross,

Blood of Christ, the price of our salvation,

Blood of Christ, without which there is no remission of sins,

Blood of Christ, drink and cleansing of souls in the Eucharist,

Blood of Christ, flood of mercy,

Blood of Christ, triumphant over demons,

Blood of Christ, strength of martyrs,

Blood of Christ, inspiration of confessors,

Blood of Christ, seed of virgins,

Blood of Christ, help of those in peril,

Blood of Christ, support in our trials,

Blood of Christ, solace in our sorrows,

Blood of Christ, hope of the repentant,

Blood of Christ, comfort the dying,

Blood of Christ, peace and delight of our hearts,

Blood of Christ, pledge everlasting life,

Blood of Christ, deliverance of the souls in purgatory,

Blood of Christ, worthy of all honor and glory,

Lamb of God, who take away the sins of the world, spare us, O Lord.

Lamb of God, who take away the sins of the world, graciously hear us, O Lord.

Lamb of God, who take away the sins of the world, have mercy on us.

P: You have redeemed us, Lord, by your blood.

All: You have made us to reign with our God.

Let us pray.
Almighty everlasting God, who appointed your only-begotten Son

as Redeemer of the world, and chose to be appeased by His blood; help us, we beg you, so to reverence this price of our salvation, that we may be protected by its power from the evils of this life, and enjoy its lasting rewards in the life to come; through
Christ our Lord.

All: Amen.

LITANY OF THE BLESSED VIRGIN MARY

Lord, have mercy.

Christ, have mercy.

Lord, have mercy.

Christ, hear us.

Christ, graciously hear us.

God, the Father in heaven, have mercy on us.

God, the Son, Redeemer of the world, have mercy on us.

God, the Holy Spirit, have mercy on us.

Holy Trinity, one God, have mercy on us.

Holy Mary, pray for us.* (After each invocation: "Pray for us.")

Holy Mother of God,

Holiest of all virgins,

Mother of Christ,

Mother of God's gift to men,

Mother, all pure,

Mother, all chaste,

Mother inviolate,

Mother undefiled,

Mother, worthy of our love,

Mother, worthy of our admiration,

Mother of good counsel,

Mother of our Creator,

Mother of our Savior,

Virgin, all prudent,

Virgin, all venerable,

Virgin, all renowned,

Virgin, all powerful,

Virgin, all mild,

Virgin, all faithful,

Mirror of justice,

Seat of wisdom,

Means of our joy,

Vessel of the Holy Spirit,

Exalted vessel,

Glorious vessel of holiness,

Mystical rose,

Tower of David,

Tower of ivory,

House of gold,

Ark of the covenant,

Gate of heaven,

Morning star,

Health of the sick,

Refuge of sinners,

Comforter of the afflicted

Help of Christians,

Queen of angels,

Queen of patriarchs,

Queen of prophets,

Queen of apostles,

Queen of martyrs,

Queen of confessors,

Queen of virgins,

Queen of all saints,

Queen conceived without original sin,

Queen taken into heaven,

Queen of the holy rosary,

Queen of peace,

Lamb of God, who take away the sins of the world, spare us, O Lord.

Lamb of God, who take away the sins of the world, graciously hear us, O Lord.

Lamb of God, who take away the sins of the , world, have mercy on us.

The following prayers are added, in accord with the season of the church year:

From the first Sunday in Advent until Christmas:

P: The angel of the Lord brought the tidings to Mary.

All: And she conceived by the Holy Spirit.

Let us pray.
God, who willed that your Word take flesh in the womb of the blessed Virgin Mary at the angel's message; grant that we, your petitioners, who believe she is truly the Mother of God, may be aided by her intercession, through Christ our Lord.
All: Amen.

From Christmas until Candlemas:

P: After childbirth you remained ever an inviolate Virgin.

All: Mother of God, intercede for us.

Let us pray.
God, who brought to mankind the gift of eternal salvation through the virginal motherhood of blessed Mary; let us be helped by her prayers, since through her we have been favored with the source of life, our Lord Jesus Christ your Son.
All: Amen.

From Candlemas until Easter, and from Trinity Sunday until Advent:

P: Pray for us, O holy Mother of God.

All: That we may be worthy of Christ's promise.

Let us pray.

We entreat you, Lord God, grant us the enjoyment of lasting health of body and mind; and by the glorious intercession of blessed Mary, ever a Virgin, free us from present sorrow and give us everlasting joy; through Christ our Lord.
All: Amen.

During Eastertime:

P: Be joyful, be glad, O Virgin Mary, alleluia.
All: For the Lord is truly risen, alleluia.

Let us pray.
God, who mercifully brought joy into the world by the resurrection of your Son, our Lord Jesus Christ; grant that we may come to the joy of everlasting life through the prayers of His Mother, the Virgin Mary; through Christ our Lord.
All: Amen.

Lord, have mercy.

Christ, have mercy.

Lord, have mercy.

Christ, hear us.

Christ, graciously hear us.

God, the Father in heaven, have mercy on us.

God, the Son, Redeemer of the world, have mercy on

God, the Holy Spirit, have mercy on us.

Holy Trinity, one God, have mercy on us.

Holy Mary, pray for us.*(After each invocation: "Pray for us.)

St. Joseph,

Illustrious son of David,

Splendor of patriarchs,

Spouse of God's Mother,

Chaste guardian of the Virgin,

Foster-father of the Son of God,

Watchful defender of Christ,

Head of the Holy Family,

Joseph, all just,

Joseph, all pure,

Joseph, all prudent,

Joseph, all courageous,

Joseph, all obedient,

Joseph, all faithful,

Model of patience,

Lover of poverty,

Model of laborers,

Glory of family life,

Protector of virgins,

Mainstay of families,

Solace of the afflicted,

Hope of the sick,

Patron of the dying,

Terror of demons,

Protector of holy Church,

Lamb of God, who take away the sins of the world, spare us, O Lord.

Lamb of God, who take away the sins of the world, graciously hear us, O Lord.

Lamb of God, who take away the sins of the world, have mercy on us.

P: God made him master of His household.

All: And ruler of all His possessions.

Let us pray.
God, who in your indescribable providence singled out St. Joseph as the spouse of your holy Mother, grant we pray, that we may merit to have him for our intercessor in heaven, whom we venerate as our defender here on earth. We ask this of you who live and reign forever and ever.
All: Amen.

13

BLESSINGS FORMERLY RESERVED TO RELIGIOUS ORDERS

Only hours before going to press we learned from the new "Instruction" of September 26, 1964 that the following blessings, except for the first, are no longer reserved. That explains why they are listed separately here.

BLESSING AND ERECTING STATIONS OF THE CROSS

(Reserved to the Bishops of the World)

(This is given under Rite for Erecting Stations of the Cross)

BLESSING AND ERECTING STATIONS OF THE SORROWFUL MOTHER IN HONOR OF OUR LADY OF THE SEVEN DOLORS

(Formerly reserved to the Order of Servites)

(Approved by the Congregation of Sacred Rites, March 10, 1883)

The priest vests in surplice and purple stole. He should be assisted by clerics or other ministrants, who hold the aspersory, thurible, and incense boat. First the priest goes up to the altar predella and addresses the people briefly on the excellence and value of this devotion of the Stations of the Sorrowful Mother. After this he kneels on the lowest step of the altar and intones the Veni Creator, which is continued by the choir. When the hymn is finished he says:

P: Send forth your Spirit and all things shall be recreated.

All: And you shall renew the face of the earth.

Let us pray.
God, who instructed the hearts of the faithful by the light of the Holy Spirit, guide us by your Spirit to desire only what is good and so always to find joy in His comfort.

Lord, we beg you to protect this people from every adversity, by the intercession of blessed Mary, ever a Virgin; and as they fervently bow down before you shield them by your benevolence from all wiles of the enemy.

We beg you, Lord, let a breath of your grace prompt our undertakings and guide them along their course, so that our least prayer and work may ever begin in you and end in you; through Christ our Lord.
All: Amen.

Then the priest blesses the paintings or images of the stations:

P: Our help is in the name of the Lord.
All: Who made heaven and earth.
P: The Lord be with you.
All: May He also be with you.

Let us pray.
Almighty everlasting God, who do not forbid us to carve or paint

likenesses of your saints, in order that whenever we look at them with our bodily eyes we may call to mind their holy lives, and resolve to follow in their footsteps; may it please you to bless and to hallow these images, which have been made in memory and honor of the Sorrowful Virgin and Mother of God. And grant that all who in their presence pay devout homage to the sorrows which the blessed Virgin Mary endured throughout the life, suffering, and death of her only-begotten Son, our Lord Jesus
Christ, may by her merits and pleading obtain your grace in this life and everlasting glory in the life to come; through Christ our Lord.
All: Amen.

The priest puts incense into the thurible and blesses it. And taking the aspersory he sprinkles the images with holy water, saying:

Purify me with hyssop, Lord, and I shall be clean of sin. Wash me, and I shall be whiter than snow.

Then taking the thurible he incenses them without saying anything. In a private oratory the incensation may be omitted.

After the blessing of the images the priest, accompanied by the clergy, goes in procession to the place where the first station is to be erected. The procession is led by the cross-bearer (who walks between two acolytes carrying lighted candles). The priest kisses the first image and then hangs it in place, either himself or with the help of another cleric. He then reads the meditation and prayers proper to this station; and the same is done at the other stations. After this he proceeds to the shrine or the image of the Sorrowful Mother, during which time the Stabat Mater is sung. At the shrine the priest says:

P: Pray for us, O Virgin of many sorrows.

All: That we may be worthy of Christ's promise.

Let us pray.
O God, during whose passion, as Simeon had foretold, a sword of

sorrow pierced the tender heart of the glorious Virgin and Mother Mary; mercifully grant that we who meditate on her sufferings may attain the blessed effect of your passion. We ask this of you who live and reign forever and ever.
All: Amen.

Next the Te Deum is sung, along with its versicles and oration.

Then the priest kneels and invokes the help of the Sorrowful Mother, saying the following words three times:

P: Virgin, most sorrowful.

All: Pray for us.

Lastly the priest goes up to the altar predella, and turning toward the people blesses them with the words:

Together with her beloved Son, may Mary, Virgin most sorrowful, bless us.

BLESSING AND INVESTITURE WITH SCAPULAR OF BLESSED TRINITY

(Formerly reserved to the Order of the Holy Trinity for the Ransoming of Captives)

The one who is to receive the scapular is kneeling. The priest, vested in surplice and white stole, says:

P: Our help is in the name of the Lord.
All: Who made heaven and earth.
P: The Lord be with you.
All: May He also be with you.

Let us pray.
Lord Jesus Christ, who condescended to clothe yourself in our mortal nature, we beg you in your boundless goodness to bless

this garment which our holy fathers have sanctioned for those who renounce the world, in token of the innocence and humility which should be theirs. May this servant of yours, who is to wear it, likewise put on you. We ask this of you who live and reign forever and ever.
All: Amen.

He sprinkles the scapular with holy water; then continues:

P: Our help is in the name of the Lord.

All: Who made heaven and earth.

P: The Lord be with you.

All: May He also be with you.

Let us pray.
Hear, Lord, our humble entreaties, and be pleased to bless   this servant of yours, whom we invest in your name with the religious garb of the Most Holy Trinity. May he (she), by your bounty, persevere in piety and deserve to attain everlasting life; through Christ our Lord.
All: Amen.

Then he invests the person with the scapular, saying:

Take this garb of the Most Holy Trinity. May it help you to grow in faith, hope, and charity; in the name of the Father, and of the Son, and of the Holy Spirit.
All: Amen.

P: The Lord be with you.

All: May He also be with you.

Let us pray.
Almighty everlasting God, who enable us, your servants, in our profession of the true faith, to acknowledge the glory of the three

Persons in the eternal Godhead, and to adore their oneness of nature, their co-equal majesty; grant, we pray, that by steadfastness in that faith we may ever be guarded against all adversity.

God, whom it has pleased to found, through your saints John and Felix, the Order of the Most Holy Trinity for ransoming captives from the power of the Saracens; grant, we pray, that by their merits and intercession, and by your aid, this servant of yours may be delivered from the slavery of both body and soul; through Christ our Lord.
All: Amen.

May the Blessed Trinity add you to the number of the brothers and sisters of our confraternity. And although we are unworthy of admitting you, yet we fervently pray that the Most Holy Trinity may help you to lead a good life, and to persevere in your resolution. And as today brotherly love joins us in a spiritual bond here on earth, so may the divine goodness, in whom all love has its origin and its growth, be pleased to unite us with His faithful in heaven; through Christ our Lord.

All: Amen.

Then he gives the blessing:

May the peace and blessing of almighty God, Father, Son, and Holy Spirit, come upon you and remain with you forever.

All: Amen.

BLESSING OF THE ROSARY OR TRISAGION OF THE MOST HOLY TRINITY

P: Our help is in the name of the Lord.
All: Who made heaven and earth.
P: The Lord be with you.
All: May He also be with you.

Let us pray.

Almighty and merciful God, whom it pleased to reveal the mystery of the Blessed Trinity through your only-begotten Son, and through the prophets and the apostles, so that we on earth, imitating the choirs of holy angels might offer devout and worthy praise to you; we appeal to your goodness, asking that you bless and hallow   these rosaries (this rosary), which the Church has sanctioned for the honor and praise of the Most Holy Trinity. Let them (it) be endowed with such power of the Holy   Spirit, that whoever carries one on his person or reverently keeps it in his home, or devoutly recites it may be protected by you from every danger to body and soul. Let him (her) share in all the graces, privileges and indulgences granted by the Holy See; and in the hour of death let him (her) deserve to be presented by your holy angels at the throne of your divine majesty; through Christ our Lord.

All: Amen.

They (it) are (is) sprinkled with holy water.

BLESSING AND INVESTITURE WITH THE BLACK SCAPULAR OF OUR LORD'S SACRED CROSS AND PASSION

(Formerly reserved to the Congregation of Passionists)

The one who is to receive the scapular is kneeling. The priest, vested in surplice and red stole, says:

P: Our help is in the name of the Lord.
All: Who made heaven and earth.
P: The Lord be with you.
All: May He also be with you.

Let us pray.
Lord Jesus Christ, who, in order to redeem the world, willed to be born of a woman, submit to circumcision, to be rejected by the Jews and betrayed by the traitor, Judas, with a kiss; to be bound in

chains and led as an innocent Lamb to the slaughter; wantonly made a spectacle of in the presence of Annas and Caiphas, Pilate and Herod; accused by false witnesses; tormented with scourges and indignities; spat upon, crowned with thorns, struck with a reed, blindfolded, stripped of your garments, nailed to the cross, and pierced with a lance. O Lord, by these your sacred sufferings and by your holy cross and death, enlighten your servant's mind and inflame his (her) heart, so that, imbued with your tender charity, he (she) may ever shed tears of compunction, love you with all his (her) heart, and devote himself (herself) wholly to whatever pleases you. We ask this of you who live and reign with God the Father, in the unity of the Holy Spirit, God, forever and ever.
All: Amen.

The foregoing prayers may be omitted at will. Then the priest says:

P: Our help is in the name of the Lord.
All: Who made heaven and earth.
P: Blessed be the name of the Lord.
All: Both now and forevermore.
P: Lord, heed my prayer.
All: And let my cry be heard by you.
P: The Lord be with you.
All: May He also be with you.

Let us pray.
Lord Jesus Christ, who condescended to clothe yourself in our mortal nature, we humbly beg you to bless and to hallow this garment, designed as a reminder of you sacred passion and death. May this servant of yours, who is to wear it, have a part in your suffering, and so deserve to attain the glory of heaven. We ask this of you who live and reign forever and ever.
All: Amen.

Next the priest sprinkles the scapular with holy water and then clothes the person with it, saying:

May the Lord clothe you as a new man, so that, wearing this insignia of a sorrowing penitent, you may keep your eyes fixed on

Jesus who was crucified at the hands of wicked men, and mourn over Him with a grief befitting the death of God's firstborn Son.
All: Amen.

The priest continues:

By the faculty granted me I make you a partaker of all the spiritual benefits which the Congregation of Passionists enjoys by privilege of the Holy See; in the name of the Father, and of the Son, and of the Holy Spirit.
All: Amen.

In conclusion he adds:

May the passion of our Lord Jesus Christ be ever in our hearts.
Amen.

BLESSING AND INVESTITURE WITH THE RED SCAPULAR OF OUR LORD'S PASSION AND SACRED HEART, AND OF THE IMMACULATE VIRGIN'S LOVING AND COMPASSIONATE HEART

(Formerly reserved to the Congregation of the Missions)

(Approved by the Congregation of Sacred Rites, June 25, 1847)

The one who is to receive the scapular is kneeling. The priest, vested in surplice and red stole, says:

P: Our help is in the name of the Lord.
All: Who made heaven and earth.
P: The Lord be with you.
All: May He also be with you.

Let us pray.

Lord Jesus Christ, who condescended to clothe yourself in our mortal nature, and to despoil yourself, taking the form of a servant and becoming obedient, even to the death of the cross; we humbly beg you in your boundless goodness to bless this garment, designed as a reminder of your bitter passion and of your Sacred Heart, as well as a reminder of the loving and compassionate heart of your immaculate Mother. May this servant of yours, who is to wear it, all the better meditate on these mysteries; and may he (she), by the merits and prayers of the blessed Virgin Mary, likewise put on you. We ask this of you who live and reign forever and ever.

All: Amen.

Then the priest sprinkles the scapular with holy water, and invests the person with it, saying:

Take, dear brother (sister), this sacred garb, and divesting yourself of the old man, put on the new man. May you wear it with honor and thus attain everlasting life.

All: Amen.

Then the priest continues:

By the faculty granted me I make you a partaker of all the spiritual benefits with which this holy scapular is endowed by privilege of the Holy See; in the name of the Father, and of the Son, and of the Holy Spirit.

All: Amen.

In conclusion the following versicle is said three times:

We therefore implore you to save your servants whom your precious blood redeemed.

BLESSING AND INVESTITURE WITH THE BLUE SCAPULAR OF THE IMMACULATE VIRGIN MARY

(Formerly reserved to the Theatines, Clerks Regular)

The one who is to receive the scapular is kneeling. The priest, vested in surplice and white stole, says:

P: Our help is in the name of the Lord
All: Who made heaven and earth.
P: The Lord be with you.
All: May He also be with you.

Let us pray.
Lord Jesus Christ, who condescended to clothe yourself in our mortal nature, we humbly beg you in your boundless goodness to bless this garment, designed in honor and memory of the Immaculate Conception of the blessed Virgin Mary, and as a reminder for those who wear it to pray for the conversion of sinners. May this servant of yours, who is to wear it, by the merits and prayers of the blessed Virgin Mary, likewise put on you. We ask this of you who live and reign forever and ever.
All: Amen.

The priest sprinkles the scapular(s) with holy water, without saying anything; and then invests the person(s) with it, saying to each one:

Take, dear brother (sister), this scapular of the Immaculate Conception of the blessed Virgin Mary, so that by her intercession you may divest yourself of the old man, and be cleansed from every stain of sin. May you keep it spotless and thus attain everlasting life; through Christ our Lord.
All: Amen.

The priest continues:

By the faculty granted me, I make you a partaker of all the spiritual benefits which the Congregation of Clerks Regular enjoys by God's grace and the privilege of the Holy See; in the name of the Father, and of the Son, and of the Holy Spirit.
All: Amen.

Then he kneels, and together with the person(s) just enrolled he says the following prayers three times:

Let praise and thanksgiving be offered at every moment to the holy and godly sacrament.

Blessed be the holy and immaculate conception of the blessed Virgin Mary, Mother of God.

The faithful should be urged to repeat these praises over and over, in order to gain the indulgences attached thereto. (Decree of Pius VII, June 30, 1818; Brief of Leo XIII, Sept. 10, 1878; Decree of Pius X, April 10, 1913).

BLESSING AND INVESTITURE WITH THE BLACK SCAPULAR OF OUR LADY OF SORROWS

(Formerly reserved to the Order of Servites)

The one who is to receive the scapular is kneeling. The priest, vested in surplice and white stole, says:

P: Our help is in the name of the Lord.
All: Who made heaven and earth.
P: The Lord be with you.
All: May He also be with you.

Almighty everlasting God, whom it pleased to lift up a fallen world by the death of your only-begotten Son, in order to deliver us from everlasting condemnation, and to lead us to the joys of the kingdom of heaven; we beg you to look with favor on this family of your servants, founded in the name of the blessed Virgin of the Seven Sorrows, of which family this servant of yours wishes to be a member. Let the number of those who faithfully serve you be increased. Let this candidate be delivered from all vexations of the world and of the flesh and of the snares of the devil; and by the prayers of the blessed Virgin Mary, of St. Augustine, of St. Philip, and of the seven holy fathers and founders of our Order, may he

(she) attain the true joys that last forever; through Christ our Lord.
All: Amen.

Turning to the scapular which lies on the altar the priest says:

Let us pray.

Lord Jesus Christ, who condescended to clothe yourself in our
mortal nature, we humbly beg you in your boundless goodness to
bless this garment, which our holy fathers have sanctioned to be
worn by us in token of innocence and lowliness, and in memory of
the Seven Sorrows of the blessed Virgin Mary. May he (she), who
is to wear it, likewise put on you, our Savior, in body and soul. We
ask this of you who live and reign forever and ever.
All: Amen.

He sprinkles the scapular with holy water, saying:

Purify me with hyssop, Lord, and I shall be clean of sin. Wash me,
and I shall be whiter than snow.

Then he blesses the rosary of the Seven Sorrows, using the prayer
"Almighty and merciful God" given below; and he sprinkles the
rosary with holy water.

After this he invests the person (who is kneeling before him) with
the scapular, saying:

Take, dear brother (sister), this habit of the blessed Virgin
Mary, the special badge of her servants, as a reminder of the Seven
Sorrows she endured during the life and death of her only-begotten
Son. And having been invested with it, may you by her patronage
attain everlasting life.
All: Amen.

Then he hands the rosary to the person, saying:

Take the rosary of the blessed Virgin Mary, designed to
commemorate her Seven Sorrows. As your lips utter her praises,

may your heart fully commiserate with her in her sufferings.
All: Amen.

Lastly he blesses the person(s), saying:

May the blessing of almighty God, Father, Son, and Holy Spirit,
come upon you and remain with you forever.
All: Amen.

BLESSING OF THE ROSARY OF THE SEVEN SORROWS

(Formerly reserved to the Order of Servites)

The priest, vested in surplice and white stole, says:

P: Our help is in the name of the Lord.
All: Who made heaven and earth.
P: The Lord be with you.
All: May He also be with you.

Let us pray.
Almighty and merciful God, who, out of exceeding love for us,
willed that your only-begotten Son, our Lord Jesus Christ, come
down on earth for our salvation, taking our flesh and submitting to
the torment of the cross; we humbly beg you in your boundless
goodness to bless   and to hallow this rosary, which your faithful
Church has consecrated to the memory of the Seven Sorrows of the
Mother of your Son. Let it be endowed with such power of the
Holy   Spirit, that whoever recites it, or carries it on his person, or
reverently keeps it in his home, may always and everywhere in this
life be shielded from all enemies, visible and invisible, and at the
hour of death attain the grace of being presented to you by the
blessed Virgin Mary, crowned with the aureole of good works
through Christ our Lord.
All: Amen.

The priest sprinkles the rosary with holy water.

SHORT FORM FOR BLESSING THE ROSARY OF THE SEVEN SORROWS

(Formerly reserved to the Order of Servites)

(Approved by the Congregation of Sacred Rites, Feb. 11, 1925)

This form may be used only in a private manner, whenever through force of circumstances it would be very inconvenient to use the longer form.

May this rosary be blessed and hallowed ~ for the praise and glory of the Virgin Mary, Mother of God, and in memory of the sorrows she endured during the life and death of her Son, our Lord Jesus Christ; in the name of the Father, and of the Son, and of the Holy Spirit.
All: Amen.

BLESSING AND INVESTITURE WITH SCAPULAR OF OUR LADY OF MOUNT CARMEL

(Formerly reserved to the Order of Discalced Carmelites)

The person who is to receive the scapular is kneeling. The priest vested in surplice and white stole, says:

The antiphon, versicles, and the prayer "May Christ," etc., for all of which see below. Then he adds the following versicles and oration:

P: Our help is in the name of the Lord.
All: Who made heaven and earth.
P: Blessed be the name of the Lord.
All: Both now and forevermore.

P: Lord, heed my prayer.
All: And let my cry be heard by you.
P: The Lord be with you.
All: May He also be with you.

Let us pray.
Almighty God and everlasting Father, who willed that your only-begotten Son be clothed in our mortal nature, we humbly beg you in your boundless goodness to let your blessing flow out on this garment, which our holy fathers have sanctioned to be worn by those who renounce the world, in token of innocence and lowliness. Let it please you to endow it with such blessing,   that he (she), who is to wear it, may likewise put on our Lord Jesus Christ, your Son, who lives and reigns with you, in the unity of the Holy Spirit, God, forever and ever.
All: Amen.

Then he says the prayer "We earnestly beg you," etc., see below; after which he sprinkles the habit with holy water. If only the habit is to be blessed, the blessing begins with the versicle Our help etc. (see above) and concludes with the aforementioned prayer "We earnestly beg you," etc. As he invests the person with the habit he says: "Take, dear brother," etc. (see below); after which he adds:

Lord, hear our humble entreaties, and help this servant of yours, whom we enroll in the holy sodality of the Carmelites, to be ever constant and true to his (her) proposal, and to serve you in all holiness. Protect your servant, Lord, with the saving grace of peace; and as he (she) confides himself (herself) to the patronage of blessed Mary, ever a Virgin, let him (her) be safe from all adversaries.

Then he blesses the new member with the sign of the cross, using the prayer "May almighty God," etc., below.

He sprinkles the person with holy water; after which he adds:

By the delegated power which I enjoy, I receive you into the confraternity of the holy order of Carmelites, and enroll you as a

partaker of all the spiritual benefits of this order; in the name of the Father, and of the Son, and of the Holy Spirit.
All: Amen.

(See the concluding rubric regarding the admonition on p. 692)

ANOTHER BLESSING AND INVESTITURE
WITH SCAPULAR OF OUR LADY OF MOUNT CARMEL

(Formerly reserved to the Order of Discalced Carmelites)

The person who is to receive the scapular is kneeling. The priest, vested in surplice and whitestole, says:

Antiphon: O God, we ponder your kindness within your temple. * As your name, O God, so also your praise reaches to the ends of the earth. Your right hand is full of justice.

Psalm 47

Psalm 132

P: Behold, how good it is, and how pleasant, * where brethren dwell at one!

All: It is as when the precious ointment upon the head runs down over the beard, the beard of Aaron, * till it runs down upon the collar of his robe.

P: It is a dew like that of Hermon, * which comes down upon the mountains of Sion;

All: For there the Lord has pronounced His blessing life forever.

P: Glory be to the Father.

All: As it was in the beginning.

All: Ant.: O God, we ponder your kindness within your temple. * As your name, O God, so also your praise reaches to the ends of the earth. Your right hand is full of justice.

P: Lord, have mercy. Christ, have mercy. Lord, have mercy. Our Father (the rest inaudibly until:)

P: And lead us not into temptation.

All: But deliver us from evil.

P: Save your servant.

All: Who trusts in you, my God.

P: Lord, send him (her) aid from your holy place.

All: And watch over him (her) from Sion.

P: Let the enemy have no power over him (her).

All: And the son of iniquity be powerless to harm him (her).

P: Lord, heed my prayer.
All: And let my cry be heard by you.
P: The Lord be with you.
All: May He also be with you.

Let us pray.
May Christ add you to the number of His faithful; and we, in spite of our unworthiness, include you in our prayers. May God, through His only-begotten Son, the Mediator of God and men, help you to live well, to do good, to persevere in your resolution, and to attain the inheritance of everlasting life. And as today brotherly love joins us in a spiritual bond here on earth, so may the divine goodness, in whom all love has its origin and its growth, be pleased to unite us with His faithful in heaven; through Christ our

Lord.

All: Amen.

Let us pray.
Hear, Lord, our humble entreaties, and be pleased to bless this servant of yours, whom we receive in your holy name as a member and a partaker of all the spiritual benefits of this holy order, dedicated in a special way to the blessed Virgin Mary, Mother of your Son. May he (she),by your bounty, remain loyal to the Church and make progress in virtue. Assisted by the prayers of Our holy order, may he (she) deserve to attain everlasting life. We ask this of you who live and reign forever and ever.
All: Amen.

Then turning to the habit he says:

P: Lord, show us your mercy.

All: And grant us your salvation.

P: Lord God of hosts, let us turn to you.

All: Show us your countenance and we will be saved.

P: Lord, heed my prayer.
All: And let my cry be heard by you.
P: The Lord be with you.
All: May He also be with you.

Let us pray.
We earnestly beg you, O Lord, to let your gracious blessing come on this garment, in which your servant is to be clothed. May it be blessed and endowed with your power to repel all vicious assaults of our visible and invisible enemies.
All: Amen.

Let us pray.
God, head of all the faithful and Savior of the human race, sanctify

by your right hand this habit, which is to be worn by your servant in love and devotion to you and your blessed Mother, Our Lady of Mount Carmel. Under your constant guidance let its mystical significance be preserved both in the body and soul of him (her) who is to wear it; and may he (she) happily attain, along with all your saints, the everlasting reward. We ask this of you who live and reign forever and ever.
All: Amen.

Let us pray.
Creator, preserver, and Savior of all men; God, the generous provider of man's well-being and the giver of all spiritual goods; pour out your blessing   on this habit, so that he (she) who is to wear it, aided from on high, may be filled with true faith, firm hope, desired charity, and may never be separated from you. We ask this of you who live and reign forever and ever.
All: Amen.

He sprinkles the habit with holy water, and invests the person with it, saying to each one:

Take, dear brother (sister), this blessed garment, and call on the most holy Virgin, that by her merits you may keep it spotless, be shielded by her from all adversity, and attain everlasting life.
All: Amen.

Then he continues:

By the power delegated to me, I receive you and enroll you as a partaker of all the prayers, penances, suffrages, almsdeeds, fasts, vigils, Masses, canonical hours, as well as all other spiritual favors which, by the merciful help of Jesus Christ, are performed day and night in various places by the members of our whole order; in the name of the Father, and of the Son,   and of the Holy Spirit.
All: Amen.

Then he blesses the new member with the sign of the cross, saying:

May almighty God, Maker of heaven and earth, bless you, He who

graciously chose you for the society and confraternity of Our Lady of Mount Carmel. We pray to her that in the hour of your death she will crush the head of your adversary, the serpent, so that you may finally and triumphantly possess the palm and crown of the everlasting inheritance; through Christ our Lord.
All: Amen.

Lastly he sprinkles the person with holy water.

If several are being received, the plural forms are used.

If only the habit is to be blessed, the blessing begins with the versicle "Lord, show us your mercy," and concludes with the prayer "Creator," etc.

At the end of the service the priest addresses a few but effectual Words of admonition to the newly enrolled member, to the effect that he order his life wisely and piously, and fulfill all the obligations, both those laid down in general for all tertiaries, as well as the special ones for members who desire to enjoy the so-called "Sabbatine" privileges (concerning which he should fully enlighten the party); moreover, that in future he be assiduous in honoring the Virgin Mother of God with devotions of a special nature, and dedicate himself in filial and sincere affection to her whom he regards in a special way as a most tender Mother.

THE SHORT FORM FOR BLESSING AND INVESTITURE
WITH THE SCAPULAR
OF OUR LADY OF MOUNT CARMEL

(Which can be used more conveniently by the officiating priest especially in a private investiture or when large numbers are being received.)

(Approved by the Congregation of Sacred Rites, July 24, 1888)

The one who is to receive the scapular is kneeling. The priest, vested in surplice and white stole or at least the latter, says:

P: Lord, show us your mercy.
All: And grant us your salvation.
P: Lord, heed my prayer.
All: And let my cry be heard by you.
P: The Lord be with you.
All: May He also be with you.

Let us pray.
Lord Jesus Christ, Savior of the human race, sanctify by your right hand this habit, which is to be worn by your servant in love and devotion to you and your blessed Mother, Our Lady of Mount Carmel. By her intercession may he (she) be defended from the evil foe and persevere in your grace until death. We ask this of you who live and reign forever and ever.

All: Amen.

Then he sprinkles the habit with holy water, and invests the person with it, saying to each one:

Take this blessed habit, and call on the most holy Virgin, that by her merits you may keep it spotless, be protected by her from all adversity, and attain everlasting life.
All: Amen.

By the power granted me I receive you as a partaker of all the spiritual favors which, by the merciful help of Jesus Christ, are enjoyed by the religious of the Order of Carmelites; in the name of the Father, and of the Son, and of the Holy Spirit.
All: Amen.

May almighty God, Creator of heaven and earth, bless you, He who graciously chose you for the confraternity of Our Lady of Mount Carmel. We pray to her that in the hour of your death she will crush the head of the ancient serpent, so that you may finally possess the palm and crown of the everlasting inheritance; through Christ our Lord.
All: Amen.

He sprinkles the person with holy water. If several are being received the plural forms are used. If only the habit is to be blessed, the blessing begins with the versicle Lord, show us your mercy, and concludes with the prayer Lord Jesus Christ, etc.

THE SHORT FORM FOR BLESSING AND INVESTITURE FOR THE FIVE FOLLOWING SCAPULARS:

Blessed Trinity, Our Lord's Sacred Passion, the Immaculate Virgin Mary, Our Lady of Sorrows, Our Lady of Mount Carmel

The ones who are to receive the scapulars are kneeling. The priest, vested in surplice and white stole, says:

P: Our help is in the name of the Lord.
All: Who made heaven and earth.
P: The Lord be with you.
All: May he also be with you.

Let us pray.
Lord Jesus Christ, head of all the faithful and Savior of the human race, who condescended to clothe yourself in our mortal nature, we humbly beg you in your boundless goodness to bless and to hallow these garments, designed in homage to the Most Blessed Trinity, in honor and in memory of your bitter passion, in honor of the Virgin Mother of God, under the titles of the Immaculate Conception, Our Lady of Sorrows, and Our Lady of Mount Carmel. Grant that those who are to wear them may deserve, by the intercession of your blessed Mother, likewise to put on you, our Savior, both in body and soul. We ask this of you who live and reign forever and ever.
All: Amen.

They are sprinkled with holy water. Then the priest invests each one singly with the scapulars, but he says the respective form only once for all in common:

1. Take this scapular of the Most Holy Trinity. May it help you to grow in faith, hope, and charity, so that you may put on the new man, created in the likeness of God in holiness and righteousness.

2. Take this scapular of the passion of our Lord Jesus Christ, and divesting yourself of the old man, put on the new man. May you wear it with honor and thus attain everlasting life.

3. Take this scapular of the devoted servants of the blessed Virgin Mary conceived without sin, so that by her intercession you may be cleansed from every stain of sin and attain everlasting life.

4. Take this scapular of the devoted servants of Our Lady of the Seven Sorrows; and by diligent meditation on her sorrows may you be marked in heart and body with the passion of our Lord Jesus Christ, and ever remain steadfast in your devotion.

5. Take this habit of the society and confraternity of Our Lady of Mount Carmel, and call on the most holy Virgin, so that by her merits you may keep it spotless, be shielded by her from all adversity, and attain everlasting life.

By the faculty delegated to me by the Holy See, I make you partakers of all the spiritual favors of these orders and congregations, as well as the indulgences granted by privilege of the Holy See to these scapulars; in the name of the Father, and of the Son, and of the Holy Spirit.
All: Amen.

P: Save your servants.

All: Who trust in you, my God.

P: Lord, send them aid from your holy place.

All: And watch over them from Sion.

P: Let them find in you, Lord, a fortified tower.

All: In the face of the enemy.

P: Let the enemy have no power over them.

All: And the son of iniquity be powerless to harm them.

P: Lord, heed my prayer.
All: And let my cry be heard by you.
P: The Lord be with you.
All: May He also be with you.

Let us pray.
Lord, hear our humble prayers, and be pleased to bless those on whom we have bestowed these sacred habits in your name. May they co-operate with your grace, and thus deserve to attain everlasting life; through Christ our Lord. All: Amen. May the blessing of almighty God, Father, Son, and Holy Spirit, come upon you and remain with you forever.
All: Amen.

The singular form is used if the scapulars are bestowed on one person only.

BLESSING OF THE SCAPULAR OF THE PRECIOUS BLOOD

This scapular should be made of wool dyed red, and it should have on it an image of the crucifixion or one of our Lord's Sacred Heart with blood flowing into a chalice.

The one who is to receive the scapular is kneeling. The priest, vested in surplice and red stole, says:

P: Our help is in the name of the Lord.

All: Who made heaven and earth.

P: You have redeemed us, Lord, in your blood.

All: You have made us to reign with our God.

P: We therefore implore you to save your servants.

All: Whom your precious blood has redeemed.

P: Lord, heed my prayer.
All: And let my cry be heard by you.
P: The Lord be with you.
All: May He also be with you.

Let us pray.
Almighty God and everlasting Father, who willed that your only-begotten Son be clothed in our mortal nature, and shed His precious blood for the salvation of the world; we humbly beg you in your boundless goodness to bless and to hallow   this garment, designed as a sign of the faithful's devotion to the price of our redemption. Let him (her), who is to wear it, deserve likewise to put on this same Lord Jesus Christ, your Son, who lives and reigns with you, in the unity of the Holy Spirit, God, forever and ever.
All: Amen.

It is sprinkled with holy water.

BLESSING OF CORDS AND SASHES OF THE PRECIOUS BLOOD

The sashes are made of wool dyed red: and if they are worn outwardly by women they ought to hang on the left. The cords too are made of wool dyed red. The versicles and responses are the same as Blessing of the Scapular of the Precious Blood; they are followed by this prayer.

Let us pray:

Almighty everlasting God, who appointed your only-begotten Son the Redeemer of the human race, and willed to be appeased by His blood; increase our love of you, and be pleased to pour out your

blessing on these cords (or sashes). Let him (her) who is to be girl with one know compunction for his (her) sins in this life, be delivered from every sin of the flesh and all dangers to body and soul, and finally attain everlasting life; through Christ our Lord.
All: Amen.

They are sprinkled with holy water.

BLESSING OF A VOTIVE GARB OF THE PRECIOUS BLOOD

This garb is black in color.

The versicles and responses are the same as Blessing of the Scapular of the Precious Blood; and they are followed by this prayer:

Let us pray.
Holy Lord, almighty Father, everlasting God, from whom every good and every gift descends on us, we offer you our thanks for having heard our prayers. By the merits of the precious blood of your beloved Son, our Lord Jesus Christ, and by the prayers of the blessed Virgin Mary, bestow on your servant who is to wear this garment well-being in body and mind. Help her to worship you in true faith as the Creator of all things; strengthen her hope in your only-begotten Son, Redeemer of the world; help her to love you above all else as the supreme good and to keep your holy commandments, until it becomes her happy lot to attain everlasting glory; through Christ our Lord.
All: Amen.

It is sprinkled with holy water.

BLESSING AND INVESTITURE WITH SCAPULAR OF THE SACRED HEART OF JESUS

(Approved by the Congregation of Sacred Rites, April 4, 1900)

The one who is to receive the scapular is kneeling. The priest, in surplice and white stole, says:

P: Our help is in the name of the Lord.
All: Who made heaven and earth.
P: Lord, show us your mercy.
All: And grant us your salvation.
P: Lord, heed my prayer.
All: And let my cry be heard by you.
P: The Lord be with you.
All: May He also be with you.

Let us pray.
Lord Jesus, who in a singular outpouring of love opened to your spouse, the Church, the indescribable treasures of your heart, be pleased to bless this scapular, ornamented with the emblem of your heart. Grant that whoever will devoutly wear it may, by the prayers of Mary, your most gracious and blessed Mother, deserve to be enriched with gifts and powers from on high. We ask this of you who live and reign forever and ever.
All: Amen.

Then the priest sprinkles the scapular with holy water, and invests the person with it, saying:

Take, dear brother (sister), this scapular of the Sacred Heart of Jesus; and thus adorned in honor and in memory of His love and sacred passion, may you deserve, by the prayers of the blessed Virgin Mary, Mother of mercy, to have the fulness of divine grace and the reward of never ending glory; through Christ our Lord.
All: Amen.

If the scapular is bestowed on several, the plural form is used. Lastly the priest says only once the following invocations, with the newly enrolled members joining in:

Jesus, meek and humble of heart, let my heart resemble yours.

Mary, Mother of grace and Mother of mercy, protect us from the enemy and receive us in the hour of our death.

BLESSING AND INVESTITURE WITH SCAPULAR OF THE IMMACULATE HEART OF MARY

The one who is to receive the scapular is kneeling. The priest, vested in surplice and white stole, says:

The antiphon, versicles and responses, and the prayer "May Christ receive you," etc. are the same as under Another Blessing and Investiture with Scapular of Our Lady of Mount Carmel. After these come the following versicles and prayer:

P: Our help is in the name of the Lord.
All: Who made heaven and earth.
P: The Lord be with you.
All: May He also be with you.

Let us pray.
God, by whose word all things are hallowed, pour out your blessing   on this habit (these habits); and grant that whoever will wear it in accord with your will and your law, as well as in gratitude to you, may, in calling on your holy name, be rewarded with health in body and protection of soul; through Christ our Lord.
All: Amen.

Lastly he sprinkles the scapular with holy water, and invests the person with it, saying:

Take, dear brother (sister), this blessed habit, and call on the most holy Virgin, so that by hermerits you may keep it spotless, be shielded by her from all adversity, and attain everlasting life.
All: Amen.

BLESSING AND INVESTITURE WITH SCAPULAR OF THE SACRED HEARTS OF JESUS AND MARY

The one who is to receive the scapular is kneeling; the priest, vested in surplice and white stole, says: first, the versicles and responses is given above, No. 18; then he adds the following:

Let us pray.
Merciful God, who for the salvation of sinners and a refuge for the afflicted willed that the heart of your Son, Jesus Christ, be full of love and mercy, and likewise the heart of the blessed Virgin Mary; be pleased to bless this scapular, which is to be worn in honor and in memory of the Sacred Hearts of Jesus and Mary. Grant that this servant of yours in wearing it may, by the prayers and merits of the Virgin and Mother of God, come to resemble the heart of Jesus; through Christ our Lord.
All: Amen.

Then the priest sprinkles the scapular with holy water, and invests the person with it, saying:

Take, dear brother (sister), this scapular of the Sacred Hearts of Jesus and Mary. Let it be for you a safeguard and shield, so that, in meditating on the virtues of their hearts and seeking to imitate them, you may be worthy of the glorious resurrection; through Christ our Lord.
All: Amen.

If the scapular is bestowed on several, the plural forms are used. Lastly the priest says only once the following invocations, with the newly enrolled members joining in:

Most Sacred Heart of Jesus, have mercy on us.

Immaculate Heart of Mary, pray for us.

BLESSING AND INVESTITURE WITH SCAPULAR OF OUR LADY OF RANSOM

(Formerly reserved to the Order of Our Lady of Mercy for

Ransoming Captives)

The one who is to receive the scapular is kneeling. The priest, vested in surplice and white stole, says: first, the versicles and responses as given under No. 18; then he adds the following:

Let us pray.
Lord Jesus Christ, who condescended to clothe yourself in our mortal nature, we beg you in your boundless goodness to bless his garment, which our holy fathers have sanctioned to be worn in token of innocence and holiness. May he (she), who is to wear it, deserve likewise to put on you, who live and reign forever and ever.
All: Amen.

Then he sprinkles the habit with holy water, and invests the person with it, saying:

By the power of our Lord Jesus Christ and that of the apostles Peter and Paul, which has been granted to me, I present you with the habit of the Order of Our Lady of Mercy. This is done in recognition of your devotion to the most holy and immaculate Mary, Mother of God, as well as to the order founded in her name. And having been so enrolled, may it be your good fortune to have the grace of the Holy Spirit in this life, and everlasting glory, the reward of the elect, in the life to come; in the name of the Father, and of the Son, and of the Holy Spirit.

All: Amen.

Then the "Veni Creator" is said), followed by the versicle:

P: Send forth your Spirit and all things shall be recreated.

All: And you shall renew the face of the earth.

P: Save your servant.

All: Who trusts in you, my God.

P: The Lord be with you.

All: May He also be with you.

Let us pray.
Lord, hear our humble prayers, and be pleased to bless this servant of yours whom we clothe in your holy name with the habit of the Order of Our Lady of Mercy. He (she) deserves out of piety to wear it as long as he (she) lives, so that by your bountiful help he (she) may remain loyal to your Church, and finally attain everlasting life through Christ our Lord.
All: Amen.

BLESSING OF THE SAME SCAPULAR WITHOUT THE INVESTITURE

(Formerly reserved to the same Order)

The priest, vested in surplice and white stole, says: first, the versicles as given under No. 18; then he adds the following prayers:

Lord Jesus Christ, who condescended to clothe yourself in our mortal nature, we beg you in your boundless goodness to bless this garment which our holy fathers have sanctioned to be worn in token of innocence and humility. May he (she), who is to wear it, likewise put on you. We ask this of you who live and reign forever and ever.
All: Amen.

Let us pray.
Father of mercy and God of all consolation, you manifest above all how wonderful you are and how worthy of all praise in the gifts you have conferred on the most holy Virgin, Mother of your only-begotten Son. You have given her to us as our merciful Mother, raising her up to be the ransomer of captives, thus showing how it pleases you to be glorified in her. And so we humbly appeal to your kindness, asking that you graciously pour out your blessing

on every part of this scapular, designed to venerate the holy Virgin. Grant that whoever offers her due veneration may experience the powerful aid of this heavenly patron, along with your tender mercy both in this life and the life to come; through Christ our Lord.
All: Amen.

Let us pray.
Lord God of clemency, who made the blessed Virgin Mary, the exalted Mother of your Son, shine forth forever in white-robed splendor and glorious array; we beg you to bless this white garment, dedicated to the honor of the Virgin Mother, under the title of Help of Captives. Grant that whoever will wear it devoutly may be delivered from all evil, and deserve finally to be robed with the garment of heavenly glory; through Christ our Lord.
All: Amen.

It is sprinkled with holy water.

BLESSING AND INVESTITURE WITH SCAPULAR OF OUR LADY, HEALTH OF THE SICK

(Formerly reserved to Clerks Regular for Care of the Sick)

The one who is to receive the scapular is kneeling. The priest, vested in surplice and white stole, says:

P: Our help is in the name of the Lord.
All: Who made heaven and earth.
P: The Lord be with you.
All: May He also be with you.

Let us pray.
Lord, we beg you to bless   this garment, and to grant that whoever will wear it in honor of Mary, God's holy Mother, who is the health of the sick, may enjoy well-being in body and mind, and be led in the hour of death to everlasting life; through Christ our Lord.
All: Amen.

It is sprinkled with holy water. After this the little red crosses that are to be attached to the scapulars are blessed:

P: Our help is in the name of the Lord.
All: Who made heaven and earth.
P: The Lord be with you.
All: May He also be with you.

Let us pray.
Lord, bless   these crosses, that they may prove a saving remedy for the faithful; and grant that in calling on your holy name all who are to wear them may experience health m body and protection in soul; through Christ our Lord.
All: Amen.

Let us pray.
Almighty everlasting God, who consecrated the cross with the precious blood of your Son, and willed to redeem the world by the death on this cross of Jesus Christ, your Son, who delivered the human race from the tyranny of the ancient foe by the power of this sacred cross; we humbly appeal to your kindness, asking that you bless these crosses and impart to them your heavenly grace and power. May he (she) who carries them on his (her) person deserve to have an abundance of heavenly grace, and to have Christ as the defender against all artifices of the devil. We ask this of Him who lives and reigns with you and the Holy Spirit forever and ever.
All: Amen.

They are sprinkled with holy water. After this the rosary of the dying is blessed:

P: Our help is in the name of the Lord.

All: Who made heaven and earth.

P: You have crowned the year with your bounty.

All: And the fields are filled with the fruits of the earth. p

Lord, heed my prayer.

All: And let my cry be heard by you.

P: The Lord be with you.

All: May He also be with you.

Let us pray.
Lord Jesus Christ, who willed to become man, to sojourn in the world, to suffer so much for the salvation of mankind, even submitting to death on the cross; be pleased, we pray, to bless and to hallow this rosary. May he (she), who will devoutly carry it on his (her) person and faithfully recite it, be enriched with your many graces and favors, and deserve to obtain an everlasting crown in heaven. May all the faithful the wide world over, who are suffering the last agony, be strengthened by your compassion, and thus come to share in your everlasting glory and splendor. We ask this through you, Jesus Christ, Savior of the world, who live and reign with God the Father, in the unity of the Holy Spirit, God, forever and ever.
All: Amen.

The rosary is sprinkled with holy water. Next he receives the person into this pious confraternity, saying:

P: Our help is in the name of the Lord.
All: Who made heaven and earth.
P: The Lord be with you.
All: May He also be with you.

Let us pray.
Almighty and merciful God, we humbly implore you to give health of body and soul to the members of this pious sodality, as often as they invoke the help of the blessed Virgin Mary, Health of the Sick, through Christ our Lord.
All: Amen.

Let us pray.

God, who in your indescribable providence chose to elect St. Joseph as spouse of your holy Mother, and appointed him, along with the immaculate Virgin, a patron of the dying; grant that by his prayers we may in the hour of death invoke your holy name and the name of Mary, and so deserve to enter into everlasting rest. We ask this of you who live and reign forever and ever.
All: Amen.

God, who endowed St. Camillus with the gift of extraordinary charity, making him the father of a new offspring for the care of the sick; grant by his merits and prayers that all who suffer from bodily illness may finally obtain everlasting health of soul; through Christ our Lord.
All: Amen.

Then he presents the scapular, saying to each one:

Take, dear brother (sister), this garment, the special emblem of the pious sodality of Our Lady, Health of the Sick, and of St. Joseph and St. Camillus; and wear it under their patronage so that you may come to everlasting life.
All: Amen.

Lastly he presents the rosary, saying to each one:

Take this rosary of our Lord Jesus Christ, which has been woven as a memorial of His passion. And as you utter His praises may all who are in their last agony bear their sufferings patiently, and finally attain everlasting life; through Christ our Lord.
All: Amen.

May the peace and blessing of almighty God, Father, Son, and Holy Spirit, come upon you and remain with you forever.
All: Amen.

BLESSING AND INVESTITURE WITH SCAPULAR OF OUR LADY OF GOODCOUNSEL

(Formerly reserved to the Hermits of St. Augustine)

(Approved by the Congregation of Sacred Rites, Dec. 21, 1893)

* This scapular is made in the usual way of two pieces of white wool joined together by double cords or bands. One part has an image of the Blessed Virgin made of silk or similar material, with the lettering: "Mother of Good Counsel," as venerated at the shrine of Genazzano. The other part has the papal arms, namely, the tiara with the keys, and the lettering: "Child, follow her counsel" (Leo XIII).

The one who is to receive the scapular is kneeling. The priest, vested in surplice and white stole, says: first, the versicles as given on which he says the following:

Let us pray.
Lord Jesus Christ, who by your incarnation dwelt among men as the Angel of Great Counsel and the Wonderful Counsellor; be pleased to bless   this scapular of Our Lady of Good Counsel. May all who are to wear this emblem be empowered by you to follow right counsel and so come to enjoy the good things of eternity. We ask this of you who live and reign forever and ever.
All: Amen.

Then he sprinkles the scapular with holy water, and invests the person with it, saying:

Take, dear brother (sister)   this emblem of the blessed Virgin Mary, Mother of Good Counsel; and by her inspiration may you always do whatever is pleasing to God, and so deserve to be numbered among His elect; through Christ our Lord.
All: Amen.

The priest continues:

P: Pray for us, O Mother of Good Counsel.

All: That we may be worthy of Christ's promise.

Let us pray.
God, who gave us the Mother of your beloved Son as our Mother,
and made her beautiful image renowned by a wondrous apparition;
grant, we pray, that we may ever follow her admonitions, and so be
disposed to pass our lives in accord with your divine heart, and
come happily to our heavenly home; through Christ our Lord.
All: Amen.

BLESSING AND INVESTITURE WITH SCAPULAR OF ST. JOSEPH, SPOUSE OF MARY AND PATRON OF THE UNIVERSAL CHURCH

(Formerly reserved to the Order of Friars Minor Capuchin)

(Approved by the Congregation of Sacred Rites on April 18, 1893)

The one who is to receive the scapular is kneeling. The priest,
vested in surplice and white stole, says:

P: Our help is in the name of the Lord.
All: Who made heaven and earth.
P: The Lord be with you.
All: May He also be with you.

Let us pray.
Lord Jesus Christ, who willed to be given over to the custody of St.
Joseph, spouse of Mary, your immaculate Mother, be pleased to
bless this garment, designed as a safeguard for the faithful of your
Church. Grant that this servant of yours may serve you steadfastly
and devoutly, under the protection of St. Joseph. We ask this of
you who live and reign forever and ever.
All: Amen.

The priest sprinkles the scapular with holy water, and invests the
person with it, saying:

Take, dear brother (sister), this scapular of St. Joseph, spouse of

the blessed Virgin Mary; and having him as a guardian and protector, may you be defended from the wickedness of the devil, and finally attain everlasting life; through Christ our Lord.
All: Amen.

Lastly the priest kneels and says three times the following invocation, with the newly enrolled joining in:

St. Joseph, our protector, pray for us.

BLESSING AND INVESTITURE WITH THE CINCTURE IN HONOR OF THE BLESSED VIRGIN MARY

(Formerly reserved to the Hermits of St. Augustine)

The priest, vested in surplice and white stole, says:

P: Our help is in the name of the Lord.
All: Who made heaven and earth.
P: The Lord be with you.
All: May He also be with you.

Let us pray.
Almighty and merciful God, who grant mercy and pardon to sinners as they seek your tender forgiveness, we appeal to your kindness, asking that you graciously bless and hallow this cincture. Let him (her) who is to be girt with it in penance for his (her) sins observe continence, which is so pleasing to you; let him (her) be obedient to your commandments; let him (her) obtain pardon for his (her) sins, by the prayers of blessed Mary, ever a Virgin, of St. Augustine and St. Monica, and finally attain everlasting life; through Christ our Lord.
All: Amen.

Let us pray.
Holy Lord, almighty Father, everlasting God, we beg you to bless this cincture, a sign of purity, reminding us to restrain the loins and

reins, to subject them under your law. Let him (her) who will wear it devoutly and implore your mercy obtain pardon and remission of sins by your exceeding great mercy; through Christ our Lord.
All: Amen.

The priest sprinkles the cincture with holy water. Then he blesses the rosary, saying:

Let us pray.
Lord Jesus Christ, who taught your disciples to pray, we beg you to accept with a blessing the prayers of your servants, so that their prayer may ever begin in you and end in you, who live and reign forever and ever.
All: Amen.

He sprinkles the rosary with holy water. Then he blesses the person saying:

Let us pray.
Lord, hear our humble prayers, and grant that this servant of yours, on whom we bestow in your name this cincture, may by your bounty always devoutly persevere in holy religion; through Christ our Lord.
All: Amen.

The priest sprinkles the person with holy water. Then he invests the person with the cincture, saying:

Take this cincture about your loins, and let them be girt in token of chastity and temperance; in the name of the Father, and of the Son, and of the Holy Spirit.
All: Amen.

Lastly the priest says:

May the Lord who has begun a good work in you also bring it to completion; and by the merits of blessed Mary, ever a Virgin, and of St. Augustine and his devoted mother, Monica, may He grant you an increase of grace and glory.

All: Amen.

By the authority I enjoy in virtue of the Apostolic indult, I receive you into the Order of St. Augustine, and make you a partaker of all the spiritual benefits of our whole Order.

May the blessing of almighty God, Father, Son, and Holy Spirit, come upon you and remain with you forever.
All: Amen.

BLESSING AND INVESTITURE WITH THE CORD IN HONOR OF ST. FRANCIS OF ASSISI

(Formerly reserved to the Order of Friars Minor Conventual)

The priest, vested in surplice and white stole, says:

P: Our help is in the name of the Lord.
All: Who made heaven and earth.
P: Pray for us, O holy Father Francis.
All: That we may be worthy of Christ's promise.
P: Lord, heed my prayer.
All: And let my cry be heard by you.
P: The Lord be with you.
All: May He also be with you.

Let us pray.
God, who willed in redeeming your servant that your Son should be bound by the hands of wicked men, we beg you to bless this cord; and grant that your servant, who will gird his body with it as with the chains of a penitent, may ever keep in mind the chains of our Lord Jesus Christ, ever persevere in the Order to which he (she) has consecrated himself (herself), and ever acknowledge himself (herself) bound in affection to your service; through Christ our Lord.

All: Amen.

Let us pray.
Almighty everlasting God, who in your loving kindness have pardoned and shown mercy to all sinners who long and seek for it; we pray that in your boundless mercy you may bless   and hallow this cord. Let him (her) who will be girt with it in penance for his (her) sins, by appealing to your goodness and by the merits and prayers of your blessed servant, Francis, obtain pardon and remission of his (her) sins and the other fruits of your holy mercy; through Christ our Lord.
All: Amen.

The priest sprinkles it with holy water, and then invests the person with it saying:

Take this cord about your loins and let them be girt in token of chastity; in the name of the Father, and of the Son, and of the Holy Spirit.
All: Amen.

BLESSING AND INVESTITURE WITH WOOL CINCTURE IN HONOR OF ST. FRANCIS OF PAULA

(Formerly reserved to the Order of Minims)

The priest, vested in surplice and white stole, says as he signs himself:

P: Our help is in the name of the Lord.
All: Who made heaven and earth.
P: The Lord be with you.
All: May He also be with you.

Let us pray.
Almighty, everlasting, and merciful God, who in your loving kindness have pardoned and shown mercy to sinners who long and

seek for it; we pray that in your boundless mercy you may bless
and hallow   this woolen cincture. Let him (her) who will be girt
with it in penance for his (her) sins, by appealing to your goodness
and by the prayers of blessed Francis, obtain the pardon and
remission of your holy mercy; through Christ our Lord.
All: Amen.

The priest sprinkles the cincture with holy water, and presents the
person with it, saying:

Take this cincture about your loins and let them be girt in token of
chastity and temperance; in the name of the Father, and of the Son,
and of the Holy Spirit.
All: Amen.

BLESSING OF CINCTURES IN HONOR OF ST. THOMAS AQUINAS FOR PRESERVATION OF CHASTITY

(Formerly reserved to the Order of Preachers)

The priest, vested in surplice and white stole, says:

P: Our help is in the name of the Lord.
All: Who made heaven and earth.
P: The Lord be with you.
All: May He also be with you.

Let us pray.
Lord Jesus Christ, Son of the living God, lover and guardian of
purity, we appeal to your boundless goodness, asking that just as
you caused St. Thomas Aquinas to be girt with the cincture of
chastity by the ministry of angels, and preserved him from every
stain of body and soul, so also you may be pleased to bless and to
hallow these cinctures in his honor and glory. Let all who
reverently bind their loins with them be cleansed of every
defilement of mind and body, and deserve to be presented to you at
the hour of death by the hands of the holy angels. We ask this of

you who live and reign forever and ever.
All: Amen.

The cinctures are sprinkled with holy water.

BLESSING AND INVESTITURE WITH SACRED MEDAL OF MARY IMMACULATE

Commonly Known as the "Miraculous Medal"

(Formerly reserved to the Congregation of the Missions)

(Approved by the Congregation of Sacred Rites, April 19, 1895)

The priest who is to bless the sacred medal of the Immaculate Conception, vested in surplice and white stole, says:

P: Our help is in the name of the Lord.
All: Who made heaven and earth.
P: The Lord be with you.
All: May He also be with you.

Let us pray.
Almighty and merciful God, who by the many appearances on earth of the Immaculate Virgin Mary were pleased to work miracles again and again for the salvation of souls; kindly pour out your blessing on this medal, so that all who devoutly wear it and reverence it may experience the patronage of Mary Immaculate and obtain mercy from you; through Christ our Lord.
All: Amen.

The priest sprinkles the medal with holy water, and presents it to the person, saying:

Take this holy medal; wear it with faith, and handle it with due devotion, so that the holy and immaculate Queen of heaven may protect and defend you. And as she is ever ready to renew her wondrous acts of kindness, may she obtain for you in her mercy

whatever you humbly ask of God, so that both in life and in death you may rest happily in her motherly embrace.
All: Amen.

The priest continues:

Lord, have mercy. Christ, have mercy. Lord, have mercy. Our Father (the rest inaudibly until:)

P: And lead us not into temptation.

All: But deliver us from evil.

P: Queen conceived without original sin.

All: Pray for us.

P: Lord, heed my prayer.
All: And let my cry be heard by you.
P: The Lord be with you.
All: May He also be with you.

Let us pray.
Lord Jesus Christ, who willed that your Mother, the blessed Virgin Mary conceived without sin, should become illustrious through countless miracles; grant that we who ever seek her patronage may finally possess everlasting joys. We ask this of you who live and reign forever and ever.
All: Amen.

BLESSING OF MEDALS OF ST. BENEDICT

(Formerly reserved to the Order of St. Benedict)

The priest who is to bless the medals of St. Benedict says:

P: Our help is in the name of the Lord.
All: Who made heaven and earth.

I cast out the demon from you, creature medals, by God the Father almighty, who made the heavens and the earth and the seas and all that they contain. May all power of the adversary, all assaults and pretensions of Satan, be repulsed and driven afar from these medals, so that they may be for all who will use them a help in mind and body; in the name of the Father   almighty, of Jesus Christ, His Son, our Lord, of the Holy Spirit, the Advocate, and in the love of our Lord Jesus Christ, who is coming to judge both the living and the dead and the world by fire.
All: Amen.

Lord, have mercy. Christ, have mercy. Lord, have mercy. Our Father (the rest inaudibly until:)

P: And lead us not into temptation.

All: But deliver us from evil.

P: Save your servants.

All: Who trust in you, my God.

P: Let us find in you, Lord, a fortified tower.

All: In the face of the enemy.

P: The Lord will give strength to His people.

All: The Lord will bless His people with His peace.

P: Lord, send us aid from your holy place.

All: And watch over us from Sion.

P: Lord, heed my prayer.
All: And let my cry be heard by you.
P: The Lord be with you.
All: May He also be with you.

Let us pray.
Almighty God, lavish dispenser of every good, we humbly ask that
by the prayers of St. Benedict you pour out your blessing on these
sacred medals, impressed with letters and signs ascribed to you.
Let all who will wear them with hearts intent on good works
deserve to obtain health of mind and body, your holy grace, and
the indulgences that have been granted to us. And may they escape
by your merciful help all attacks and wiles of the devil, and finally
appear in your presence sinless and holy; through Christ our Lord.
All: Amen.

Let us pray.
Lord Jesus Christ, who willed in redeeming the whole world to be
born of a Virgin, to be circumcized, rejected by the Jews, betrayed
with a kiss by Judas, bound in chains, crowned with thorns, pierced
with nails, crucified between robbers, wounded with a lance, and
to die at last on the cross; I humbly ask, by this your sacred
passion, that you expel all attacks and wiles of the devil from the
person who devoutly calls on your holy name, using these words
and signs ascribed to you. May it please you to lead him (her) to
the harbor of everlasting salvation, you who live and reign forever
and ever.
All: Amen.

May the blessing of almighty God, Father, Son, and Holy Spirit,
come upon you and remain with you forever.
All: Amen.

The priest sprinkles the medals with holy water.

SHORT FORM FOR BLESSING MEDALS OF ST. BENEDICT

(Formerly reserved to the same Order)

(Approved by the Congregation of Sacred Rites, Dec. 13, 1922)

The first versicle and the exorcism are the same as those given under No. 31. Then follow the versicles beginning with "Lord, heed my prayer," etc. and the oration "Almighty God," etc.; after which the medals are sprinkled with holy water.

BLESSING OF THE ROSARY OF OUR LORD

(Formerly reserved to the Order of Camaldulese)

The versicles and responses are the same as those given under No. 23 and they are followed by this prayer:

Let us pray.
Lord Jesus Christ, who became man, sojourning in the world for thirty-three years, suffering many things for the salvation of men, and who willed finally to die on the cross; be pleased, we pray, to bless and to hallow this rosary (these rosaries), which you directed St. Michael the Hermit of Camaldulese to introduce for the purpose of commemorating your life, passion, and death. May all who devoutly carry it (them) on their person and faithfully recite it (them) be enriched with your many graces and mercies, and deserve to obtain an everlasting crown in heaven; through Christ our Lord.
All: Amen.

It (they) is (are) sprinkled with holy water.

BLESSING OF ROSARIES OF THE PRECIOUS BLOOD

(Formerly reserved to the Congregation of Missionaries of the Precious Blood)

The rosary is made up of thirty-three beads divided into seven parts, six of which have five beads each, and the seventh only three. In this way the sevenprincipal sheddings of Christ's blood are honored by the recitation of thirty-three Our Fathers and seven

Glory be to the Fathers.

The versicles and responses are the same as those given under No. 15; and they are followed by this prayer:

Let us pray.
Almighty and merciful God, who, out of exceeding love for us, willed that your only-begotten Son, our Lord Jesus Christ, come down from heaven to earth, taking flesh at the angel's message in the sacred womb of Our Lady, the blessed Virgin Mary, in order to snatch us from Satan's tyranny; we humbly beg you in your boundless goodness to bless and to hallow these rosaries, which your faithful Church has consecrated to the honor and praise of the precious blood of your Son. Let them be endowed with such power of the Holy Spirit, that whoever carries one on his person or reverently keeps one in his home, may always and everywhere in this life be shielded from all enemies, visible and invisible, and at his death, by the merits of the precious blood, happily attain everlasting blessedness; through Christ our Lord.
All: Amen.

They are sprinkled with holy water.

BLESSING OF ROSARIES OF OUR LADY

(Formerly reserved to the Order of Preachers)

P: Our help is in the name of the Lord.
All: Who made heaven and earth.
P: The Lord be with you.
All: May He also be with you.

Let us pray.
Almighty and merciful God, who, out of exceeding love for us, willed that your only-begotten Son, our Lord Jesus Christ, come down from heaven to earth, take flesh at the angel's message in the sacred womb of Our Lady, the blessed Virgin Mary, submit to death on the cross, and rise gloriously from the dead on the third

day, in order to snatch us from Satan's tyranny; we humbly beg you in your boundless goodness to bless and to hallow these rosaries, which your faithful Church has consecrated to the honor and praise of the Mother of your Son. Let them be endowed with such power of the Holy Spirit, that whoever carries one on his person or reverently keeps one in his home, or devoutly prays to you, while meditating on the divine mysteries, according to the rules of this holy society, may fully participate in all the graces, privileges, and indulgences which the Holy See has granted to this society. And may he always and everywhere in this life be shielded from all enemies, visible and invisible, and at his death deserve to be presented to you by the blessed Virgin Mary, Mother of God, laden with the merits of good works; through Christ our Lord.
All: Amen.

The rosaries are sprinkled with holy water.

SHORT FORM FOR BLESSING ROSARIES OF OUR LADY

(Formerly reserved to the same Order)

(Approved by the Congregation of Sacred Rites, Nov. 23, 1918)

To the honor and glory of the Virgin Mary, Mother of God, and in memory of the mysteries of the life, death, and resurrection of our Lord Jesus Christ, may these rosaries be blessed and hallowed ; in the name of the Father, and of the Son, and of the Holy Spirit.
All: Amen.

BLESSING OF ROSES FOR THE SOCIETY OF THE ROSARY

(Formerly reserved to the same Order)

P: Our help is in the name of the Lord.
All: Who made heaven and earth.
P: The Lord be with you.

All: May He also be with you.

Let us pray.
God, the Creator and preserver of the human race, giver of
heavenly grace, and lavish dispenser of everlasting salvation; with
your holy benediction bless   these roses which we present to you
today in gratitude for your favors, and in devotion and veneration
of blessed Mary, ever a Virgin. By the power of the holy cross
pour out a heavenly blessing   on these roses, which you have
given to man to enjoy their sweet fragrance and to alleviate the
sufferings of the sick. By the sign of the holy cross let them be
endowed with such blessing that the sick to whom they are brought
and whose homes they adorn may be healed of their infirmities;
and let them drive away in fear and trembling the devil with all his
followers, nevermore to molest the people who are your servants;
through Christ our Lord.
All: Amen.

The roses are sprinkled with holy water.

BLESSING OF CANDLES FOR ROSARY SOCIETY

(Formerly reserved to the same Order)

P: Our help is in the name of the Lord.
All: Who made heaven and earth.
P: The Lord be with you.
All: May He also be with you.

Let us pray.
Lord Jesus Christ, the true light that enlightens every man who
comes into the world, by the prayers of the blessed Virgin Mary,
your Mother, and the fifteen mysteries of her rosary, pour out your
blessing on these candles and tapers, and hallow them by the light
of your grace. Mercifully grant that as these lights with their
visible fire dispel the darkness of the night, so may the Holy Spirit
with His invisible fire and splendor dispel the darkness of our
transgressions. May He help us ever to discern with the pure eye of

the spirit the things that are pleasing to you and beneficial to us, so that in spite of the darkness and pitfalls of this world we may come at last to the unending light. We ask this of you who live and reign forever and ever.
All: Amen.

They are sprinkled with holy water.

BLESSING OF ROSARIES OF ST. BRIDGET

(Formerly reserved to the Order of the Holy Savior)

P: Our help is in the name of the Lord.
All: Who made heaven and earth.
P: The Lord be with you.
All: May He also be with you.

Let us pray.
Almighty and merciful God, who, out of exceeding love for us, willed that your only-begotten Son, our Lord Jesus Christ, come down from heaven to earth for our salvation taking flesh at the angel's message in the sacred womb of the blessed Virgin, in order to snatch us from Satan's tyranny; we humbly beg you in your boundless goodness to bless and to hallow these rosaries, which your faithful Church has consecrated to the honor and praise of the Mother of your Son. Let them be endowed with such power of the Holy Spirit, that whoever carries one on his person, or recites it, or reverently keeps it in his home, may always and everywhere be shielded from every foe and adversity, may gain the indulgences granted by the holy Roman Church, and at his death deserve to be presented to you by the blessed Virgin, laden with the merits of good works; through Christ our Lord.
All: Amen.

May the blessing of almighty God, Father, Son, and Holy Spirit, come upon you and remain with you forever.
All: Amen.

They are sprinkled with holy water.

BLESSING OF THE ROSARY OF ST. JOSEPH

(Formerly reserved to the Order of Carmelites)

The versicles are followed by this prayer:

Let us pray.
Almighty and merciful God, who, out of exceeding love for us,
willed that your only-begotten Son, our Lord Jesus Christ, come
down from heaven to earth for our salvation, taking flesh at the
angel's message in the sacred womb of the blessed Virgin, in order
to snatch us from Satan's tyranny; we humbly beg you in your
boundless goodness to bless this rosary, made and dedicated to the
honor and praise of the Mother of your Son and of St. Joseph, her
devoted spouse. Let it be endowed with such power of the Holy
Spirit, that whoever carries it on his person, or reverently keeps it
in his home, may always and everywhere in this life be shielded
from every visible and invisible foe, and at his death deserve to be
presented to you by these holy spouses, laden with the merits of
good works; through Christ our Lord.
All: Amen.

It is sprinkled with holy water.

BLESSING OF THE RING OF ST. JOSEPH

(Formerly reserved to the same Order)

The versicles are the same as #39; and they are followed by this
prayer:

Let us pray.God, whose word sanctifies everything that we
possess, we beg you to pour out your blessing on us and on this
ring; and by the prayers of the blessed Mary, ever a Virgin, and her

spouse, St. Joseph, may we mercifully obtain whatever is necessary for us in this life and be grateful for it; through Christ our Lord.
All: Amen.

It is sprinkled with holy water.

BLESSING OF THE SICK WITH RELIC OF TRUE CROSS OR THE SIGN OF ST. MAURUS THE ABBOT

(Formerly reserved to the Order of St. Benedict)

Before the ceremony a relic of the true cross of our Lord is exposed. with at least two lighted candles beside it. Then the sick person is encouraged to make an act of contrition, as well as an act of firm faith that, by the merits and prayers of St. Benedict and St. Maurus, he will be restored to health, God willing. Three Our Fathers, Hail Marys and Glory be to the Father are said in honor of the Most Holy Trinity. Following this the priest, vested in surplice and red stole, holds the relic in his right hand before the sick person, and says:

P: Blessing, and glory, and wisdom, and thanksgiving and honor, and power, and strength to our God forever and ever.
All: Amen.

P: My foot is set on the right path.

All: I will praise you, Lord, in the assemblies.

Invocation

As I call on the holy name of the Lord, may you be restored to desired good health by that faith with which St. Maurus healed the sick with the following words; and I, unworthy sinner though I am, in similar faith now humbly say this prayer over you:

367

In the name of the all holy and undivided Trinity, and aided by the merits of our holy father, St. Benedict, I say to you: "Arise, N., fully restored to health"; in the name of the Father, and of the Son, and of the Holy Spirit.
All: Amen.

Antiphon: Surely He has born our grief and endured our sorrows; and by His stripes we are healed.

P: He who pardons man's iniquities.

All: May He heal your infirmities.

P: Lord, heed my prayer.
All: And let my cry be heard by you.
P: The Lord be with you.
All: May He also be with you.

Let us pray.
God, Creator of all things, who ordained that your only-begotten Son, by the co-operation of the Holy Spirit, take flesh in the womb of the Virgin Mary, in order to redeem the human race; and who in redeeming us were pleased to heal the wounds and infirmities of our souls by the holy and glorious wood of the life-bearing cross; grant that your servant, N., be restored to former good health by the power of this same life-giving sign; through Christ our Lord.
All: Amen.

Let us pray.
Lord Jesus Christ, who gave to St. Benedict, my master, the power to obtain from you whatever he would ask in your name; be pleased to expel by his prayers all suffering from this servant of yours, so that restored to health he (she) may offer thanksgiving to your holy name. We ask this of you who live and reign with the Father and the Holy Spirit forever and ever.
All: Amen.

The Sign

By the intercession of the immaculate Mother of God, ever a Virgin, and by the prayers of St. Benedict and St. Maurus, may the power of God the Father, the wisdom of God the Son, andthe might of the Holy Spirit, deliver you from this infirmity.
All: Amen.

May God's will be done in all things, and so may it be done in your case, just as you seek and desire only the praise and honor of the all holy cross of our Lord Jesus Christ.

Lastly he blesses the sick person with the relic of the holy cross, saying:

May the blessing of almighty God, Father, Son, and Holy Spirit, come upon you and remain with you forever.
All: Amen.

He then presents the relic to be kissed. This "sign" may be repeated three times if necessary, either the same day or on different days, as the case requires. Also, if desired, three votive Masses may be celebrated one of the Passion, one of St. Maurus the Abbot, and one of the dead. Otherwise the sick person will recite the rosary of the blessed Virgin Mary, if he is able, or will have it recited for him, distributed in three parts and for the aforementioned intention.

BLESSING OF WATER FOR THE SICK IN HONOR OF THE B.V.M. AND ST. TORELLUS

(By a Brief dated December 16, 1628)

P: Our help is in the name of the Lord.
All: Who made heaven and earth.
P: The Lord be with you.
All: May He also be with you.

Let us pray.

God, who in your heavenly mercy keep harmful things from man, giving him only the things that are for his good; who at the pool of Probatica moved the waters by the hand of your angel, thus destroying sickness and conferring health; pour out the dew of your blessing on this water, so that all the sick who drink it may, by the merits and prayers of the blessed Virgin Mary and the holy confessor, Torellus, regain their health. May women who are with child be spared every dire misfortune, and have the happiness of bringing their offspring to the grace of holy baptism; through Christ our Lord.
All: Amen.

The water is sprinkled with holy water.

BLESSING OF WATER WITH THE RELICS OF ST. PETER THE MARTYR

(Formerly reserved to the Order of Preachers)

The versicles are the same as those given above; and they are followed by this prayer:

Let us pray.
God, who for man's salvation instituted the most wonderful mysteries in the element of water, hearken to our prayer, and pour forth your blessing on this element, water, which we now make holy in the name of St. Peter the Martyr. By the intercession of this martyr of yours let it prove a salutary remedy for your faithful, driving out evil spirits and warding off illness and suffering of body and spirit. May all who drink of it or are sprinkled with it be delivered from every affliction of body and soul and regain health in their whole being; through Christ our Lord.
All: Amen.

Let us pray.
Almighty everlasting God, we humbly appeal to your mercy and goodness to graciously bless by your indescribable power these

your faithful people, who come to venerate the relics of St. Peter the Martyr and beg his intercession. Delivered by your martyr's prayers from every affliction of mind and body, protected by your mercy here and everywhere, and saved by your grace, may they deserve, after this life has run its course, to attain the joys that are unending; through Christ our Lord.
All: Amen.

BLESSING OF PALMS OR OTHER FOLIAGE ON THE FEAST OF ST. PETER THE MARTYR

(Formerly reserved to the same Order)

The versicles are the same as those given under #43; and they are followed by this prayer:

Let us pray.
Lord Jesus Christ, Son of the living God, we beg you to bless these tree-branches, to pour out on them a heavenly blessing, by the power of the holy cross and the prayers of St. Peter the Martyr; for when you once went forth to triumph over the enemy of mankind, you willed that little children pay honor to you, waving palms and tree-branches before you. By the sign of the holy cross, let these branches be so endowed with your blessing, that wherever they are kept the prince of darkness with all his followers may flee in fear and trembling from such homes and places; no damage may be done there from lightning and storm; no inclement weather consume or destroy the fruits of the earth; no happening disturb or molest those who serve you, the almighty God, who live and reign forever and ever.
All: Amen.

They are sprinkled with holy water.

BLESSING OF WATER FOR THE SICK IN HONOR OF ST. VINCENT FERRER

(Formerly reserved to the same Order)

P: Our help is in the name of the Lord.

All: Who made heaven and earth.

P: Blessed be the name of the Lord.

All: Both now and forevermore.

P: Lord, heed my prayer.
All: And let my cry be heard by you.
P: The Lord be with you.
All: May He also be with you.

Let us pray.
We humbly appeal to your majesty, O Lord, asking that as you
once blessed the rock in the desert, letting a copious flow of water
come forth when Moses struck it twice with his rod, thus typifying
by this double stroke the mystery of your passion and the two
wooden beams of the cross; so now you may again hallow with
your bounteous blessing this water by the mystery of the same holy
cross. And let every sick person who drinks of it or is sprinkled
with it forthwith experience the healing effect of your blessing;
through Christ our Lord.
All: Amen.

I bless this water in the name of God   the Father almighty, who
created this pleasing element for man's use ennobling it by His
wondrous power to wash away the stains of both body and soul; to
be drink for the thirsty cool refreshment for those suffering from
the heat; a means of travel for seafarers; and who in water and by
the water in the universal deluge--when the cataracts of heaven
poured down rain for forty days and forty nights, yet sparing the
lives of the eight people in the Ark--prefigured the sacrament of
the New Covenant. May He now bless and hallow this water, so
that by the invocation of His holy name and that of St. Vincent, it
may heal the sick, strengthen the infirm, cheer the downcast, purify
the unclean, and give full well-being to those who seek it; in the

name of the Father, and of the Son, and of the Holy Spirit.
All: Amen.

The priest, touching the vessel of water with a relic or image of St.
Vincent, says:

Let us pray.

Lord, hear our entreaties, and by the merits of St. Vincent, whose
relic (or image) we apply to it, pour out your constant blessing on
this element, water, and let it be a health-giving drink to those who
use it.
All: Amen.

In the name of the Father, and of the Son, and of the Holy Spirit.
All: Amen.

This sign of the cross should be traced with the relic or image.
Then the priest says;

Antiphon: May St. Vincent be with us in the twilight of life to lead
us on the sure path to Christ.

P: Pray for us, St. Vincent.

All: That we may be worthy of Christ's promise.

Let us pray.
God, who has granted that a multitude of people acknowledge your
name through the preaching of your confessor, Vincent; we beg
you that it be our lot to have Him as our reward in heaven whom
he announced on earth as the Judge who is to come; through Christ
our Lord.
All: Amen.

BLESSING OF WATER FOR THE SICK IN HONOR OF ST. RAYMOND NONNATUS

(Formerly reserved to the Order of Our Lady of Ransom)

The versicles are the same as those given under No. 43; and they are followed by this prayer:

Let us pray.
God, the health and strength of all the faithful, who once completely cured the mother-in-law of your apostle, Peter, of her high fever, as you perceived her devout desire; be pleased to bless and to hallow this creature, water, in your own holy name and that of your confessor, Raymond, whom you called to forsake the world and to enter the order of the exalted Virgin Mary, Mother of God. Grant, we pray, by her glorious merits and prayers, that all who suffer from fever may be delivered from every infirmity of body and soul when they bathe in this water, or drink it, or are sprinkled with it, and so deserve to be restored unharmed to your Church, where they will always offer their prayers of gratitude. We ask this of you who live and reign forever and ever.
All: Amen.

Let us pray.
By the merits of St. Raymond, bless,　O Lord, this creature, water, as you once consecrated the waters of the Jordan through contact with your sacred body. And grant that all who taste of it or touch it may regain health in body and soul; you who live and reign forever and ever.
All: Amen.

Antiphon: O Blessed Raymond, model of purity, chastity continency; intercede with the Mother of mercy that she may keep us from evildoing in this vale of tears, and help us to attain everlasting rest after we have laid aside this mortal body.

Let us pray.
Almighty God, grant, we pray, that, by the power of this blessed water, by the merits of the passion of our Lord Jesus Christ, by the prayers of the blessed Virgin Mary, St. Raymond, and all the saints, the faithful who reverently drink of this water or touch it may regain health in body and soul, and so persevere in your holy

service; through Christ our Lord.
All: Amen.

Let us pray.
Almighty everlasting God, who enable us, your servants, in our
profession of the true faith, to acknowledge the glory of the three
Persons in the eternal Godhead, and to adore their oneness of
nature, their co-equal majesty; grant, we pray, that by steadfastness
in that faith we may ever be guarded against all adversity; through
Christ our Lord.
All: Amen.

Let us pray.
We entreat you, Lord God, grant us the enjoyment of lasting health
of body and mind; and by the glorious intercession of blessed
Mary, ever a Virgin, free us from present sorrow and give us
everlasting joy; through Christ our Lord.
All: Amen.

Let us pray.
God, who endowed Blessed Raymond, your confessor, with the
wondrous power to deliver your faithful from captivity under
impious men; grant by his intercession that we may be absolved
from the bonds of our sins, and then tranquilly perform only those
things that are pleasing to you; through Christ our Lord.
All: Amen.

May the blessing of almighty God, Father, Son, and Holy Spirit,
come upon you and remain with you forever.
All: Amen.

It is sprinkled with holy water.

BLESSING OF CANDLES IN HONOR OF ST. RAYMOND NONNATUS

(meant especially to be lit for a safe delivery)

(Formerly reserved to the same Order)

The versicles are the same as those given under No. 43; and they are followed by this prayer:

Let us pray.
Lord Jesus Christ, Son of the living God, light of everlasting life, who have given us candles to dispel the darkness; we humbly beg you to bless these candles by the merits of Blessed Raymond, your confessor. By the power of the holy cross bestow a heavenly blessing on them. Let them be so empowered by the sign of the holy cross, that the spirits of darkness will flee in fear and trembling from all places where their light shines, and nevermore disturb or molest those who serve you, the almighty God, who live and reign forever and ever.
All: Amen.

Then saying again "Let us Pray" the priest adds the three orations given on pp. 732-33; after which he continues:

May the blessing of almighty God, Father, Son, and Holy Spirit, come upon you and remain with you forever.
All: Amen.

He sprinkles them with holy water.

BLESSING OF OIL IN HONOR OF ST. SERAPION, MARTYR

(Formerly reserved to the same Order)

The versicles are the same as those given under "BLESSING OF WATER FOR THE SICK IN HONOR OFTHE B.V.M. AND ST. TORELLUS" ; and they are followed by this prayer:

Let us pray.
Almighty everlasting God, the healer and solace of all men, be pleased to hallow this creature, oil, as we bless it in your name and in the name of the illustrious and valiant athlete of Christ,

Serapion. Let all who suffer from sores, fractures, or other painful ailments, by the anointing with this holy oil and the prayers and aid of the Saint, who endured such intense and excruciating torment at his martyrdom, experience alleviation in this life, and attain perfect well-being in the life to come; through Christ our Lord.
All: Amen.

Antiphon: O Blessed Serapion, noble athlete and standard-bearer in the legion of Mary, beloved of the Virgin Mother, illustrious by your martyrdom; pray for us to the Lord who made you brave and strong in the crucible of your suffering.

Let us pray.
O Jesus our Redeemer, inflame our hearts with the fire of your love. And as Blessed Serapion followed your example, even to death on a cross, in order to ransom the faithful, so by his intercession may we never be broken by any kind of adversity, but always have strength to embrace your cross. We ask this of you who live and reign forever and ever.
All: Amen.

Let us pray.
Lord of mercy and of clemency, by the illustrious merits of the bitter suffering of your martyr, Serapion, a Machabee of the New Covenant, bless   this oil and hallow it by the power of your benediction. Grant that, by the devout anointing with this oil in honor of your martyr, all who are suffering from any kind of pain may experience by your help alleviation in body, and by your grace solace of mind, and thus fully restored in health, be able to offer you thanksgiving in your Church; through Christ our Lord. All: Amen.

May the blessing of almighty God, Father, Son, and Holy Spirit, come upon you and remain with you forever.
All: Amen.

It is sprinkled with holy water.

BLESSING OF WATER IN HONOR OF ST. ALBERT, CONFESSOR

(Formerly reserved to the Order of Discalced Carmelites)

The priest is vested in surplice and stole, or at least in a stole. Assisted by a server who carries a lighted candle, he goes to the place where the relics of St. Albert are reserved and reverently exposes them. The water to be blessed is at hand in a fitting vessel. First the priest says the versicle as given under BLESSING OF WATER FOR THE SICK IN HONOR OF ST. VINCENT FERRER, after which he adds the following:

Let us pray.
Lord Jesus Christ, health and strength of all the faithful, who once completely cured the mother-in-law of your apostle, Peter, of her high fever; be pleased to bless and to hallow this creature, water. By the prayers of Blessed Albert, your confessor, whom you called to forsake the world and to enter the Order of your Mother, the Virgin Mary, and by the humble use of this water, may all who suffer from fever be delivered from every infirmity of body and soul, and so deserve to be restored unharmed to your Church, where they will always offer their prayers of gratitude. We ask this of you who live and reign forever and ever.
All: Amen.

Then he reverently takes the relics and immerses them in the water tracing with them the sign of the cross, and saying:

By the merits of St. Albert, bless, O Lord, this creature, water, as you once consecrated the waters of the Jordan through contact with your sacred body. And grant that all who taste of it may regain health in body and soul; you who live and reign forever and ever.

All: Amen.

Antiphon: O Blessed Albert, model of purity, chastity, continency; intercede with the Mother of mercy that she may keep us from evildoing in this vale of tears, and help us to attain everlasting rest after we have laid aside this mortal body.

P: Pray for us, O Blessed Albert.

All: That we may be worthy of Christ's promise.

Let us pray. Almighty and merciful God, grant, we beg you, that by the prayers of Blessed Albert, your confessor, all the faithful who reverently drink of this water may regain health in body and soul, and so persevere in your holy service; through Christ our Lord.
All: Amen.

BLESSING OF WATER IN HONOR OF ST. IGNATIUS, CONFESSOR

(Formerly reserved to the Society of Jesus)

Holy Lord, almighty Father, everlasting God, who, in pouring out the grace of your blessing on the bodies of the sick, encompass your creatures with your generous love; hearken as we call on your holy name, and by the prayers of Blessed Ignatius, your confessor, free your servants from illness and restore them to health, and then hasten their convalescence by your sure hand, strengthen them by your might, shield them by your power, and give them back in full vigor to your holy Church; through Christ our Lord.
All: Amen.

He then immerses a medal or a reliquary of St. Ignatius in the water, and holds it so until the following prayer is concluded:

Lord, bless   this water, that it be a saving remedy for men; and grant that, by the prayers of Blessed Ignatius, whose medal (or relics) is (are) now immersed in it, all who will drink this water may have health in body and protection in soul; through Christ our Lord.
All: Amen.

He then removes the medal or reliquary from the water, and says:

Let us pray.
God, who through Blessed Ignatius have strengthened the Church militant with new reserves for promoting the greater glory of your name; grant that we who fight for your cause here on earth by his help and example may win the crown with him in heaven; through Christ our Lord.
All: Amen.

BLESSING OF WATER FOR THE SICK IN HONOR OF ST. VINCENT DE PAUL

(Formerly reserved to the Congregation of the Missions)

(Approved by the Congregation of Sacred Rites, March 16, 1882)

The versicles and responses are the same as those given on No. 46 and they are followed by this prayer:

Let us pray.
Holy Lord, almighty Father, everlasting God, who, in pouring out the grace of your blessing on the bodies of the sick, encompass your creatures with your generous love; hearken as we call on your holy name, and by the prayers of Blessed Vincent, your confessor, free your servants from illness and restore them to health, and then hasten their convalescence by your sure hand, strengthen them by your might, shield them by your power, and give them back in full vigor to your holy Church; through Christ our Lord.
All: Amen.

He then immerses a medal or a reliquary of St. Vincent de Paul in the water, and holds it so until the following prayer is concluded:

Lord, bless this water, that it be a saving remedy for men; and grant that, by the prayers of Blessed Vincent, your confessor, whose relics (or medal) are (is) now immersed in it, all who will

drink this water may have health in body and protection in soul; through Christ our Lord.
All: Amen.

He then removes the medal or reliquary from the water, and says:

Antiphon: The poor of Sion I will sate with bread, and I will let my blessing overflow on her priests, and her saints will exult exceedingly.

P: God, you have provided in your kindness for the poor.

All: The Lord gives orders to his messengers with great authority.

Let us pray.
God, who through Blessed Vincent have added to your Church a new community to serve the poor and to train the clergy; grant, we pray, that we may be imbued with the same fervor, so as to love what he loved and to carry out what he inculcated; through Christ our Lord.
All: Amen.

14

RECEPTION OF CONVERTS AND PROFESSION OF FAITH

(As prescribed by the Sacred Congregation of the Holy Office on July 20, 1859; with the new form for abjuration of errors and profession of faith, approved by the Holy Office for the use of converts, and communicated through the Apostolic Delegate to the U. S. on March 28, 1942.)

In the case of a convert from heresy, inquiry should first be made about the validity of his former baptism. If after careful investigation it is discovered that the party was never baptized or that the supposed baptism was invalid, he must now be baptized

unconditionally. However, if the investigation leaves doubt about
the validity of baptism, then it is to be repeated conditionally,
using the ceremony for baptism of adults. Thirdly, if ascertained
that the former baptism was valid, reception into the Church will
consist only in abjuration of former errors and profession of faith.
The reception of a convert will, consequently, take place in one of
the following three ways:

I

If baptism is conferred unconditionally, neither abjuration of
former errors nor absolution from censures will follow, since the
sacrament of rebirth cleanses from all sin and fault.

II

If baptism is to be repeated conditionally, the order will be: (1)
abjuration or profession of faith; (2) baptism with conditional
form; (3) sacramental confession with conditional absolution.

III

If the former baptism has been judged valid, there will be only
abjuration or profession of faith, followed by absolution from
censures. But if the convert greatly desires that the full rites of
baptism lacking hitherto be supplied on this occasion, the priest is
certainly free to comply with his devout request. In this case he
ought to use the form of baptism for adults, making those changes
necessitated by the fact that baptism has already been validly
conferred.

The priest vested in surplice and purple stole is seated in the
middle of the altar predella, unless the Blessed Sacrament is
reserved in the tabernacle--in which case he takes a place at the
epistle side. The convert kneels before him, and with his right hand
on the book of Gospels makes the profession of faith as given
below. If the person is unable to read, the priest reads it for him

slowly, so that he can understand and repeat the words after him.

Profession of Faith

I, N.N., ... years of age, born outside the Catholic Church, have
held and believed errors contrary to her teaching. Now,
enlightened by divine grace, I kneel before you, Reverend Father
...., having before my eyes and touching with my hand the holy
Gospels. And with firm faith I believe and profess each and all the
articles contained in the Apostles' Creed, that is: I believe in God,
the Father almighty, Creator of heaven and earth; and in Jesus
Christ, His only Son, our Lord, who was conceived by the Holy
Spirit, born of the Virgin Mary, suffered under Pontius Pilate, was
crucified, died, and was buried; He descended into hell, the third
day He arose again from the dead; He ascended into heaven, and
sits at the right hand of God, the Father almighty,from there He
shall come to judge the living and the dead. I believe in the Holy
Spirit; the holy Catholic Church; the communion of saints; the
forgiveness of sins; the resurrection of the body, and life
everlasting. Amen.

I firmly admit and embrace the apostolic and ecclesiastical
traditions and all the other constitutions and ordinances of the
Church.I admit the Sacred Scriptures in the sense which has been
held and is still held by holy Mother Church, whose duty it is to
judge the true sense and interpretation of Sacred Scripture, and I
shall never accept or interpret them in a sense contrary to the
unanimous consent of the fathers.

I also must profess that the sacraments of the New Law are truly
and precisely seven in number, instituted for the salvation of
mankind, though all are not necessary for each individual: baptism,
confirmation, holy Eucharist, penance, anointing of the sick, holy
orders, and matrimony. I profess that all confer grace, and that
baptism, confirmation, and holy orders cannot be repeated without
sacrilege. I also accept and admit the ritual of the Catholic Church
in the solemn administration of all the aforementioned sacraments.

I accept and hold in each and every part all that has been defined and declared by the Sacred Council of Trent concerning original sin and justification. I profess that in the Mass there is offered to God a true, real, and propitiatory sacrifice for the living and the dead; that in the holy sacrament of the Eucharist the body and blood together with the soul and divinity of our Lord Jesus Christ is really, truly, and substantially present, and that there takes place in the Mass what the Church calls transubstantiation, which is the change of all the substance of bread into the body of Christ and of all substance of wine into His blood. I confess also that in receiving under either of these species one receives Jesus Christ whole and entire.

I firmly hold that Purgatory exists and that the souls detained there can be helped by the prayers of the faithful.

Likewise I hold that the saints, who reign with Jesus Christ, should be venerated and invoked, that they offer prayers to God for us, and that their relics are to be venerated.

I firmly profess that the images of Jesus Christ and of the Mother of God, ever a Virgin, as well as of all the saints should be given due honor and veneration. I also affirm that Jesus Christ left to the Church the faculty to grant indulgences, and that their use is most salutary to the Christian people. I recognize the holy, Roman, Catholic, and apostolic Church as the mother and teacher of all the churches, and I promise and swear true obedience to the Roman Pontiff, successor of St. Peter, the prince of the apostles and vicar of Jesus Christ.

Moreover, without hesitation I accept and profess all that has been handed down, defined, and declared by the sacred canons and by the general councils, especially by the Sacred Council of Trent and by the Vatican General Council, and in special manner all that concerns the primacy and infallibility of the Roman Pontiff. At the same time I condemn and reprove all that the Church has condemned and reproved. This same Catholic faith, outside of which none can be saved, I now freely profess and I truly adhere to it. With the help of God, I promise and swear to maintain and profess this faith entirely, inviolately, and with firm constancy until the last breath of life. And I shall strive, as far as possible, that this same faith shall be held, taught, and publicly professed by all who depend on me and over whom I shall have charge.

So help me God and these holy Gospels.

The convert remains kneeling, and the priest, still seated, says psalm 50, or psalm 129, concluding with "Glory be to the Father."

After this the priest stands and says:

Lord, have mercy. Christ, have mercy. Lord, have mercy. Our Father (the rest inaudibly until:)

P: And lead us not into temptation.
All: But deliver us from evil.
P: Save your servant.
All: Who trusts in you, my God.

P: Lord, heed my prayer.
All: And let my cry be heard by you.
P: The Lord be with you.
All: May He also be with you.

Let us pray.
God, whose nature is ever merciful and forgiving, accept our prayer that this servant of yours, bound by the fetters of sin, may be pardoned by your loving kindness: through Christ our Lord.
All: Amen.

The priest again sits down, and facing the convert pronounces the absolution from excommunication, inserting the word perhaps if in doubt as to whether it has been incurred:

By the authority of the Holy See which I exercise here, I release you from the bond of excommunication which you have (perhaps) incurred; and I restore you to communion and union with the faithful, as well as to the holy sacraments of the Church; in the

name of the Father, and of the Son, and of the Holy Spirit.
Amen.

Lastly the priest imposes some salutary penance, such as prayers,
visits to a church, or the equivalent.

SHORT FORM FOR PROFESSION OF FAITH

(In case of grave necessity only)

I, N.N., reared in the Protestant religion (or another religion as the
case may be) but now by the grace of God brought to the
knowledge of the truth, sincerely and solemnly declare that I
firmly believe and profess all that the holy, Catholic, apostolic, and
Roman Church believes and teaches, and I reject and condemn
whatever she rejects and condemns.

After this the priest says psalm 50 and the rest as above.

SHORT FORM FOR CONDITIONAL BAPTISM OF ADULT CONVERTS

(To be used only in dioceses that have received this special indult)

{On January 4, 1914, Pope Pius X granted permission to the
archdiocese of Philadelphia and to all dioceses of that province to
use the following short form of conditional baptism, in the case of
converts who had received baptism in the sect to which they
formerly belonged, with the provision that the faculty would have
to be renewed as circumstances require.}

P: N., what are you asking of God's Church?

Convert: Faith.

P: Do you believe in God the Father almighty, Creator of heaven and earth?

C: I do believe.

P: Do you believe in Jesus Christ, His only Son, our Lord, who was born into this world and suffered for us?

C: I do believe.

P: And do you believe in the Holy Spirit, the holy Catholic Church, the communion of saints, the forgiveness of sins, the resurrection of the body, and life everlasting?

C: I do believe.

P: N., do you wish to be baptized if you are not validly baptized?

C: I do.

P: N., if you are not baptized I baptize you in the name of the Father, and of the Son, and of the Holy Spirit.

The ceremonies of anointing with chrism and the bestowal of the white robe and of the lighted candle are not of obligation in this case, but a matter of edification. Because of their mystic signification they ought not to be omitted if they can be carried out. The preceding rite is followed by sacramental confession with conditional absolution.

THE ITINERARIUM

Or Invoking God's Blessing When Starting on a Journey

A cleric when starting on a journey says the following in the singular if he is to travel alone; but in the plural if he has companions:

Antiphon: May the almighty and merciful Lord lead us in the way of peace and prosperity. May the Angel Raphael be our companion on the journey and bring us back to our homes in peace, health, and happiness.

Then the Canticle of Zachary is said; and after the canticle the above antiphon is repeated. Then the priest continues:

Lord, have mercy. Christ, have mercy. Lord, have mercy. Our Father (the rest inaudibly until:)

P: And lead us not into temptation.

All: But deliver us from evil.

P: Save your servants.

All: Who trust in you, my God.

P: Lord, send us aid from your holy place.

All: And watch over us from Sion.

P: Let us find in you, Lord, a fortified tower.

All: In the face of the enemy.

P: Let the enemy have no power over us.

All: And the son of iniquity be powerless to harm us.

P: May the Lord be praised at all times.

All: May God, our helper, grant us a happy journey.

P: Lord, show us your ways.

All: And lead us along your paths.

P: Oh, that our life be bent.

All: On keeping your precepts.

P: For the crooked ways will be made straight.

All: And the rough places plain.

P: God has given His angels charge over you.

All: To guard you in all your undertakings.

P: Lord, heed my prayer.
All: And let my cry be heard by you.
P: The Lord be with you.
All: May He also be with you.

Let us pray.
God, who led the children of Israel dry-shod through the sea, and showed the way to the three Magi by the guidance of a star; grant us, we pray, a happy journey and peaceful days, so that, with your holy angel as our guide, we may safely reach our destination and finally come to the haven of everlasting salvation.

God, who led your servant, Abraham, out of Ur of the Chaldeans, and kept him safe in all his wanderings; may it please you, we pray, also to watch over us, your servants. Be to us, Lord, a help in our preparations, comfort on the way, shade in the heat, shelter in the rain and cold, a carriage in tiredness, a shield in adversity, a staff in insecurity, a haven in accident; so that under your guidance we may happily reach our destination, and finally return safe to our homes.

Lord, we beg you to hear our request that you guide the steps of your servants along the path of well-being that comes from you, and that in the midst of this fickle world we may always live under your protection.

Grant, we pray, O Almighty God, that your party of travellers find a safe route; and heeding the admonitions of blessed John, the

precursor, come finally to Him whom John foretold, your Son, Jesus Christ our Lord, who lives and reigns with you, in the unity of the Holy Spirit, God, forever and ever.
All: Amen.

P: Let us go forth in peace.
All: In the name of the Lord. Amen.

BLESSING AT MEALS

Before the Noonday Meal

The priest, or the father of the family, who is to bless the table says:

P: Bless the Lord.

All: Bless the Lord.

P: The eyes of all hope in you, Lord.

All: You give them food in due time. You open your hand and fill all creatures with your blessing. Glory be to the Father, etc.

P: Lord, have mercy.

All: Christ, have mercy. Lord, have mercy.

P: Our Father (the rest inaudibly until:)

P: And lead us not into temptation.

All: But deliver us from evil.

P: Let us pray. Bless us, O Lord, and these your gifts which we are about to receive from your bounty; through Christ our Lord.

All: Amen.

One of the family: Please, Father, give us a blessing.

P: May the King of everlasting glory give us a place at His heavenly table.

All: Amen.

After the Noonday Meal

If there has been reading at table the reader concludes "But you, O Lord, have mercy on us. All: Thanks be to God." Then all rise.

P: Let all your works praise you, O Lord.

All: Let all your saints glorify you. Glory be to the Father, etc.

P: We give you thanks, almighty God, for all your benefits; you who live and reign forever and ever.

All: Amen.
P: Praise the Lord, all you nations; * glorify Him, all you peoples.

All: His love for us is enduring; * He is faithful forever.

P: Glory be to the Father.

All: As it was in the beginning.

P: Lord, have mercy.

All: Christ, have mercy. Lord, have mercy.

P: Our Father (the rest inaudibly until:)

P: And lead us not into temptation.

All: But deliver us from evil.

P: He has been generous to the poor.

All: His goodness is everlasting.

P: I will bless the Lord at all times.

All: His praises are ever on my lips.

P: My soul will exult in the Lord.

All: The meek will hear it with gladness.

P: Praise the Lord with me.

All: Let us heighten our praise of His name.

P: Blessed be the name of the Lord.

All: Both now and forevermore.

P: Lord, be pleased to award everlasting life to all who do good to us in your name.

All: Amen.

P: Let us bless the Lord.

All: Thanks be to God.

P: May the souls of the faithful departed through the mercy of God rest in peace.

All: Amen.

Then an Our Father may be said silently, after which this conclusion is added:

P: May the Lord grant us His peace.
All: Amen.

Before the Evening Meal

P: Bless the Lord.

All: Bless the Lord.

P: The poor will eat and receive their fill.

All: Those who seek the Lord will praise Him and will live forever. Glory be to the Father, etc.

P: Lord, have mercy.

All: Christ, have mercy. Lord, have mercy.

P: Our Father (the rest inaudibly until:)

P: And lead us not into temptation.

All: But deliver us from evil.

P: Let us pray. Bless us, O Lord, and these your gifts which we are about to receive from your bounty; through Christ our Lord.

All: Amen.

One of the family: Please, Father, give us a blessing.

P: May the King of everlasting glory bring us to His heavenly banquet.

All: Amen.

After the Evening Meal

P: The kind and compassionate Lord has left us a memorial of His wondrous deeds.

All: He has given food to all who live in holy fear. Glory be to the Father, etc.

P: Blessed is God in His gifts and holy in all His works; He who lives and reigns forever and ever.

All: Amen.

Then they alternate in saying Ps. 116 "Praise the Lord, all you nations" and the rest as given above after the noonday meal.

If only one meal is taken the prayers are those of the evening meal.

The preceding manner of blessing and giving thanks at meals is used at all times of the year, except on the days noted below, when there are some variations.

On the Feast of Christmasuntil supper on the eve of Epiphany exclusive

P: The Word was made flesh, alleluia.

All: And dwelt among us, alleluia. Glory be to the Father, etc., and the rest as above.

At the end of the meal:

P: The Lord has manifested Himself to us, alleluia.

All: The Savior has appeared to us, alleluia. Glory be to the Father, etc., and the rest as above.

On Epiphany and throughout the following week

Before and after meals:

P: The kings of Tarsis and the islands pay tribute, alleluia.

All: The kings of Arabia and Saba bring gifts, alleluia.

And the rest as above.

On Maundy Thursday

Before meals:

P: For our sake Christ was obedient unto death.

Then the Our Father is said silently by all; after which the priest makes the sign of the cross over the table without saying anything.

P: For our sake Christ was obedient unto death.

P: Have mercy on me, God, in your goodness; * in the greatness of your compassion wipe out my offense.

All: Thoroughly wash me of my guilt, * and cleanse me of my sin.

The rest of psalm 50 can be said; but the doxology is:

P: Lord, we beg you to look with favor on this family of yours, for which our Lord Jesus Christ did not hesitate to be handed over to wicked men and to submit to death on the cross.

Then all say the Our Father silently; the rest is omitted.

On Good Friday

At both meals all is said as on Maundy Thursday, except that the versicle is:

P: For our sake Christ was obedient unto death, even to death on the cross.

On Holy Saturday

Before the noonday meal:

P: For our sake Christ was obedient unto death, even to death on the cross.

All: This is why God has exalted Him, and given Him the name above all names.

The rest as on Maundy Thursday.

After the noonday meal: the same versicle and response is said as before the meal; then follow the verses of psalm 50 as above on Maundy Thursday. Lastly the priest says:

Grant, we beg you, almighty God, that we who devoutly anticipate the resurrection of your Son may partake of the glory of His resurrection.

Then all say the Our Father silently; the rest is omitted.

Before the evening meal:

P: The chief priests and the Pharisees went and secured the grave.

All: By sealing the slab and setting the guard.

The rest as on Maundy Thursday.

After the evening meal the same versicle and response is said as before the meal; then follow the verses of psalm 116:

P: Praise the Lord, all you nations; * glorify Him, all you peoples.

All: His love for us is enduring; * He is faithful forever.

After this the Our Father is said silently; and then the prayer "Grant, we beg you, almighty God" as after the noonday meal.

On Easter

And throughout the octave

Before meals:

P: This day was made by the Lord, alleluia.

All: We rejoice and are glad, alleluia. Glory be to the Father, etc., and the rest as under Blessing at Meals.

After meals:

The same versicle and response are said as before the meal, and the rest is the same as Blessing at Meals.

On Ascension and throughout the following week

Before meals:

P: God mounts His throne amid shouts of joy, alleluia.

All: The Lord rises on high amid trumpet blast, alleluia. Glory be to the Father, etc., and the rest as Blessing at Meals.

After meals:

P: Christ rises on high, alleluia.

All: He leads the onetime captives to freedom, alleluia. Glory be to the Father, etc., and the rest as Blessing at Meals.

On Pentecost

Starting on the eve and throughout the octave

Before meals:

P: The Spirit of the Lord has filled the whole world, alleluia.

All: He sustains all things and knows man's words, alleluia. Glory be to the Father, etc., and the rest as Blessing at Meals.

After meals:

P: They were all filled with the Holy Spirit, alleluia.

All: They spoke in foreign tongues, alleluia. Glory be to the Father, etc., and the rest as Blessing at Meals.

HOME ENTHRONEMENT OF THE SACRED HEART

{His Eminence Albert Cardinal Meyer, in a televised talk given on May 31, 1964, said: "The enthronement of the Sacred Heart in a home is not just a pretty ceremony once performed and then forgotten. It is a way of life. It is the official and social recognition of the loving kingship of the Heart of Jesus in a Christian family." The Cardinal also noted that the presence of a priest is not necessary at the enthronement; that the father of the family may

conduct the ceremony; but that if a priest were present he could
bless the picture or statue of the Sacred Heart during the rite. The
present suggested ceremony may be adapted according to
circumstances, depending on whether a priest or the father of the
family presides at the enthronement.}

On entering the home the priest sprinkles holy water in the living
room and on the members of the family, saying:

Purify me with hyssop, Lord, and I shall be clean of sin. Wash me,
and I shall be whiter than snow. Have mercy on me, God in your
great kindness. Glory be to the Father, and to the Son, and to the
Holy Spirit.

All: As it was in the beginning, etc.
P: Our help is in the name of the Lord.
All: Who made heaven and earth.
P: Lord, heed my prayer.
All: And let my cry be heard by you.
P: The Lord be with you.
All: May He also be with you.

Let us pray.
Hear us, holy Lord and Father, almighty everlasting God, and in
your goodness send your holy angel from heaven to watch over
and protect all who live in this home, to be with them and give
them comfort and encouragement; through Christ our Lord.
All: Amen.

Let us pray.
Lord Jesus Christ, as I, in all humility, enter this home, let there
enter with me abiding happiness and God's choicest blessings. Let
serene joy pervade this home and charity abound here and health
never fail. Let no evil spirits approach this place but drive them far
away. Let your angels of peace take over and put down all wicked
strife. Teach us, O Lord, to recognize the majesty of your holy
name. Sanctify our humble visit and bless   what we are about to
do; you who are holy, you who are kind, you who abide with the

Father and the Holy Spirit forever and ever.
All: Amen.

An Early Christian Inscription on a Home

The victory is Christ's. Begone, Satan.Our Lord Jesus Christ, God's
Son and Word, lives here.
Nothing evil may come inside.Jesus Christ, King of kings and Lord
of lords, in your mercy keep your eyes on this house day and night.
This is the Lord's door.Those who come through it must be
just.God the holy, God the strong, God the undying, crucified for
us, have mercy on us. You have our trust, Lord; may we have your
mercy.

The priest then blesses the picture or statue of the Sacred Heart
using the blessing of an image of our Lord. Afterward he says:

Prayer of Christ the High Priest

At that time Jesus raised His eyes to heaven and said: "Father, the
hour is come. Glorify your Son, that your Son may glorify you.
You have given Him authority over all mankind, that He might
give eternal life to all you have entrusted to Him. And this is the
sum of eternal life--their knowing you, the only true God, and your
ambassador Jesus Christ.

I have glorified you on earth by completing the work you gave me
to do. And now, for your part, Father, glorify me in your bosom
with the glory I possessed in your bosom before the world existed.
I have made your name known to all men whom you singled out
from the world and entrusted to me. Yours they were, and to me
you have entrusted them; and they cherish your message.

I am offering a prayer for them; not for the world do I pray, but for
those whom you have entrusted to me; for yours they are. All that
is mine is yours, and yours is mine; and they are my crowning
glory. Holy Father, keep them loyal to your name which you have

given me. May they be one as we are one. I have delivered to them your message; and the world hates them, because they do not belong to the world, just as I do not. I do not pray you to take them out of the world, but only to preserve them from its evil influence. The world finds nothing kin in them, just as the world finds nothing kin in me. Consecrate them to the service of the truth. Your message is truth. As you have made me your ambassador to the world, so I am making them my ambassadors to the world; and for their sake I consecrate myself, that they, in turn, may in reality be consecrated.

O Father, I will that those whom you have entrusted to me shall be at my side where I am. I want them to behold my glory, the glory you bestowed on me because you loved me before the world was founded. Just Father! The world does not know you, but I know you, and thus these men have come to know that I am your ambassador. I have made known to them your name, and will continue to make it known. May the love with which you loved me dwell in them, as I dwell in them myself.

Prayer to the Sacred Heart

Lord Jesus Christ, we acknowledge you as King of the universe. All that has been made exists for your glory. Exercise over us your sovereign rights. We now renew the promises of our baptism; we again renounce Satan and all his works and attractions; we again promise to lead a truly Christian life. And in a very special way we undertake to bring about the triumph of your rights and the rights of your Church. Sacred Heart of Jesus, we offer you our poor actions to obtain that all men acknowledge your sacred kingly power. May the kingdom of your peace be firmly established throughout the world.
All: Amen.

Lord Jesus Christ, who, while you were subject to Mary and Joseph, sanctified family life by your unexcelled virtues; grant that we, aided by Mary and Joseph, may be inspired by the example of your holy family, and so attain the happiness of living with them in

heaven. We ask this of you who live and reign forever and ever.
All: Amen.

Lastly the priest blesses the family:

May the blessing of almighty God, Father, Son, and Holy Spirit,
come upon you and remain with you forever.
All: Amen.

OATH AGAINST MODERNISM

I, N.N., firmly accept and embrace each and every doctrine defined
by the Church's unerring teaching authority, and all that she has
maintained and declared, especially those points of doctrine which
directly oppose the errors of our time. In the first place I profess
that God, the beginning and the end of all things, can be known
with certitude and His existence demonstrated by the natural light
of reason from the things that are made, that is, from the visible
works of creation, as a cause is known from its effects. Secondly, I
acknowledge and admit the external arguments for revelation,
namely, divine facts, especially miracles and prophecies, as most
certain signs of the divine origin of the Christian religion, and I
hold that these are perfectly suited to the intelligence of every age
and of all men, including our own times. Thirdly, I also firmly
believe that the Church, the guardian and teacher of God's revealed
word, was directly and absolutely instituted by Christ Himself, the
true Christ of history, while He lived among us; and that the same
Church was founded on Peter, the prince of the apostolic hierarchy,
and on his successors to the end of time. Fourthly, I sincerely
accept the doctrine of faith in the same sense and with always the
same meaning as it has been handed down to us from the apostles
through the officially approved fathers. And therefore I wholly
reject the heretical notion of the evolution of dogmas, according to
which doctrines pass from one sense to another sense alien to that
which the Church held from the start. I likewise condemn every
erroneous notion to the effect that instead of the divine deposit of

faith entrusted by Christ to His spouse, the Church, and to be faithfully guarded by her, one may substitute a philosophic system or a creation of the human mind gradually refined by men's striving and capable of eventual perfection by indefinite progress. Fifthly, I hold as certain and sincerely profess that faith is not a blind religious sense evolving from the hidden recesses of subliminal consciousness, and morally formed by the influence of heart and will, but that it is a real assent of the intellect to objective truth learned by hearing, an assent wherein we believe to be true whatever has been spoken, testified, and revealed by the personal God, our Creator and Lord, on the authority of God who is the perfection of truth.

Furthermore, in all due reverence I submit to and fully uphold all the condemnations, declarations, and directions contained in the encyclical letter "Pascendi" and in the decree "Lamentabili," especially as regards what is called the history of dogmas. I also reject the error of those who allege that the faith proposed by the Church may conflict with history, and that Catholic dogmas, in the sense in which they are now understood, cannot be reconciled with the actual origins of Christianity. I condemn and reject, moreover, the opinion put forth that a more learned Christian can assume a dual personality, one as believer and another as historian, thus making it permissible for the historian to maintain what his faith as a believer contradicts, or to lay down premises from which there follows the falsity or the uncertainty of dogmas, provided only that these are not directly denied. I likewise reject that method of determining and interpreting Sacred Scripture which, setting aside the Church's tradition and the analogy of faith and the norms of the Holy See, adopts the principles of the rationalists, and with equal arbitrariness and rashness regards textual criticism as the sole supreme rule. Moreover, I reject the opinion of those who hold that a teacher of the science of historical theology or a writer on the subject must first put aside any preconceived notions about the supernatural origin of Catholic tradition or about the divine aid promised for the continual preservation of each revealed truth; or that the writings of individual fathers must be interpreted solely by the data of science, without any reference to sacred authority, and with the same freedom of judgment usually accorded to any profane records.

Finally, I profess that I am far removed in general from the error of the modernists, who hold that there is nothing inherently divine in sacred tradition; or who--which is far worse--admit it in a pantheistic sense. For then there would remain only a bare simple fact, like the ordinary facts of history, to the effect that the system started by Christ and His apostles still finds men to support it by their energy, shrewdness, and ability. Therefore, I most firmly retain and will retain to my last breath the faith of the fathers of the Church, which has the supernatural guarantee of truth, and which is, has been, and ever will be residing in the bishops who are the successors of the apostles (St. Irenaeus 4). And this is not to be so understood that we may hold what seems better suited to the culture of a particular age, but rather that we may never believe nor understand anything other than the absolute and unchangeable truth preached from the beginning by the apostles

All this I promise to keep faithfully, entirely, and sincerely, and to guard inviolably, and never to depart from it in any way in teaching, word, or writing. So I promise, so I swear, so help me God and His holy Gospels.

ABOUT THE AUTHOR

K.W.Kesler was born in Ohio, lives life much like you do, loves to go places and see and do many things. He has gained communication degrees, worked at places such as everything from fast food, to museums. He has been interested and studied the Occult for the better degree of his life, and is constantly still investigating incidents and occurrences of paranormal situations whenever they are presented to him.

Milton Keynes UK
Ingram Content Group UK Ltd.
UKHW010458210224
438187UK00001B/305